○ ○ ○ ○ ○

Presented To:

_____

By:

_____

Date:

_____

○ ○ ○ ○ ○

God's Little Devotional Journal for Teens

Honor Books
Tulsa, Oklahoma

God's Little Devotional Journal for Teens
ISBN 1-56292-456-7
Copyright © 2001 by Honor Books
P.O. Box 55388
Tulsa, Oklahoma 74155

God's Little Devotional
Journal for Teens

Introduction

Keeping a journal is a valuable and time-honored tradition. It has been practiced by kings and queens and philosophers for centuries. In recent times, the therapeutic benefits of journaling have once again come to the forefront. Psychologists tell us that it's a great way to work through emotional issues and learn more about our deepest motivations, thoughts, and desires. Teachers encourage journaling as a proven method of improving communication skills. Business leaders suggest using a journal for setting and keeping goals. And regular journaling is a boost to spiritual growth as well.

In the opening words of his first journal entry on September 3, 1822, Eugene Delacroix—a nineteenth-century French artist—writes: "I am carrying out my plan, so long formulated, of keeping a journal. What I most keenly wish is not to forget that I am writing for myself alone. Thus I shall always tell the truth, I hope, and thus I shall improve myself."

God's Little Devotional Journal for Teens has been designed with the special needs and interests of teenagers in mind. It provides an uplifting story, an inspirational scripture, a thought-provoking quotation, and journaling space for each day of the year. We hope you will read it daily and jot down your thoughts. At the end of the year, you will be amazed at how much you have matured. Read and write with an open heart, and let God teach you remarkable things about yourself, your spiritual life, and your relationships with others.

Sharing God's Love

The story is told of a small dog that was struck by a car and tossed to the edge of the road. A doctor, who just happened to be driving by, noticed that the dog was still alive, so he stopped his car, picked up the dog, and took it home with him. He discovered the dog had suffered only a few minor cuts and abrasions. Reviving the dog, the doctor cleaned its wounds, then carried it to the garage, where he intended to provide a temporary bed.

However, the dog wriggled free from his arms, jumped to the ground, and scampered off. "What an ungrateful dog," the doctor said to himself. He was glad that the animal had recovered so quickly, but he was a little miffed that it had shown so little appreciation for his expert, gentle care.

The doctor thought no more about the incident until the next evening. When he answered the "scratch" at the door, he found the little dog he had treated, with an injured doggie friend at its side.

Be encouraged! You may never see the difference you make in someone's life or the difference that person will make in the lives of others; nevertheless, those with whom you share your love and encouragement will *never* be the same.

○ ○ ○ ○ ○

No one is useless in this world who lightens the burden of anyone else.

Whom can I lend a hand to today?

_____ .
_____ .
_____ .
_____ .
_____ .
_____ .
_____ .
_____ .
_____ .
_____ .
_____ .
_____ .
_____ .
_____ .
_____ .

Whatever you do or say, let it be as a representative of the Lord Jesus, all the while giving thanks through him to God the Father.

COLOSSIANS 3:17 NLT

Don't Let Fear Stop You

How can I develop the courage to "take the shot" when it's needed?

_____

_____

_____

_____

_____

_____

_____

_____

_____

_____

_____

_____

_____

_____

_____

T. R. was having a terrible basketball game. He'd heard enough crowd taunts of "Airball!" and "Brick" to last him all season. He just hoped he could avoid making any more mistakes. His team was behind but gradually started to pull closer to the opposition. T. R. kept looking to the bench, expecting his coach to pull him from the game. But the coach stuck with his lineup.

Eventually, T. R. glanced at the scoreboard. His team was down by two points. Five seconds remained, and T. R.'s team had the ball. Given his poor shooting percentage, he was sure no one would pass him the ball.

Wrong.

Because of his poor shooting average, T. R. found himself wide open just behind the half-court line. A teammate fired him the ball. He looked desperately for someone to pass to, but no one was open. As a defender charged him, T. R. fired an off-balance half-court shot in the general direction of the basket. His shot was another brick. It bounced hard off the backboard—and through the hoop.

As he accepted the congratulations from his teammates, T. R. didn't dare tell them that he almost didn't shoot the ball at all because he didn't want to face the prospect of missing. He merely nodded and smiled the smile of a winner.

○ ○ ○ ○ ○

Be strong! Be courageous! Do not be afraid of them! For the Lord your God will be with you. He will neither fail you nor forsake you.

DEUTERONOMY 31:6 TLB

The only man who never makes mistakes is the man who never does anything.

Run toward the Goal with Excellence

During the days when the United States was taking shape as a nation, Andrew Bradford had an enviable business contract. His company was given the responsibility of doing all the public printing for the new state of Pennsylvania.

Bradford's company had a reputation for sometimes producing shoddy work, and unfortunately, that was the verdict when Bradford was asked to print an important address the governor was planning to deliver. The document was put together in a careless, unimpressive manner.

Another young printer saw this example of sloppy work as a great opportunity. He prepared an elegant document of the speech and forwarded it with his compliments to the governor and each member of the assembly. He was soon awarded the contract for all of Pennsylvania's public printing. His name? Benjamin Franklin.

Franklin replaced what was inferior with something that was of quality and excellence. That's the mark of a successful product, no matter what it is—even your own emerging life.

o o o o

Give me a stock clerk with a goal, and I will give you a man who will make history. Give me a man without a goal, and I will give you a stock clerk.

What do my finished tasks say about me?

_____.

_____.

_____.

_____.

_____.

_____.

_____.

_____.

_____.

_____.

_____.

_____.

_____.

_____.

This one thing I do: forgetting what lies behind and straining forward to what lies ahead, I press on toward the goal.

PHILIPPIANS 3:13-14 NRSV

It Pays to Persevere

What can I do today to invest in my dreams?

_____

_____

_____

_____

_____

_____

_____

_____

_____

_____

_____

_____

_____

_____

_____

Victor Villasenor remained illiterate until adulthood because of dyslexia. Then a woman in his native country of Mexico taught him to read. Ironically, Victor decided he wanted to become a great writer and asked God to help him fulfill his dream.

For ten years, Victor worked hard at manual labor, digging ditches and cleaning houses. As he worked, he thought of interesting characters and plots. At night, he read voraciously—devouring more than five thousand books, memorizing favorite opening lines, and analyzing literary styles. Then he started writing: nine novels, sixty-five short stories, and ten plays. He sent them all to publishers—and all were rejected. One publisher sent a two-word response: "You're kidding."

Instead of being discouraged, Victor was happy that the publisher had read his work! In 1972, after 260 rejections, Victor sold his first novel, _Macho_. He then published a nonfiction book and an award-winning screenplay. He is best known for his saga about his own family, _Rain of Gold_, which took twelve years to write.

Be encouraged to dream big! You can turn those dreams into reality![1]

o o o o o

Most of the important things in the world have been accomplished by people who have kept on trying when there seemed to be no hope at all.

Do not throw away your confidence; it will be richly rewarded.

HEBREWS 10:35 NIV

Don't Neglect the Details

can I be more
diligent to tend to the
details in my life?

Noel Borja of Malaybalay, Bukidnon, Philippines, would have been the youngest Philippine multimillionaire on record. Alas, it was not to be.

Borja had thirty days in which to appear before his grandfather's executor so that he might receive the $116 million that his grandfather left him as his sole heir. Unfortunately, the letter from the executor ended up in the dead-mail section of the Bureau of Post, and the deadline expired. Borja never appeared.

Why didn't Borja receive the notice? He had moved from a boarding house in Manila without leaving a forwarding address. His own negligence left him without a solid basis on which to appeal.

The opposite of diligence is not necessarily laziness, but often negligence. We should be certain to take care of routine tasks, follow normal procedures, and fill out necessary forms. Borja lost far more than money because of his lack of diligence. A new standard of living, a new opportunity for giving, and a new outlook on life were all within his grasp.

○ ○ ○ ○ ○

The leading rule for a man of every calling is diligence; never put off until tomorrow what you can do today.

Don't procrastinate—
there's no time to lose.

PROVERBS 6:4 THE MESSAGE

What random act of kindness can I commit today?

_____

_____

_____

_____

_____

_____

_____

_____

_____

_____

_____

_____

_____

_____

_____

One night while watching the news, Chuck Wall—a human relations instructor at Bakersfield College in California—heard a cliché that stuck in his mind: "Another random act of senseless violence . . ."

Wall got an idea. He assigned his students to perform an out-of-the-ordinary act of kindness and then write an essay about it. One student paid his mother's utility bills. Another bought thirty blankets from the Salvation Army and took them to homeless people who had gathered under a bridge.

For his part, Wall created a bumper sticker that read, "Today, I will commit one random act of senseless KINDNESS . . . Will you?" A bank and a union printed the bumper stickers, and some of the students sold them for a dollar each. The profits went to the county Braille center. The bumper stickers were pasted on all 113 patrol cars in the county, and the message was repeated in pulpits, schools, and professional associations.

Wall commented later, "I had no idea our community was in such need of something positive."

Every community—and especially every school—needs those who will give their best efforts, creative ideas, and kindness. As a student and teen, will you lead the way?[2]

o   o   o   o   o

"Let your light shine before men, that they may see your good deeds and praise your Father in heaven."

MATTHEW 5:16 NIV

You get the best out of others when you give the best of yourself.

See beyond the Obstacles

Napoleon saw Italy but not the Alps. He had an objective, and he knew where he was going. The Alps were simply something to be crossed en route.

Washington saw the Hessians massed at Trenton. He didn't see the Delaware choked with ice. A frozen river was simply a challenge to be overcome on the way to a victory.

Young people intent on improving their lives and earning college degrees will hold a strong image of "graduation day" in their minds. The exams, long nights of study, and jobs that must be done to pay for tuition and room and board are simply the price that is paid in exchange for a great reward.

A mother about to give birth has her mind and heart wrapped around the baby she will soon hold in her arms. The agony of childbirth is simply something that must be endured to experience the joy of new life.

Many people have a tendency to focus on the obstacles that loom in front of them. But the truly successful will focus on the objectives—the goals, the reasons, the dreams—that lie beyond the obstacles.

o o o o o

Ah, but a man's reach should exceed his grasp.

Where am I headed, and what are the obstacles in my path?

_____.

_____.

_____.

_____.

_____.

_____.

_____.

_____.

_____.

_____.

_____.

_____.

_____.

_____.

_____.

_____.

Faith is the assurance of things hoped for, the conviction of things not seen.

HEBREWS 11:1 NRSV

What is my part, and what do I need to trust God to handle?

_____
_____
_____
_____
_____
_____
_____
_____
_____
_____
_____
_____
_____
_____
_____
_____

In *God: A Biography*, Steven Mosley tells a story about Robert Foss and his Aunt Lana, who experienced a vision that intruded her prayers. Upon reflection and research, they concluded this "picture from God" was of a quiet cove near the Quinault Indian reservation.

Since the family had clothes to deliver to the reservation, Robert and his aunt decided to deliver them immediately. On the way, they found the exact spot Aunt Lana had seen in her vision. However, nothing unusual happened when they stopped at the beach she had seen.

Upon arrival at the reservation, an old Indian grandmother said happily, "You've come! I've been expecting you." As they unloaded the clothes, she told about the trouble in her family and the lack of warm clothing for her grandchildren. One day she had gone to a quiet place on the beach to ask for God's help. As they compared notes, they discovered that her prayer had occurred on the exact day and hour the "picture" first came to Aunt Lana's mind!

Every person has finite vision, unable to see all that is going on backstage in God's unfolding plan. We need to keep our attention on the current situations and then trust God daily that He is arranging all things for our eternal benefit—and for the benefit of those we love.[3]

○ ○ ○ ○ ○

They that know thy name will put their trust in thee: for thou, LORD, hast not forsaken them that seek thee.

PSALM 9:10

My job is to take care of the possible and trust God with the impossible.

Finish What You Start

Henry Ford was once asked, "How can I become a success?"

Ford replied, "If you start something, finish it!"

Ford learned this lesson early in his career. When he began work on his first automobile, he worked many long but exciting hours in a little brick building behind his home. Such enthusiasm overtook him that he found it hard to take time out to eat or sleep. Before he had completed his first car, however, he became acutely aware that he could build an even better car.

He was so sure of the need for improvements that the thrill and enthusiasm for his first car began to lessen. *Why spend all that time finishing a car that he already knew was inferior?* Still, something inside him forced him to continue—to focus his total energy on the first car and finish what he had started—before he allowed himself to fantasize about a second car.

As it turned out, Ford said he learned even more about how to improve the second car by finishing every detail of his original car. If he had given in to the temptation to quit building the first car, he may never have made any car at all.

Many people strive to be perfectionists, but the *completionists* usually accomplish more in life.

o o o o o

No plan is worth the paper it is printed on unless it starts you doing something.

HOW can I keep from getting distracted and finish what I start?

_____.
_____.
_____.
_____.
_____.
_____.
_____.
_____.
_____.
_____.
_____.
_____.
_____.
_____.
_____.

None of these things move me, neither count I my life dear unto myself, so that I might finish my course with joy.

ACTS 20:24

Put a Lid on It

Do I try to impress others, or am I genuine?

_____

_____

_____

_____

_____

_____

_____

_____

_____

_____

_____

_____

_____

A young attorney, just out of law school and beginning his first day on the job, sat down in the comfort of his brand-new office with a great sigh of satisfaction. He had worked long and hard to savor such a moment. Then, noticing a prospective client coming toward his door, he began to look busy and energetic.

Opening his legal pad and uncapping his pen, he picked up the telephone, and cradling it under his chin, he began to write furiously as he said, "Look, Harry, about that amalgamation deal, I think I better run down to the factory and handle it personally. . . . Yes. . . . No. I don't think three million dollars will swing it. We better have Smith from Los Angeles meet us there. Okay. Call you back later."

Hanging up the phone, he put down his pen, looked up at his visitor, stood, extended his hand, and said in his most polite but confident attorney's voice, "Good morning. How might I help you?"

The prospective "client" replied, "Actually, I'm just here to hook up your phone."

Many a foible or flaw
Need not show . . . for
If you don't say so,
Others won't know!

There's an old saying that goes, "A shut mouth gathers no foot." Sometimes the best thing to do is just keep your mouth shut!

○ ○ ○ ○

Don't talk so much. You keep putting your foot in your mouth. Be sensible and turn off the flow!

PROVERBS 10:19 TLB

I have never been hurt by anything I didn't say.

See Them through God's Eyes

NikolaTesla is the scientist who invented the method of generating electricity that is called "alternating current." Many scientists regard him as an even greater genius than the more widely recognized Alexander Graham Bell.

Tesla had an unusual habit. During thunderstorms, he would sit on a black mohair couch by the window and applaud each lightning strike. It was as though one genius was recognizing and appreciating the work of another! Tesla knew better than anyone the wonder of lightning because he had spent years researching electricity.

For thousands of years, lightning was feared and avoided. There was nothing in lightning strikes that would lead one to conclude that a similar power might be generated and harnessed and that such a power might be used for good purposes.

Rather than applauding the workmanship of God in others, we too often are critical, unloving, and even fearful. What a difference it makes when we see others—fellow students, teachers, parents, and friends—as bearers of God's grace, love, and goodness![4]

○ ○ ○ ○

There is nothing in a caterpillar that tells you it's going to be a butterfly.

Today, I will look for God's workmanship in . . .

——————————————————.
——————————————————.
——————————————————.
——————————————————.
——————————————————.
——————————————————.
——————————————————.
——————————————————.
——————————————————.
——————————————————.
——————————————————.
——————————————————.
——————————————————.

The LORD seeth not as man seeth; for man looketh on the outward appearance, but the LORD looketh on the heart.

I SAMUEL 16:7

Practice Believing Impossible Things

What impossible thing do I need to believe?

. _____

. _____

. _____

. _____

. _____

. _____

. _____

. _____

. _____

. _____

. _____

. _____

. _____

. _____

In Lewis Carroll's famous book, *Through the Looking Glass,* he presents a conversation between Alice and the queen:

"I can't believe that!" said Alice.

"Can't you?" the queen said in a pitying tone. "Try again, draw a long breath, and shut your eyes."

Alice laughed. "There's no use trying," she said. "One can't believe impossible things."

"I daresay you haven't had much practice," said the queen. "When I was your age, I always did it for half an hour a day. Why, sometimes I've believed as many as six impossible things before breakfast."

One of the things we must recognize is that most of the inventions and major achievements of the past century have been rooted in what was once considered to be impossible.

Can a person fly? Can a machine process information faster than someone can write? Can a human walk on the moon? Can a person's voice and picture be sent around the world without that person moving an inch? Can you become the person you truly would LIKE to be? It's not impossible![5]

o o o o

Expect great things from God.
Attempt great things for God.

"The things which are impossible with men are possible with God."

LUKE 18:27

Whom do I need to "get back at" with a kind gesture?

_____ .

_____ .

_____ .

_____ .

_____ .

_____ .

_____ .

_____ .

_____ .

_____ .

_____ .

_____ .

_____ .

_____ .

One day a boy at summer camp received a box of cookies from his mother. He ate a few, then placed the box under his bed. The next day, he discovered the cookies were gone. Later, a counselor who had been told of the theft saw a boy sitting behind a tree eating the stolen cookies. He sought out the victim and said, "Bill, I know who stole your cookies. Will you help me teach him a lesson?"

The boy replied, "Well, I guess—but aren't you going to punish him?"

The counselor said, "Not directly—that would only make him hate you. I have an idea. But first I want you to ask your mother to send some more cookies." The boy did as the counselor asked, and a few days later, another box of cookies arrived.

The counselor then said, "The boy who stole your cookies is by the lake. I suggest you go down there and share your cookies with him."

The boy protested, "But he's the one who stole the first ones from me!"

"I know," said the counselor. "Let's see what happens."

An hour later, the counselor saw the boys come up the hill—the thief earnestly trying to get his new friend to accept his compass in payment for the stolen cookies, and the victim just as adamantly refusing, saying a few old cookies didn't matter all that much!

Often the best way to "get back at someone" is to show that person God's love. You can usually make a friend in the process.

○ ○ ○ ○ ○

The safe and sure way to destroy an enemy is to make him or her your friend.

If thine enemy hunger, feed him; if he thirst, give him drink: for in so doing thou shalt heap coals of fire on his head.

ROMANS 12:20

Let Good Replace Evil

What can I learn from these two people?

· _____
· _____
· _____
· _____
· _____
· _____
· _____
· _____
· _____
· _____
· _____
· _____
· _____
· _____

Velazquez Polk and Janet Kuzmaak both grew up in Portland, Oregon, but the two couldn't have been more different. Polk was a tough street kid who joined a gang at age ten and was eventually arrested for selling drugs.

Kuzmaak was an honor-roll student from an upper-class neighborhood. In 1980, Kuzmaak's sister was raped and strangled to death. Authorities never found her killer. She came to regard every criminal as her sister's murderer.

Kuzmaak eventually became a nurse at a major medical center. Polk, released from jail in 1990, was given a job as her surgical aide. Kuzmaak was furious. She didn't believe in rehabilitation for criminals. But she noticed that when Polk's gang-member friends tried to entice him to rejoin their ranks, he refused. He told Kuzmaak he wanted to flee his old life and join a program to become a nurse's aide. She remembered that her sister had once befriended a man on parole, so she lobbied the hospital to pay Polk's tuition while she continued to monitor him.

Today, she and Polk are great friends. She helped him gain entrance into a world he did not know existed. He helped sweep away the bitterness that had once poisoned her heart.

Change and growth are always possible if you first turn away from evil and are determined not to return.

○ ○ ○ ○ ○

Be not overcome of evil, but overcome evil with good.

ROMANS 12:21

Evil can never be undone, but only purged and redeemed.

In *A Closer Walk*, Catherine Marshall writes:

One morning last week He gave me an assignment: for one day I was to go on a "fast" from criticism. I was not to criticize anybody about anything. For the first half of the day, I simply felt a void, almost as if I had been wiped out as a person. This was especially true at lunch . . . I listened to the others and kept silent. . . . In our talkative family no one seemed to notice. Bemused, I noticed that my comments were not missed. The federal government, the judicial system, and the institutional church could apparently get along fine without my penetrating observations. But still I didn't see what this fast on criticism was accomplishing—until mid-afternoon. That afternoon, a specific, positive vision for this life was dropped into my mind with God's unmistakable hallmark on it—joy! Ideas began to flow in a way I had not experienced in years. Now it was apparent what the Lord wanted me to see. My critical nature had not corrected a single one of the multitudinous things I found fault with. What it had done was to stifle my own creativity.

Before you are tempted to criticize someone, examine your own life. While you may not commit the same act or have the same habit you're about to criticize, you probably have some behavior that *could* be criticized. Don't stifle your creativity with criticism!

o o o o o

*Man who beef too much
find himself in stew.*

Today, instead of eing critical, I will . . .

_____.

_____.

_____.

_____.

_____.

_____.

_____.

_____.

_____.

_____.

_____.

_____.

_____.

_____.

_____.

_____.

_____.

Think about the things that are good and worthy of praise. Think about the things that are true and honorable and right and pure and beautiful and respected.

PHILIPPIANS 4:8 NCV

Shoot for the Moon

What is the first step of faith toward the dream in my heart?

_____

_____

_____

_____

_____

_____

_____

_____

_____

_____

_____

_____

_____

_____

A young man who was confused about his future and was in a quandary as to which direction to take with his life sat in a park watching squirrels scamper among the trees. Suddenly, a squirrel jumped from one high tree to another. It appeared to be aiming for a limb so far out of reach that the leap looked like suicide. As the young man had anticipated, the squirrel missed its mark, but it landed, safe and unconcerned, on a branch several feet lower. Then it climbed to its goal, and all was well.

An old man sitting on the other end of the bench remarked, "Funny, I've seen hundreds of 'em jump like that, especially when there are dogs all around and they can't come down to the ground. A lot of 'em miss, but I've never seen any hurt in trying." Then he chuckled and added, "I guess they've got to risk it if they don't want to spend their whole lives in one tree."

The young man thought, _A squirrel takes a chance. Do I have less nerve than a squirrel?_ He made up his mind in that moment to take the risk he had been thinking about. Sure enough, he landed safely, in a position higher than he had even dared to imagine.

What dream are you aiming for? Does it seem out of reach? Take a leap of faith. God will always catch you if you fall.

o o o o

Do not fear, for I am with you, do not be afraid, for I am your God; I will strengthen you, I will help you, I will uphold you with my victorious right hand.

ISAIAH 41:10 NRSV

Shoot for the moon. Even if you miss it, you will land among the stars.

Do the Common Things Well

What common thing can I do uncommonly well today?

Helping the deaf to communicate was Alexander Graham Bell's motivation for his life's work, perhaps because his mother and wife were both deaf. "If I can make a deaf-mute talk," Bell said, "I can make metal talk." For five frustrating and impoverished years, he experimented with a variety of materials in an effort to make a metal disk that, vibrating in response to sound, could reproduce those sounds and send them over an electrified wire.

During a visit to Washington, DC, he called on Joseph Henry, a scientist who was a pioneer in research related to electricity. He presented his ideas to him and asked his advice: should he let someone else perfect the telephone, or should he do it himself? Henry encouraged him to do it himself, to which Bell complained that he lacked the necessary knowledge of electricity. Henry's brief solution was, "Get it."

So Bell studied electricity. A year later when he obtained a patent for the telephone, the officials in the patent office credited him with knowing more about electricity than all the other inventors of his day combined.

Hard work. Study. Hope. Persistence. These are all "common things." They are the keys, however, to doing uncommonly well.

o o o o o

The secret of success is to do the common things uncommonly well.

Seest thou a man diligent in his business? he shall stand before kings; he shall not stand before mean men.

PROVERBS 22:29

Whom Are You Trying to Impress?

What need am I trying to meet by impressing others?

. _____

. _____

. _____

. _____

. _____

. _____

. _____

. _____

. _____

. _____

. _____

. _____

. _____

. _____

. _____

. _____

Guy de Maupassant's "The Necklace" is the story of a young woman, Mathilde, who desires desperately to be accepted into high society. One day her husband, an ordinary man, is given an invitation to an elegant ball. Mathilde borrows a necklace from a wealthy friend to wear to the occasion. During the course of the evening, she receives many compliments from the aristocracy present. Unfortunately, later that night, she realizes she has lost the necklace.

In order to restore the lost jewelry, Mathilde's husband borrows thirty-six thousand francs, tapping every resource available to him. A look-alike necklace is created, and Mathilde gives it to her friend without telling her what had happened.

For ten years the couple slaves to pay back the borrowed francs, each of them working two jobs. They are forced to sell their home and live in a slum. One day after the debt has finally been paid, Mathilde runs into her well-to-do friend. She confesses that the necklace she returned is not the one she borrowed, and she learns that the necklace loaned to her had been made from fake gemstones! The borrowed necklace had been worth less than five hundred francs.

Trying to "keep up appearances" almost always leads to "falling flat on your face."

○ ○ ○ ○

> "They do all their deeds
> to be noticed by men."
>
> MATTHEW 23:5 NASB

Definition of status: Buying something you don't need with money you don't have to impress people you don't like.

Let's Go!

A man once took his three-year-old daughter to an amusement park. It was her first visit to such a place, and she was in awe at the sights and sounds. But the most thrilling part to her was the whirl and whiz of the rides. She begged her dad to let her ride one particular ride, even though it was considered the "scariest" ride for kids her age.

As she whipped around the corners in her kiddy car, she suddenly wrinkled up her face and let loose a terrified cry. Her father, who was riding in the car with her, struggled to get her attention. With a big smile, he shouted over the roar of the ride, "This is fun!" When the little girl saw that he was not terrified, she began to laugh. The new experience that was initially terrifying had suddenly become enjoyable. In fact, she insisted on riding the same ride three more times!

What a comfort it is to know that our Heavenly Father will not only ride the new rides in life with us, but also will never be scared by the future! He has good things planned for us. When we look into the future from our perspective, we may become frightened. But when we look at the future from God's perspective, we are far more likely to shout, "Let's go! Isn't this going to be fun?"

○ ○ ○ ○ ○

I like the dreams of the future better than the history of the past.

What fear is keeping me from enjoying God's plan?

Remember ye not the former things, neither consider the things of old. Behold, I will do a new thing.

ISAIAH 43:18-19

Keep at It

What hard work does my dream require?

_____
_____
_____
_____
_____
_____
_____
_____
_____
_____
_____
_____
_____
_____

How long will you lie down, O sluggard?
When will you arise from your sleep?

PROVERBS 6:9 NASB

One day in the fall of 1894, Guglielmo retreated to his room on the third floor of his parent's home. He had just spent his entire summer vacation reading books and filling notebooks with squiggly diagrams. Now the time had come to *work*.

He rose early every morning. He worked all day and long into the night, to the point that his mother became alarmed. He had never been a robust person, but now he was appallingly thin. His face was drawn, and his eyes were often glazed over with fatigue.

Finally the day came when he announced his instruments were ready. He invited the family to his room, and pushing a button, he succeeded in ringing a bell on the first floor! While his mother was amazed, his father was not. He saw no use in being able to send a signal so short a distance. So Guglielmo labored on. Little by little, he made changes in his invention so that he could send a signal from one hill to the next and then beyond the hill. Eventually his invention was perfected, partly by inspiration, but mostly by perseverance.

Guglielmo Marconi eventually was hailed as the inventor of wireless telegraphy—the forerunner of the radio. He not only received a Nobel Prize in physics for his efforts, but also a seat in the Italian senate and many honorary degrees and titles.

You can accomplish anything you set your heart on by combining your vision with hard work.

○ ○ ○ ○ ○

The way to get to the top is to get off your bottom.

Work as if for Yourself and God

Joe Smith was a loyal carpenter who worked almost two decades for a successful contractor. The contractor called him into his office one day and said, "Joe, I'm putting you in charge of the next house we build. I want you to order all the materials and oversee the job from the ground up."

Joe accepted the assignment with great enthusiasm. He studied the blueprints and checked every measurement and specification. Suddenly, he had a thought. *If I'm really in charge, why couldn't I cut a few corners, use less expensive materials, and put the extra money in my pocket? Who will know? Once the house is painted, it will look great.*

So Joe set about his scheme. He ordered second-grade lumber and inexpensive concrete, put in cheap wiring, and cut every corner he could. When the home was finished, the contractor came to see it.

"What a fine job you've done!" he said. "You've been such a faithful carpenter to me all these years that I've decided to show you my gratitude by giving you a gift—this house."

Build well today. You will have to live with the character and reputation you construct.

o o o o o

*You are only what you are
when no one is looking.*

What improvements
can I make to the building
of my life?

_____

_____

_____

_____

_____

_____

_____

_____

_____

_____

_____

_____

_____

_____

_____

Serve wholeheartedly, as if you
were serving the Lord, not men, because
you know that the Lord will reward
everyone for whatever good he does.

EPHESIANS 6:7-8 NIV

The Six Most Important Things

The six most important things I will do today are . . .

- _____
- _____
- _____
- _____
- _____
- _____
- _____
- _____
- _____
- _____
- _____
- _____
- _____
- _____
- _____
- _____

Charles Schwab, one of the first presidents of Bethlehem Steel Company, once told efficiency expert Ivy Lee, "If you can give us something to pep us up to do the things we ought to do, I'll gladly pay you anything you ask within reason."

"Fine," Lee said, "I can give you something in twenty minutes that will step up your 'doing' by at least 50 percent." He then handed Schwab a piece of paper and said, "Write down the six most important tasks you have to do tomorrow, and number them in the order of their importance." Then Lee said, "Now put this paper in your pocket, and first thing tomorrow morning, look at item one and start working on it until it is finished. Then tackle item two in the same way; then item three and so on. Do this until quitting time. . . . Do this every working day. After you've convinced yourself of the value of this system, have your men try it . . . and then send me a check for what you think it is worth."

A few weeks later Schwab sent Lee a check for $25,000, calling his advice the most profitable lesson he had ever learned. In just five years, Lee's plan was largely responsible for turning Bethlehem Steel Company into the biggest independent steel producer in the world.[6]

○ ○ ○ ○

Precept must be upon precept, precept upon precept, Line upon line, line upon line, Here a little, there a little.

ISAIAH 28:10 NKJV

Success in life is a matter, not so much of talent or opportunity, as of concentration and perseverance.

Plan B

What can I do to develop the flexibility I need?

In the 1984 Olympics, heavyweight boxer Henry Tillman planned out a very careful strategy. He decided he would fight defensively, simply warding off his opponent's blows until he saw an opening for a strike of his own. Minutes into the fight, it became obvious to Tillman that his opponent had planned the same strategy! After the bell sounded, ending the first round, Tillman stepped back, dropped his hands, and mentally shifted gears. He recognized that his initial game plan might not work, but he had come prepared with a second plan. He switched to a take-the-offensive mode of fighting, won the match, and ultimately won a gold medal.

Figure skater Kristi Yamaguchi also had a "plan B" for her Olympic bid. Originally, she had planned to perform her most difficult jump—three revolutions in the air and a graceful single-skate landing known as the triple salchow. A slight stumble in the early portion of her routine led her to make a change. She cut the triple salchow to a double, regained her balance, caught up with her music, and then went on to perform another triple jump—the lutz.[2]

No matter how much we rehearse or plan, things don't always go as we desire. True champions are those who are prepared to adapt if necessary and switch to what works.[7]

o o o o

We cannot direct the wind,
but we can adjust the sails.

Be ready at all times.
2 TIMOTHY 4:2 NCV

Always Do Your Best

What determines the quality of my performance?

_____
_____
_____
_____
_____
_____
_____
_____
_____
_____
_____
_____
_____
_____
_____

Long ago, a band of minstrels lived in a faraway land. They traveled from town to town, singing and playing their music in hopes of making a living. But they had not been doing well financially. Times were hard, and the common people had little money to spend on concerts, even though their fee was small.

The group met one evening to discuss their plight. "I see no reason for opening tonight," one said. "It's snowing, and no one will come out on a night like this."

Another said, "I agree. Last night we performed for just a handful. Even fewer will come tonight."

The leader of the troupe responded, "I know you are discouraged. I am too. But we have a responsibility to those who might come. We will go on, and we will do the best job of which we are capable. It is not the fault of those who come that others do not. They should not be punished with less than our best."

Heartened by his words, the minstrels gave their best performance ever. After the show, the old man called his troupe to him again. In his hand was a note, given to him by one of the audience members just before the doors closed behind him. Slowly the man read, "Thank you for a beautiful performance." It was signed simply, "Your king."

Everything you do is performed before your King—the King of kings. Are all of your words and deeds worthy of His audience?

o o o o o

Daniel was preferred above the presidents and princes, because an excellent spirit was in him.

DANIEL 6:3

Every job is a self-portrait of the person who does it. Autograph your work with excellence.

Give with Both Hands

For years Arthur Blessit has carried a six-by-ten-foot, eighty-pound cross on his shoulders through towns and cities around the world. "It blows people's minds," he says. Once he has gained people's attention, he finds he has a unique opportunity to share the Gospel.

Blessit first became well known for preaching to the hippies of Hollywood's Sunset Strip. He gained national attention when he undertook a cross-carrying journey—along with four members of his rock group, the Eternal Rush—to Washington, DC. The thirty-five-hundred-mile trip took seven months to complete.

As the group traveled, they held rallies. Blessit urged fellow Christians to meet him at the Washington Monument at the end of his trip—but not with empty hands. "Christians need to come and give something," he preached. He asked that people bring or send two gifts for the nation's needy, gifts given openly with "both hands." Those who went to the capital to meet him found a third oppor-tunity to give. This gift was to be made with an open heart and an open vein—at a blood-mobile parked on the site.

While the Gospel message is free to all who will receive it, the giving of the Gospel costs, and continues to cost, a great deal!

○ ○ ○ ○ ○

He who bestows his goods upon the poor, Shall have as much again, and ten times more.

HOW can I share God's love both in word and in deed?

_____

_____

_____

_____

_____

_____

_____

_____

_____

_____

_____

_____

_____

_____

_____

_____

You shall remember the LORD your God, for it is He who gives you power to get wealth, that He may establish His covenant.

DEUTERONMY 8:18 NKJV

Learn to Be a Thinker

HOW have I taken my education for granted?

_____

_____

_____

_____

_____

_____

_____

_____

_____

_____

_____

_____

_____

_____

_____

At Princeton, Woodrow Wilson was first a teacher and later the president of the university. Although he was popular with the students, he did have a reputation for cracking down on students who were not serious in their pursuit of an education.

The mother of one young man who was expelled for cheating made a trip to Princeton to talk with Wilson. She pleaded with him to reinstate her son because of the possible adverse reaction his expulsion would have on her own health and reputation. She told him of an impending operation and said she felt certain she would die if her son were not readmitted. Wilson heard her pleas and then responded, taking a very tough stance, "Madam, you force me to say a hard thing. If I had to choose between your life or my life or anybody's life and the good of this college, I should choose the good of the college."

Failure to study and to apply oneself fully to one's studies is a form of rebellion. The same holds for cheating. Do your best in school. Don't blame a teacher for being too hard on you when the blame actually lies in your being too easy on yourself. Learn to be a thinker!

○ ○ ○ ○

You can lead a boy to college, but you cannot make him think.

It is senseless to pay tuition to educate a rebel who has no heart for truth.

PROVERBS 17:16 TLB

Christlike Living

In an extensive opinion survey, *The Day America Told the Truth,* James Patterson and Peter Kim reported some startling findings:

Only 13 percent saw all Ten Commandments as binding and relevant.

Ninety-one percent lied regularly, both at work and home.

Most workers admitted to goofing off an average of seven hours a week.

About half of the workforce admitted they regularly called in sick even when they were healthy.

When they were asked what they would be willing to do for ten million dollars, 25 percent said they would abandon their families, 23 percent would be prostitutes for a week, and 7 percent would murder a stranger!

Lest you conclude that the people they surveyed were all ungodly criminals, two other statisticians, Doug Sherman and William Hendricks, found that Christians were almost as likely as unbelievers to do such things as steal from the workplace, falsify their income tax, and selectively obey laws.

To truly claim to be a Christian, a person must do far more than go to church occasionally. He or she must strive to be Christlike 24 hours a day, 365 days a year, in all situations and all circumstances.

o o o o

If a man cannot be a Christian in the place where he is, he cannot be a Christian anywhere.

HOW would a stranger know I was a Christian?

_____ .

_____ .

_____ .

_____ .

_____ .

_____ .

_____ .

_____ .

_____ .

_____ .

_____ .

_____ .

_____ .

_____ .

_____ .

Provide things honest in the sight of all men.

ROMANS 12:17

Have Thine Own Way Lord

God is wanting to have His way in me by . . .

_____

_____

_____

_____

_____

_____

_____

_____

_____

_____

_____

_____

_____

_____

"After this manner therefore pray ye. . . . Thy kingdom come. Thy will be done in earth, as it is in heaven."

MATTHEW 6:9-10

During a prayer meeting one night, an elderly woman pleaded, "It really doesn't matter what You do with us, Lord, just have Your way with our lives." Adelaide Pollard, a rather well-known itinerant Bible teacher, overheard her prayer. At the time, she was deeply discouraged because she had been unable to raise the money she needed to go to Africa for missionary service. She was moved by this woman's sincere request of God, and when she went home that evening, she meditated on Jeremiah 18:3-4:

> Then I went down to the potter's house, and behold, he wrought a work on the wheel, and the vessel that he made of clay was marred in the hand of the potter; so he made it again another vessel, as seemed good to the potter to make it.

Before retiring, Adelaide took pen in hand and wrote in hymn form her own prayer:

"Have Thine own way, Lord! Have Thine own way! Thou art the potter, I am the clay. Mold me and make me after Thy will, while I am waiting, yielded and still.

"Have Thine own way, Lord! Have Thine own way! Search me, and try me, Master, today! Whiter than snow, Lord, wash me just now, as in Thy presence humbly I bow."

The best way to discover the purpose for your life and how to do it is to give your whole life to God. Then he can fulfill His plan for you.

○ ○ ○ ○

Don't ask God for what you think is good; ask Him for what He thinks is good for you.

In 1970, Wally started baking chocolate chip cookies for his friends using a recipe and procedure that had been passed down from his Aunt Della. For five years he gave away every batch he made, even though people often told him that his cookies were so good that he should go into business and sell them. Wally had other ideas though. He was determined to become a big-time show-business manager.

Then one day a friend, B.J. Gilmore, told him that she had a friend who could put up the money for a cookie-making business. Her friend never made the investment, but Wally got some of his own friends—including Jeff Wall, Helen Reddy, and Marvin Gaye—to put up some money. Then Wally was off and running.

Originally, he intended to open up only one store on Sunset Boulevard, just enough to "make a living." After all, his was the only store in the world dedicated to the sale of nothing but chocolate chip cookies. But business grew virtually overnight. Wally's "Famous Amos Chocolate Chip Cookies" were soon distributed worldwide. Wally himself became a spokesman for other products, from eggs to airlines to a telephone company. While he once dreamed of managing stars, he now is one in his own right!

Sometimes dreams come through the back door. Keep it unlocked!

○ ○ ○ ○ ○

Opportunities are seldom labeled.

What can I do to develop the gifts others observe in me?

_____.
_____.
_____.
_____.
_____.
_____.
_____.
_____.
_____.
_____.
_____.
_____.
_____.
_____.
_____.

In his heart a man plans his course, but the LORD determines his steps.

PROVERBS 16:9 NIV

Don't Delay

What am I tempted to put off that God wants me to do?

. _____
. _____
. _____
. _____
. _____
. _____
. _____
. _____
. _____
. _____
. _____
. _____
. _____
. _____
. _____

An old legend recounts how Satan once called three of his top aides to a special meeting so that they might devise a plan to stop the effectiveness of a particular group of Christians. One of the aides, Resentment, proposed, "We should convince them there is no God."

Satan sneered at Resentment and replied, "That would never work. They know there's a God."

Bitterness then spoke up. "We'll convince them that God does not really care about right or wrong."

Satan thought about the idea for a few moments but then rejected it. "Too many know that God does care," he finally said.

Malice then proposed his idea. "We'll let them go on thinking there is a God and that He cares about right and wrong. But we will keep whispering that there is no hurry, there is no hurry, there is no hurry."

Satan howled with delight! The plan was adopted, and Malice was promoted to an even higher position in Satan's malevolent hierarchy.

Who can tell how many souls have been lost or lives sorely wounded because someone has held to the commonly acceptable notion: *Delay is okay.*

o o o o

Don't put it off. Do it now.
Don't rest until you do.

PROVERBS 6:4 TLB

*The wise does at once
what the fool does at last.*

Passionate Enthusiasm

After years of working in Rome on life-size sculptures, Michelangelo went to Florence, where a large block of splendid white Carrara marble had been obtained for a colossal statue. Within weeks, he had signed an agreement to complete a rendition of David for the cathedral. Contract in hand, he started in at once, working with a furious energy so great that he often slept in his clothes, resenting the time it took to take them off and put them on again. He faultlessly examined and precisely measured the marble to see what pose it could accommodate. He made sketches of possible attitudes and careful, detailed drawings from models. He tested his ideas in wax on a small scale. When he was finally satisfied with his design, only then did he pick up a chisel and mallet.

Michelangelo approached painting the ceiling of the Sistine Chapel with the same intensity. He took only a month to develop the theme, then launched with a fury into the final design—building scaffolding and hiring helpers. Lying at uncomfortable angles on hard boards, breathing the suffocating air just under the vault—plaster dust inflaming his eyes and irritating his skin—he spent much of the next four years literally sweating in physical distress as he worked.

May you do your work with the same passionate enthusiasm!

o o o o o

Nothing great was ever achieved without enthusiasm.

I need an infusion of God's passion to . . .

_____
_____
_____
_____
_____
_____
_____
_____
_____
_____
_____
_____
_____
_____
_____
_____

Never be lacking in zeal, but keep your spiritual fervor, serving the Lord.

ROMANS 12:11 NIV

God Never Disappoints

Is there any reason why I <u>wouldn't</u> trust God with my future?

. _____

. _____

. _____

. _____

. _____

. _____

. _____

. _____

. _____

. _____

. _____

. _____

. _____

. _____

. _____

The Scriptures tell us that no one who believes in Christ will ever be disappointed.

ROMANS 10:11 TLB

Marian had her sights set on becoming a concert singer—a challenge that was doubly difficult because of the color of her skin. Her mother, however, had a patient trust in God. Marian later said, "Mother's religion made her believe that she would receive what was right for her to have if she was conscientious in her faith. If it did not come, it was because He had not considered it right for her. We grew in this atmosphere of faith that she created. . . . We believed as she did because we wanted the same kind of haven in the time of storm."

When Marian was denied admission to a famous music conservatory because of her race, her mother calmly said, "Someone would be raised up" to help her accomplish what she had hoped to do at the conservatory. That someone arrived only a few weeks later. One of Philadelphia's most outstanding voice teachers, Guiseppe Boghetti, made room for her to become one of his students.

Marian Anderson was on her way to becoming one of the most magnificent singers of the twentieth century. On Easter Sunday in 1939, she sang for more than 75,000 people gathered in front of the Lincoln Memorial and gave a performance never forgotten by those who were there. Trusting her future to God, she accomplished more than she could have dreamed.

Regardless of the opposition you encounter in reaching your dream, always remember that God is on your side.

○ ○ ○ ○ ○

Trust in yourself, and you are doomed to disappointment; but trust in God, and you are never to be confounded in time or eternity.

Take the First Step

What will I do today to make my tomorrow better?

During the late 1960s, a couple was vacationing in the California mountains one day, and they noticed a pleasant-looking young man sitting by a bridge near their hotel. Day after day they saw him sitting in that same spot. At first they assumed he was fishing, but after taking a closer look, they realized he was doing nothing—just sitting and staring into space. Finally, on the last day of their vacation, they couldn't stand it anymore. They just had to ask: "Why do you sit in that one spot all day, every day?"

He replied with a smile, "I happen to believe in reincarnation. I believe that I have lived many times before and that I will have many lives following this one. So this life I'm sitting out."

In reality, it's impossible for any of us to "sit out" life. Each day, we are either moving forward or backward, getting stronger or weaker, moving higher or lower. Each of us begins every new day with a fresh opportunity to change tomorrow's "starting point."

You only have one chance at life, so make it count.

○ ○ ○ ○ ○

Don't be discouraged; people who got where they are, started where they were.

Leave behind your foolishness and begin to live; learn how to be wise.

PROVERBS 9:6 TLB

What are the areas in which I need to mature?

. _____
. _____
. _____
. _____
. _____
. _____
. _____
. _____
. _____
. _____
. _____
. _____
. _____
. _____
. _____

A number of definitions of maturity have been offered by experts, but these are perhaps among the best understood by the average person:

- Maturity is when you not only want to have a puppy to call your own, but you remember on your own to give it food and water every day.
- Maturity is when you not only know how to dress yourself, but you remember to put your dirty clothes in the laundry hamper after you've taken them off.
- Maturity is when you not only are capable of using a telephone to call a friend, but you know how to keep your calls short so others can have access to the phone.
- Maturity is when you not only are old enough to stay at home alone, but you can be trusted to stay at home and even have friends over.
- Maturity is when you are not only old enough to drive the car by yourself, but you pay for the gasoline you use.
- Maturity is when you are not only old enough to stay up late, but you are wise enough to go to bed early.

The more you learn to accept responsibility for your life, the more you will grow in maturity. With greater responsibility and maturity come greater privileges.

o o o o

Our greatest wish and prayer is that you will become mature Christians.

2 CORINTHIANS 13:9 TLB

Maturity doesn't come with age; it comes with acceptance of responsibility.

Get Back Up

The difference between success and failure is often the ability to get up just one more time than you fall down!

Moses easily could have given up. He had an "interrupted" childhood and lived with a foster family. He also had a strong temper, a stammering tongue, and a criminal record, but when God called to him, Moses ultimately said yes.

Joshua had seen the Promised Land and believed they could conquer their enemies and possess the land. Yet he was forced to wander in the wilderness for forty years with cowards who didn't believe. He could have given up in discouragement, but he was willing to go when God said to go.

Peter had a hard time making the transition from fisherman to fisher *of* men. He sank while trying to walk on water, was strongly rebuked by Jesus for trying to tell Him what to do, and denied knowing Jesus in that hour when Jesus needed him most. He easily could have seen himself as a hopeless failure. But when the opportunity came to preach the Gospel before thousands on the Day of Pentecost, he rose to the occasion.

No matter what you've done, what mistakes you may have made, what errors you may have committed, you're not a failure until you lie down and quit.

○ ○ ○ ○ ○

HOW can I increase my courage to go on when I feel like quitting?

The man who wins may have been counted out several times, but he didn't hear the referee.

Though a righteous man falls seven times, he rises again.
PROVERBS 24:16 NIV

Make the Most of Your Situation

HOW can I develop a more positive outlook on life?

. _____

. _____

. _____

. _____

. _____

. _____

. _____

. _____

. _____

. _____

. _____

. _____

. _____

. _____

A story is told of identical twins. One was a hope-filled optimist who often said, "Everything is coming up roses!" The other was a sad and hopeless pessimist who continually expected the worst to happen. The concerned parents of the twins brought them to a psychologist in hopes he might be able to help them balance their personalities.

The psychologist suggested that on the twins' next birthday, the parents put them in separate rooms to open their gifts. "Give the pessimist the best toys you can afford," the psychologist said, "and give the optimist a box of manure." The parents did as he said.

When they peeked in on the pessimistic twin, they heard him complaining, "I don't like the color of this toy. I'll bet this toy will break! I don't like to play this game. I know someone who has a bigger toy than this!"

Tiptoeing across the corridor, the parents peeked in and saw their optimistic son gleefully throwing manure up in the air. He was giggling as he said, "You can't fool me! Where there's this much manure, there's gotta be a pony!"

o o o o

The happiest people don't necessarily have the best of everything. They just make the best of everything.

I have learned to be content in whatever circumstances I am.

PHILIPPIANS 4:11 NASB

Look for Examples

Famous World War II general, George S. Patton Jr., was an avid reader and student of history. He wrote to his son in 1944: "To be a successful soldier, you must know history. Read it objectively. . . . In Sicily I decided as a result of my information, observations, and a sixth sense that I have that the enemy did not have another large scale attack in his system. I bet my shirt on that, and I was right." His sixth sense may very well have been formed by thousands of hours of reading history, biographies, and autobiographies.

Historical parallels were constantly on Patton's mind. When he observed the situation in Normandy on July 2, 1944, he immediately wrote Eisenhower that the German Schlieffen Plan of 1914 could be applied. A month later, an operation such as he had described brought about the German defeat in Normandy.

The book that perhaps influenced Patton most was Ardant du Picque's *Battle Studies*. Patton used it to help solve the problem of getting infantry to advance through enemy artillery fire. He recommended it to Eisenhower: "First read *Battle Studies* by du Pique (you can get a copy at Leavenworth) then put your mind to a solution."

Most of the successful men in the world are avid readers, especially of biographies. If you are interested in being a success in life, immerse yourself in the life stories of successful people. You will learn from their mistakes and failures as well as their successes and triumphs.

o o o o o

Learn by experience— preferably other people's.

Who are the people I'd most like to learn about and why?

_____.

_____.

_____.

_____.

_____.

_____.

_____.

_____.

_____.

_____.

_____.

_____.

_____.

_____.

_____.

_____.

All these things happened to them as examples—as object lessons to us—to warn us against doing the same things.

I CORINTHIANS 10:11 TLB

Develop "Won't" Power

What is my plan of escape when temptation rises?

_____

_____

_____

_____

_____

_____

_____

_____

_____

_____

_____

_____

_____

_____

In *Sin, Sex and Self-Control,* Norman Vincent Peale writes:

Martha took the kids away to the mountains for a month, so I was a summer bachelor. And about midway through that month I met a girl, a beautiful girl looking for excitement. She made it clear that I had a green light . . . so for one weekend I put my conscience in mothballs and arranged a meeting with her for Saturday night.

I woke up early Saturday morning with a bit of a hangover; I'd played poker until late the night before. I decided to get up, put on my swimming trunks, and take a walk on the beach to clear my head. I took an ax along, because the wreck of an old barge had come ashore down the beach, and there was a lot of tangled rope that was worth salvaging. . . . There was something about the freshness of the morning and the feel of the ax that made me want to keep on swinging it. So I began to chop in earnest.

I felt as if I were outside myself, looking at myself through a kind of fog that was gradually clearing. And suddenly I knew that what I had been planning for that evening was so wrong, so out of key with my standards and my loyalties and the innermost me that it was out of the question.

Have you exercised your "won't" power lately?

◦ ◦ ◦ ◦ ◦

Run from anything that stimulates youthful lust. Follow anything that makes you want to do right.

2 TIMOTHY 2:22 NLT

Many men have too much willpower. It's "won't" power they lack.

Can You Look Yourself in the Eye?

When you get what you want in your
struggle for self,

    And the world makes you king for a day,
    Just go to a mirror and look at yourself,
    And see what that man has to say.

    For it isn't your father or mother or
        wife,
    Whose judgment upon you must pass;
    The fellow whose verdict counts most in
        your life,
    Is the one staring back from the glass.

    Some people may think you are a
        straight-shooting chum,
    And call you a wonderful guy,
    But the man in the glass says you're only
        a bum,
    If you can't look him straight in the eye.

    He's the fellow to please, never mind all
        the rest,
    For he's with you clear up to the end,
    And you have passed your most danger-
        ous, difficult test,
    If the man in the glass is your friend.

    You may fool the whole world down
        your pathway of years,
    And get pats on the back as you pass,
    But your final reward will be heartache
        and tears,
    If you've cheated the man in the glass.

        —Anonymous

Learn to conquer yourself by developing
your self-control, and you'll be able to look
yourself straight in the eye and know you've
done your best.

o o o o o

Conquer yourself rather than the world.

Is there anything keeping me
from looking myself in the eye?

———————————————.
———————————————.
———————————————.
———————————————.
———————————————.
———————————————.
———————————————.
———————————————.
———————————————.
———————————————.
———————————————.
———————————————.
———————————————.
———————————————.
———————————————.

A man's conscience is the Lord's searchlight
exposing his hidden motives.

PROVERBS 20:27 TLB

What do I believe is my part in the body of Christ?

._____

._____

._____

._____

._____

._____

._____

._____

._____

._____

._____

._____

._____

._____

._____

Jewish physician Boris Kornfeld was imprisoned in Siberia. There he worked in surgery, helping both the staff and prisoners. He met a Christian whose name is unknown but whose quiet faith and frequent reciting of the Lord's Prayer had an impact on Dr. Kornfeld.

One day while repairing the slashed artery of a guard, Dr. Kornfeld seriously considered suturing the artery in such a way that the guard would slowly die of internal bleeding. The violence he recognized in his own heart appalled him, and he found himself saying, "Forgive us our sins as we forgive those who sin against us." Afterward, he began to refuse to obey various inhumane, immoral, prison-camp rules. He knew his quiet rebellion put his life in danger.

One afternoon, he examined a patient who had undergone an operation to remove cancer. He saw in the man's eyes a depth of spiritual misery that moved him with compassion, and he told him his entire story, including a confession of his secret faith. That very night, Dr. Kornfeld was murdered as he slept. But his testimony was not in vain. The patient who had heard his confession became a Christian as a result. He survived the prison camp and went on to tell the world about life in the gulag. That patient was Aleksandr Solzhenitsyn, who became one of the leading Russian writers of the twentieth century. He revealed to the world the horrors of the prison camps and perils of Russian communism.

One person can truly make a difference. There is something you can do, and only you can do it. God created you with a destiny.

o o o o o

Under [Christ's] direction the whole body is fitted together perfectly, and each part in its own special way helps the other parts.

EPHESIANS 4:16 TLB

I am only one; but still I am one. I cannot do everything, but still I can do something; I will not refuse to do the something I can do.

Manners Matter

In 1865, after General Ulysses S. Grant had moved his occupying army into Shiloh, he ordered a seven-o'clock curfew for the city. One distinguished Southern lady, a Mrs. Johnson, was seen walking near the army's downtown headquarters near the curfew time.

General Grant approached her and said, "Mrs. Johnson, it's a little dangerous out there. I am going to ask two of my officers to escort you home."

She replied determinedly, "I won't go."

Grant smiled, went back into his headquarters, and returned in a few minutes wearing an overcoat that covered his insignia and rank, and therefore the fact that he was a Northerner.

"May I walk with you, Mrs. Johnson?" he asked.

"Why, yes," Mrs. Johnson replied, nearly blushing. "I'm always glad to have a gentleman as an escort."

Mrs. Johnson would walk with a man she saw as a *gentleman,* even though she would not walk with a Union solider. Good manners and genuine politeness go a long way toward "covering" many of our faults, mistakes, and differences.

○ ○ ○ ○ ○

Politeness goes far, yet costs nothing.

HOW do I rate in the art of being courteous?

A kind man benefits himself.

PROVERBS 11:17 NIV

Be a Friend

HOW can I be a better friend?

. _____
. _____
. _____
. _____
. _____
. _____
. _____
. _____
. _____
. _____
. _____
. _____
. _____
. _____
. _____

President Harry Truman had a reputation for having never been sly or disloyal in his life. He stood by a friend even when he risked public ridicule for it.

One of Truman's friends from his army days was Jim Pendergast, whose uncle Tom was the head of the Democratic Party in Kansas City. Jim and his dad urged Truman to run for office—a judgeship in rural Jackson County. A year later Truman did so, and with Pendergast's support, he won the election. As judge, he didn't always agree with Pendergast's practices. Tom once said to a group of contractors who had asked him to influence Truman, "I told you he was the hardheadedest, orneriest man in the world; there isn't anything I can do."

Unfortunately, Pendergast's penchant for horse races caused him to be investigated for income-tax evasion. He confessed, was fined, and was sentenced to serve fifteen months in a federal penitentiary. When Pendergast died during Truman's vice-presidency, Truman didn't hesitate to fly to Kansas City for the funeral. "He was always my friend," Truman said of him, "and I have always been his."

True friendship is not based on what a friend does for you but on what he or she means to you.

o o o o

We should behave to our friends as we would wish our friends to behave to us.

"As ye would that men should do to you, do ye also to them likewise."

LUKE 6:31

A Friend Is a Friend at All Times

In *Lessons from Mom,* Joan Aho Ryan writes the following about loyalty in friendship:

We went to one of the local shopping malls recently where Mom ran into two women who live in her development. . . . They greeted her effusively. It was a brief exchange, during which she introduced me, and they were on their way. "What phony baloney," she said when they were well ahead of us. Since her remark came from nowhere, I asked her what she meant.

With obvious disdain, she explained that she has sat under the canopy at her pool on several occasions with these two women and one of their friends, Sylvia. One day, she said, she sat nearby and heard the three of them talking about the wedding reception of Sylvia's daughter the week before. They raved about the food, the flowers, the elegant country club location, the beautiful bride. . . . Mom said Sylvia was obviously beaming with pride.

"Well, then Sylvia left, and you should have heard them," Mom said. . . . "I couldn't believe friends could be that two-faced. They ripped her apart, talking about how cheap she was, her homely son-in-law, the music they couldn't dance to. It was awful. And they call themselves friends," she clucked. "Who needs friends like that?"

Speaking well of others is not only a good way to acquire friends but to keep them.

○ ○ ○ ○

Who ceases to be a friend,
never was one.

What kind of friend am I behind others' backs?

"'These people honor me with their lips, but their hearts are far from me.'"

MARK 7:6 NIV

Don't Let Failures Keep You Down

What are my responses to mistakes, failure, and rejection?

_____

_____

_____

_____

_____

_____

_____

_____

_____

_____

_____

_____

_____

_____

_____

Did you fall down the first time you tried to walk? Most likely. Did you feel as if you were drowning the first time you ventured into deep water? Probably. Did you hit the ball the first time you swung a bat? Probably not.

R.H. Macy failed seven times before his store in New York became popular.

English novelist John Creasey received 753 rejection slips prior to publishing 564 books.

Babe Ruth struck out 1,330 times, yet he is best known for hitting 714 home runs.[8]

Michael Jordan didn't make the cut for his high-school basketball team when he was a sophomore. He cried over his failure but then tried harder. The next year he made the team and never looked back.[9]

One salesman noted that he made one sale for about every ten "cold calls" he made. Each sale averaged about $1,000. Rather than be discouraged when he was turned down, he'd simply say, "Well, I just made $100." He saw himself as one-tenth closer to a commission.

Don't expect _never_ to fail. Expect occasional failure, learn from it, and move a little closer to your goal.

o o o o

Failure is the halfway mark on the road to success.

Rejoice not against me, O mine enemy: when I fall, I shall arise.

MICAH 7:8

Break Free from Limitations

As a senior in high school, Jim averaged a .427 at bat and led his team in home runs. He also quarterbacked his football team to the state semifinals. Jim later went on to pitch professionally for the New York Yankees.

That's a remarkable achievement for any athlete. But it's an almost unbelievable one for Jim, who was born without a right hand.

A little boy who had only parts of two fingers on one of his hands once came to Jim in the clubhouse after a Yankees game and said, "They call me 'Crab' at camp. Did kids ever tease you?"

"Yeah," Jim replied. "Kids used to tell me that my hand looked like a foot." And then he asked the boy an all-important question: "Is there anything you can't do?" The boy answered no.

"Well, I don't think so either," Jim responded.

Today, what others see as a limitation is only a limitation if *you* think it is. God certainly doesn't see you as limited—He sees you as having unlimited potential. When we begin to see ourselves the way God sees us, there are no records that we can't break!

o o o o o

Adversity causes some men to break, others to break records.

What can I do to succeed in spite of my limitations?

_____ .
_____ .
_____ .
_____ .
_____ .
_____ .
_____ .
_____ .
_____ .
_____ .
_____ .
_____ .
_____ .
_____ .
_____ .

I can do everything with the help of Christ who gives me the strength I need.

PHILIPPIANS 4:13 NLT

Keep Your Promises

When tempted to break my word, I will . . .

_____

_____

_____

_____

_____

_____

_____

_____

_____

_____

_____

_____

_____

_____

The former president of Baylor University, Rufus C. Burleson, once told the following to an audience:

How often I have heard my father paint in glowing words the honesty of his old friend Colonel Ben Sherrod. When he was threatened with bankruptcy and destitution in old age and was staggering under a debt of $850,000, a contemptible lawyer told him, "Colonel Sherrod, you are hopelessly ruined, but if you will furnish me $5,000 as a witness fee, I can pick a technical flaw in the whole thing and get you out of it."

The grand old Alabamian said, "Your proposition is insulting. I signed the notes in good faith, and the last dollar shall be paid if charity digs my grave and buys my shroud." [My father] carried me and my brother Richard once especially to see that incorruptible old man, and his face and words are imprinted upon my heart and brain.

People will remember you for your kept promises and your honesty, especially when you could have profited from not telling the truth. The character of your word is your greatest asset, and honesty is your best virtue.

○ ○ ○ ○

> Who may worship in your sanctuary, LORD? . . . Those who . . . keep their promises even when it hurts.
>
> PSALM 15:1,4 NLT

Integrity is the first step to true greatness.

Being a Leader

In 1643, a young shoemaker's apprentice went to Leicestershire, England, for a business fair. While there, a cousin invited him to share a jug of beer with him and another friend in the pub where they had gone to eat. Being thirsty, he joined them.

After each of the men had drunk a glass apiece, the man's cousin and friend began to drink to the health of first this one and then the other. They agreed that the person who didn't join in with their toasts would have to pay for the jug. This shocked the serious shoemaker's apprentice. He rose from the table, took out a coin, and said simply, "If it be so, I will leave you."

At that, he left the pub and spent much of the night walking up and down the streets of the city, praying and crying to the Lord. The Lord spoke to him these words as recorded in his journal: "Thou seest how young people go together into vanity and old people into the earth. Thou must forsake all—young and old—keep out of all, and be as a stranger unto all." In obedience to this command, the young man left his relations and his home and became a wanderer in England. His name? George Fox, the founder of the Quakers.

If you want to be a leader in life, you will reach a day when you will have to turn your back on people who want to waste their lives. Turn, instead, toward those who will be a positive influence in your life, and turn most of all to the One who will always lead you— your Father God.

○ ○ ○ ○ ○

Learn to say "No"; it will be of more use to you than to be able to read Latin.

Do I need to change whom I'm following?

_____ .

_____ .

_____ .

_____ .

_____ .

_____ .

_____ .

_____ .

_____ .

_____ .

_____ .

_____ .

_____ .

_____ .

_____ .

Just say a simple yes or no, so that you will not sin.

JAMES 5:12 TLB

HOW can I make sure my words and actions are consistent?

—————————————————————
—————————————————————
—————————————————————
—————————————————————
—————————————————————
—————————————————————
—————————————————————
—————————————————————
—————————————————————
—————————————————————
—————————————————————
—————————————————————
—————————————————————
—————————————————————
—————————————————————

When Teddy Roosevelt was asked to give a speech to the Naval War College in Newport, Rhode Island, on June 2, 1897, his theme was "readiness." He insisted the only way to keep peace was to be ready for war, and the only way to be ready for war was to enlarge the navy. It was a rousing, patriotic speech. The following February, the *Maine* was blown up, killing 264 sailors, and Americans across the land cried, "Remember the *Maine!*" In April, President McKinley asked Congress to declare war.

For obvious reasons, Americans were not surprised that Roosevelt backed the war effort. Most Americans *were* surprised, however, when Teddy Roosevelt resigned from his position as assistant secretary of the navy, three weeks after the war declaration, so that he'd be ready to fight. His friends told him he was crazy for throwing away his political future. His wife was against it. Yet all who knew Roosevelt well, knew that their protests were in vain, even as they made them. He had to join the effort. He later wrote that he wanted to be able to tell his children why he had fought in the war not why he hadn't fought in it. As far as he was concerned, a person simply couldn't preach one thing and then do another.

That kind of attitude is what will separate you from the pack and cause you to be a great man or woman in life. When your actions line up with your words, a tremendous reputation will follow.

o o o o o

Many a man claims to have unfailing love, but a faithful man who can find?

PROVERBS 20:6 NIV

Men are alike in their promises. It is only in their deeds that they differ.

Staying Cool

During the four-week siege of Tientsin, during the Boxer Rebellion of June 1900, Herbert Hoover helped erect barricades around the foreign compound and organized all the able-bodied men into a protective force to man them. Mrs. Hoover went to work, too, helping set up a hospital, taking her turn nursing the wounded, rationing food, and serving tea every afternoon to those on sentry duty. Like her husband, she remained calm and efficient throughout the crisis and even seemed to enjoy the excitement.

One afternoon, while sitting at home playing solitaire to relax after her work at the hospital, a shell suddenly burst nearby. She ran to the back door and discovered a big hole in the backyard. A little later, a second shell hit the road in front of the house. Then came a third shell. This one burst through one of the windows of the house and demolished a post by the staircase.

Several reporters covering the siege rushed into the living room to see if she was all right and found her calmly seated at the card table. "I don't seem to be winning this hand," she remarked coolly, "but that was the third shell and therefore the last one for the present anyway. Their pattern is three in a row." Then she suggested brightly, "Let's go and have tea."

If you think about it, you will realize most of the things you worry about never happen. Instead of worrying, relax and use your mental energy for more important things.

o o o o o

Peace is not the absence of conflict from life, but the ability to cope with it.

HOW can I keep cool and not be moved?

_____.
_____.
_____.
_____.
_____.
_____.
_____.
_____.
_____.
_____.
_____.
_____.
_____.
_____.
_____.

I have set the LORD always before me: because he is at my right hand, I shall not be moved.

PSALM 16:8

Ready Obedience

HOW quick am I to obey?

_____

_____

_____

_____

_____

_____

_____

_____

_____

_____

_____

_____

_____

_____

The story is told of a great military captain who, after a full day of battle, sat by a warming fire with several of his officers and began talking over the events of the day.

He asked them, "Who did the best today on the field of battle?"

One officer told of a man who had fought bravely all day and then just before dusk had been severely wounded. Another told of a man who had taken a hit for a fellow soldier, sparing his friend's life but possibly losing his own. Yet another told of the man who had led the charge into battle. Still another told of a solider who had risked his life to pull a fellow soldier into a trench.

The captain heard them out and then said, "No, I fear you are all mistaken. The best man in the field today was the soldier who was just lifting up his arm to strike the enemy, but, upon hearing the trumpet sound the retreat, checked himself, dropped his arm without striking the blow, and retreated. That perfect and ready obedience to the will of his general is the noblest thing that was done today on the battlefield."

That's the kind of obedience God desires from us—immediate and complete.

○ ○ ○ ○ ○

The wise in heart accept commands, but a chattering fool comes to ruin.

PROVERBS 10:8 NIV

Obedience is not servitude of man to man, but submission to the will of God who governs through the medium of men.

In 1877, George Eastman dreamed that the wonderful world of photography might be accessible to the average person. At the time, photographers working outdoors had to carry multiple pieces of bulky equipment and a corrosive agent called silver nitrate. Eastman theorized that if he could eliminate most of this equipment, he could make his dream a reality.

Working in a bank by day, he spent his nights reading books on chemistry and magazines about photography. He took foreign language lessons so he could read information published in France and Germany. Then with a partner, he began his own company in 1881. Almost immediately, a problem arose with the new "dry plates" he had invented. Eastman refunded the money to those who had purchased them and returned to his lab. Three months and 472 experiments later, he came up with the durable emulsion for which he had searched!

Eastman spent many nights sleeping in a hammock at his factory after long days designing equipment. To replace the glass used for photographic plates, he created a roll of thin, flexible material now known as film. To replace heavy tripods, he developed a pocket camera. By 1895, photography was at last available to the "common man."

George Eastman's long-term vision kept him motivated even when 471 experiments failed. Keeping your ultimate dream in mind, set short, attainable goals, and before you even know it, your vision will become a reality!

o o o o o

You must have long-range goals to keep you from being frustrated by short-range failures.

What short, attainable goals can I set?

Let us fix our eyes on Jesus, the author and perfecter of our faith, who for the joy set before him endured the cross, scorning its shame, and sat down at the right hand of the throne of God.
HEBREWS 12:2 NIV

Believe in Your Dream

What is hindering me from believing in my dream?

. _____
. _____
. _____
. _____
. _____
. _____
. _____
. _____
. _____
. _____
. _____
. _____
. _____
. _____

"Anything is possible if you have faith."

MARK 9:23 TLB

Grace Hopper was born with a desire to discover how things worked. At age seven, her curiosity led her to dismantle every clock in her childhood home! When she grew up, she eventually completed a doctorate in mathematics at Yale University. During World War II, Grace joined the navy and was assigned to the navy's computation project at Harvard University. There she met "Harvard Mark I," the first fully functional, digital computing machine. Once again, Grace set about to learn how something worked.

Unlike the clocks in her childhood home, however, "Harvard Mark I" was composed of 750,000 parts and 500 miles of wire! While most experts believed computers were too complicated and expensive for anyone but highly trained scientists to use, Grace had her own idea. Her goal was to make them easier to operate, so more people could use them. Her work gave rise to the programming language COBOL.

As late as 1963, each large computer had its own unique master language. Grace became an advocate for a universally accepted language. She had the audacity to envision a day when computers would be small enough to sit on a desk, more powerful than Harvard Mark I, and useful in offices, schools, and at home. At the age of seventy-nine, she retired from the navy with a rank of rear admiral. But more important to her, she had lived to see her dream of personal computers come true!

Believe in your dreams. With God, all things are possible.

o o o o o

The future belongs to those who believe in the beauty of their dreams.

Look for Possibilities

Eniac was one of the first computers to use electronic circuits, which made for lightning-fast calculations. At first, Thomas J. Watson Jr., the former chairman of IBM, saw no use for it. He said, "I reacted to Eniac the way some people probably reacted to the Wright brothers' airplane. It didn't move me at all. . . . I couldn't see this gigantic, costly, unreliable device as a piece of business equipment."

A few weeks later, he and his father wandered into a research office at IBM and saw an engineer with a high-speed punch-card machine hooked up to a black box. When asked what he was doing, he said, "Multiplying with radio tubes." The machine was tabulating a payroll at one-tenth the time it took the standard punch-card machine to do so. Watson recalls, "That impressed me as though somebody had hit me on the head with a hammer." He said, "Dad, we should put this thing on the market! Even if we only sell eight or ten, we'll be able to advertise the fact that we have the world's first commercial electronic calculator."

That's how IBM got into electronics. Within a year, they had electronic circuits that both multiplied and divided, and at that point, electronic calculators became truly useful. Thousands of the IBM 604 were sold.

What wasn't yet obvious to Thomas Watson was obvious to the engineer working in the research department. Always keep your eyes and ears open; you never know what you might discover. Look for the possibilities around you.

o o o o o

The future belongs to those who see possibilities before they become obvious.

What ordinary things could be seeds of greatness in my life?

The vision is yet for an appointed time . . . it will surely come, it will not tarry.

HABAKKUK 2:3

Don't Give Up; Work Harder

What price am I willing to pay to turn my failures into successes?

_____

_____

_____

_____

_____

_____

_____

_____

_____

_____

_____

_____

_____

He becometh poor that dealeth with a slack hand: but the hand of the diligent maketh rich.

PROVERBS 10:4

Early in the 1989 basketball season, Michigan faced Wisconsin. With just seconds left in the fourth quarter, Michigan's Rumeal Robinson found himself at the foul line. His team was trailing by one point, and he knew that if he could sink both shots, Michigan would win. Sadly, Rumeal missed both shots. Wisconsin upset the favored Michigan, and Rumeal went to the locker room feeling devastated and embarrassed.

His dejection, however, spurred him into action and ignited his determination. He decided that at the end of each practice for the rest of the season, he was going to shoot one hundred extra foul shots. Shoot 'em he did!

The moment came when Rumeal stepped to the foul line in yet another game, again with the opportunity to make two shots. This time, there were only three seconds left in overtime, and the game was the NCAA finals! _Swish_ went the first shot! And _swish_ went the second. Those two points gave Michigan the victory and the Collegiate National Championship for the season.

Have you just failed at something? Don't give up. Instead, work harder. Success is possible!

o o o o

When I was a young man, I observed that nine out of ten things I did were failures. I didn't want to be a failure, so I did ten times more work.

Dig for the Facts

Ted Turner is one of the conspicuous personalities of the twentieth century. He turned Channel 17 in Atlanta into the first "Super Station," transmitting its signal to cable systems nationwide via satellite. Soon after, he purchased the Atlanta Braves baseball team and the Atlanta Hawks basketball team. In 1980, he originated CNN, the world's first live, 'round-the-clock, all-news television network. He organized the Inaugural Goodwill Olympic Games in Moscow, has won numerous awards, and has held national and world sailing titles.

About making choices and decisions, Ted has given this advice: "There is a saying, 'Be sure of your information, then go ahead.' My father was the first one who pointed this out to me.... Get all the information you can, along with the advice and counsel of people you think are wise. This is a prerequisite for success in the long haul. You should not make decisions until you have complete knowledge about things. [When] you have to form opinions without as much information as you should have, or without firsthand knowledge ... don't hold hard and fast opinions. When new information becomes available, you should be able to change your mind."

That is wise advice. Jumped-to conclusions are usually based on speculation—not truth. The person who comes out on top is going to be the one who not only knows all the facts, but, most importantly, knows the truth.

o o o o o

Jumping to conclusions is not half as good an exercise as digging for facts.

How can I get all the facts and counsel I need to ensure my next project is a success?

Study to shew thyself approved unto God, a workman that needeth not to be ashamed, rightly dividing the word of truth.

2 TIMOTHY 2:15

If You Don't Have Anything to Say, Don't Talk!

Could I improve on only stating words of value?

_____

_____

_____

_____

_____

_____

_____

_____

_____

_____

_____

_____

_____

_____

_____

Albert Einstein is reputed to have had a wholesome disregard for the tyranny of custom. One evening, the president of Swarthmore College hosted a dinner held in Einstein's honor. Although he was not scheduled to speak during the event—only to receive an award—after the award was given, the audience clamored, "Speech, speech!" The president turned the podium over to him. Einstein reluctantly came forward and said only this: "Ladies and gentlemen, I am very sorry, but I have nothing to say." And then he sat down.

A few seconds later, he stood back up and said, "In case I do have something to say, I'll come back."

Some six months later, Einstein wired the president of the college with this message: "Now I have something to say."

Another dinner was held, and this time, Einstein made a speech.

If you have nothing to say, it's wise to say nothing. If you do have something to say, it's wise to say it in as few words as possible. As the old saying goes, "If your mind should go blank, don't forget to turn off the sound."

o o o o

The most valuable of all talents is that of never using two words when one will do.

In the multitude of words there wanteth not sin: but he that refraineth his lips is wise.

PROVERBS 10:19

A Lesson from the Lobster

Henry Ward Beecher, one of the most powerful preachers in American history, gave this illustration in one of his sermons:

The lobster, when left high and dry among the rocks, has no sense and energy enough to work his way back to the sea, but waits for the sea to come to him. If it does not come, he remains where he is, and dies, although the slightest exertion would enable him to reach the waves, which are perhaps tossing and tumbling within a yard of him.

There is a tide in human affairs that casts men into "tight places," and leaves them there, like stranded lobsters. If they choose to lie where the breakers have flung them, expecting some grand billow to take them on its big shoulders and carry them to smooth water, the chances are that their hopes will never be realized.

Laziness is doing nothing, hoping nothing, being nothing. Patience, on the other hand, doesn't mean not doing anything. It means working on in hope that what you're waiting for will eventually come to pass, but you will continue to work on, even if it doesn't.

o o o o o

Don't loaf away your time and depend on the Lord for your daily bread; He isn't running a bakery.

What is my responsibility, and what is God's?

Work hard and become a leader; be lazy and never succeed.

PROVERBS 12:24 TLB

Be Careful What You Promise

How can I apply the principles of reliability and wisdom to my life?

_____

_____

_____

_____

_____

_____

_____

_____

_____

_____

_____

_____

_____

_____

_____

A man who had been quite successful in the manufacturing business decided to retire. He called in his son to tell him of his decision, saying, "Son, it's all yours as of the first of next month."

The son, while eager to take over the firm and exert his own brand of leadership, also realized what a big responsibility he was facing. "I'd be grateful for any words of advice you have to give me," he said to his father.

The father advised, "Well, I've made a success of this business because of two principles: reliability and wisdom. First, take reliability. If you promise goods by the tenth of the month, no matter what happens, you must deliver by the tenth. Your customers won't understand any delay. They'll see a delay as failure. So even if it costs you overtime, double time, or golden time, you must deliver on your promise."

The son mulled this over for a few moments and then asked, "And wisdom?"

The father shot back: "Wisdom is never making such a stupid promise in the first place."

Carefully weigh your ability to back up your words with evidence, and be sure you can deliver on a promise before you make it. A large part of your reputation is your ability to keep your word.

o o o o o

Seest thou a man that is hasty in his words? there is more hope of a fool than of him.

PROVERBS 29:20

One-half the trouble of this life can be traced to saying "yes" too quickly, and not saying "no" soon enough.

The Courage to Speak Out

When Honorious was emperor of Rome, the great Coliseum was often filled to overflowing with spectators who came from near and far to watch the state-sponsored games. Part of the sport consisted of human beings doing battle with wild beasts or one another—to the death. The assembled multitudes made holiday of such sport and found the greatest delight when a human being died.

One such day, a Syrian monk named Telemachus was part of the vast crowd in the arena. Telemachus was cut to the core by the utter disregard he saw for the value of human life. He leaped from the spectator stands into the arena during a gladiatorial show and cried out, "This thing is not right! This thing must stop!"

Because he had interfered, the authorities commanded that Telemachus be run through with a sword, which was done. He died but not in vain. His cry kindled a small flame in the nearly burned-out conscience of the people, and within a matter of months, the gladiatorial combats came to an end.

The greater the wrong, the louder we must cry out against it. The finer the cause, the louder we must applaud.

o o o o o

I would rather fail in the cause that someday will triumph than triumph in a cause that someday will fail.

Is there a cause about which I cannot keep silent?

_____.
_____.
_____.
_____.
_____.
_____.
_____.
_____.
_____.
_____.
_____.
_____.
_____.

I eagerly expect and hope that I will in no way be ashamed but will have sufficient courage so that now as always Christ will be exalted in my body, whether by life or death.
PHILIPPIANS 1:20 NIV

Leave a Lasting Impression

HOW can I leave a lasting impression of God's love on others?

_____

_____

_____

_____

_____

_____

_____

_____

_____

_____

_____

_____

_____

_____

_____

When Salvation Army officer Shaw saw the three men before him, tears sprang to his eyes. Shaw was a medical missionary who had just arrived in India. He had been assigned to a leper colony the Salvation Army was taking over. The three men before him had manacles and fetters binding their hands and feet. Their bonds were painfully cutting into their diseased flesh. Captain Shaw turned to the guard and said, "Please unfasten the chains."

"It isn't safe," the guard protested. "These men are dangerous criminals as well as lepers!"

"I'll be responsible," Captain Shaw said. "They are suffering enough." He then reached out, took the keys, knelt, tenderly removed the shackles from the men, and treated their bleeding ankles and wrists.

About two weeks later, Shaw had to make an overnight trip. He dreaded leaving his wife and child alone. The words of the guard came back to him, and he was concerned about the safety of his family. When Shaw's wife went to the front door the morning she was alone, she was startled to see the three criminals lying on her steps. One of them explained, "We know the doctor go. We stay here all night so no harm come to you."

Even dangerous people are capable of responding to an act of love! Touched lives are the most important monuments you can leave. When you treat people with that kind of love, you are impressing your name upon their hearts.

The only letter I need is you yourselves! . . . They can see that you are a letter from Christ, written by us. . . . not one carved on stone, but in human hearts.

2 CORINTHIANS 3:2-3 TLB

o o o o

Carve your name on hearts and not on marble.

Plant Seeds from God's Book

A Bible—carefully read and well worn—was the most important book in Gerrit's house. His home was a house of prayer, where many tears were shed in intercession for revival in his church in Heemstede. Almost a generation later, his prayers were answered as that very church became the center of an upsurge of faith in Holland—part of the Great Awakening in Europe.

When she was about eighteen years old, Gerrit's great-granddaughter had a dream about him. He was walking through a beautiful park with her, and he said, "When you sow some seed and put it in the ground, this seed will make a plant, and this plant will give seed again. . . . You, my dear Corrie, are the daughter of my grandson. . . . You are a plant, blooming from my seed. I will show you something that will never be changed. It is the Word of God." In the dream, he opened his Bible and said, "This book will be the same forever." He then told her, "Plant the seeds from God's Book, and they will grow from generation to generation."

Corrie ten Boom did just that. She planted God's Word in hearts and minds around the world. Information learned in textbooks is continually updated, and courses of study change. But the truths of the Bible are absolutes. Its promises are sure. Plant its seeds in your heart.

o o o o o

A knowledge of the Bible without a college course is more valuable than a college course without the Bible.

Where can I plant seeds of God's Word today?

_____.
_____.
_____.
_____.
_____.
_____.
_____.
_____.
_____.
_____.
_____.
_____.
_____.
_____.
_____.

All scripture is given by inspiration of God, and is profitable for doctrine, for reproof, for correction, for instruction in righteousness: That the man of God may be perfect, thoroughly furnished unto all good works.

2 TIMOTHY 3:16-17

He Will Walk with You

What is the first step I need to take to conquer my problems?

_____

_____

_____

_____

_____

_____

_____

_____

_____

_____

_____

_____

_____

A young reporter once interviewed a successful businessman. The reporter asked the man to give him a detailed history of his company. As the man talked at length, the reporter began to be amazed at the enormity of the many problems the man had overcome. He finally asked him, "But how did you overcome so many problems of such great magnitude?"

The old gentleman leaned back in his chair and said, "There's really no trick to it." Then he added, "You know . . . there are some troubles that seem so high you can't climb over them." The reporter nodded in agreement, thinking of several he was currently facing. "And," the wise businessman went on, "there are some troubles so wide you can't walk around them." Again, the reporter nodded. The man went on, raising his voice dramatically, "And there are some problems so deep you can't dig under them." Eager for a solution, the reporter said, "Yes? Yes?"

"It's then," the man concluded, "that you know the only way to beat the problem is to duck your head and wade right through it."

A problem rarely will decrease in size if you merely stand and stare at it. But when you diligently pursue a solution, your problem is guaranteed to shrink.

o O o O o

When you pass through the waters, I will be with you; and through the rivers, they shall not overwhelm you; when you walk through fire you shall not be burned, and the flame shall not consume you.

ISAIAH 43:2 NRSV

A problem is an opportunity to prove God.

Keep Going

American sports fans watched in awe on Sunday, March 4, 1979, as Phil took to the giant-slalom slopes at Whiteface Mountain, New York. He exploded onto the course and then settled into a powerful carving of the mountainside. Nonetheless, at gate thirty-five, tragedy struck. Phil hooked his inside ski on a pole, went flying head over heels, and crashed in a crumpled heap. The ski team physician described the injury as "the ultimate broken ankle"—a break of both the ankle and lower leg. He had to put the bones back together with a three-inch metal plate and seven screws.

The question was, not whether Phil would ever ski again, but if he would ever walk again. Looking back, Phil describes the months after his injury as a time of deep despair. Still, he never entertained doubts about walking or skiing.

After two months on crutches and a highly disciplined exercise program, he forced himself to walk without limping. In August, he began skiing gentle slopes. Less than six months after the accident, he entered a race in Australia and finished second. In February of 1980, less than a year after his agonizing injury, Phil Mahre took on the same mountain where he had fallen and won an Olympic silver medal.

When defeat and despair threaten to overtake you and squash your dreams, keep on going. Eventually, you will overtake defeat with victory and despair with joy!

o o o o o

Never despair; but if you do,
work on, in despair.

What are the primary obstacles in my life that I will trust God to help me overcome?

_____.
_____.
_____.
_____.
_____.
_____.
_____.
_____.
_____.
_____.
_____.
_____.
_____.
_____.
_____.
_____.
_____.

As for you, be strong and do not give up, for your work will be rewarded.

2 CHRONICLES 15:7 NIV

HOW can I learn to hear God's voice?

The Lord appeared to a man named Ananias in a vision and asked him to undertake what Ananias must surely have perceived as a dangerous mission. He directed him to go to the house of a man named Judas, lay his hands on a man named Saul of Tarsus, and pray that he might receive his sight. Saul had been blinded while traveling to Damascus to persecute the Christians there, having the full intent of taking them captive to Jerusalem for trial, torture, and death. Even so, Ananias did as the Lord asked him, and within the hour, Saul's sight was restored.

According to Christian legend, Ananias was a simple cobbler who had no idea what happened to Saul after that day or how he had changed the course of human history by obeying God in a simple act that was part of Saul's transformation into the apostle Paul. As he lay on his deathbed, Ananias looked up toward Heaven and whispered, "I haven't done much, Lord: a few shoes sewn, a few sandals stitched. But what more could be expected of a poor cobbler?"

The Lord spoke in Ananias's heart, "Don't worry, Ananias, about how much you have accomplished—or how little. You were there in the hour I needed you, and that is all that matters."

Being in the right place at the right time, even if it's only for one hour, can give you the opportunity to change history. In order to be there, you must simply listen and obey.

○ ○ ○ ○ ○

Thine ears shall hear a word behind thee, saying, This is the way, walk ye in it, when ye turn to the right hand, and when ye turn to the left.

ISAIAH 30:21

You can accomplish more in one hour with God than one lifetime without Him.

Stand Firm in Your Faith

Former President Harry S Truman once remarked that no president of our nation has ever escaped abuse and even libel from the press. He noted that it was far more common than rare to find a president publicly called a traitor. Truman further concluded that the president who had not fought with Congress or the Supreme Court hadn't done his job.

What is true for an American president is also true for everyone else. No matter how small people's jobs may be—no matter how low they may be on a particular organizational chart or strata of society—there will be others who oppose them, ridicule them, and perhaps even challenge them to a fight. That is why people cannot expect to conduct themselves as if they were trying to win a popularity contest. Rather, people need to chart the courses they feel compelled to walk in life, and then they need to do so with heads held high and their convictions intact. It's simply a matter of taking life in stride and recognizing that all people will eventually face the test of ridicule and criticism as they uphold their principles or defend their morals.

It's inevitable that you will be criticized or attacked sometime in your life. But collapsing from *fear* of an attack isn't inevitable. Stand firm in your faith, and the Lord will stand with you!

o o o o o

What will I do in the face of criticism or ridicule?

_____ .
_____ .
_____ .
_____ .
_____ .
_____ .
_____ .
_____ .
_____ .
_____ .
_____ .
_____ .
_____ .
_____ .
_____ .
_____ .
_____ .

If you don't stand for something, you'll fall for anything!

If you do not stand firm in your faith, you will not stand at all.

ISAIAH 7:9 NIV

Be Extraordinary

What ordinary task can I do extraordinarily well today?

_____
_____
_____
_____
_____
_____
_____
_____
_____
_____
_____
_____
_____
_____
_____

Country-music star Randy Travis and his manager, Lib, remember the lean days of his career—all 3,650 of them. For ten years, Lib did whatever it took to keep her club open long enough for somebody to discover Travis's talent. For his part, Randy sang his heart out, and when he wasn't singing, he fried catfish or washed dishes in the kitchen. Then it happened. Everything seemed to click for him. He had a hit called "On the Other Hand," an album contract, a tour offer, and a movie deal. He was hot! Everyone seemed to be calling him an overnight success.

Travis notes, "We were turned down more than once by every label in Nashville. But I'm kind of one to believe that if you work at something long enough and keep believing, sooner or later it will happen."

In many instances in life, it's extra effort that makes the difference. Cleaning your room may be one of your chores, but doing it joyfully and without having to be asked will make it a blessing. A thoughtful gesture for another person can turn an otherwise dull day into a day worth celebrating. Money can buy a present, but a loving note to accompany it can make it a gift that touches the heart. Do more than is required of you today. Give the extra that makes life truly extraordinary.

o o o o

Whatever work you do, do your best.
ECCLESIASTES 9:10 NCV

The difference between ordinary and extraordinary is that little extra.

Take the Risk and Experience Life

Two baseball coaches were commiserating about the difficulty of recruiting quality players for their teams. Said one coach, "If only I could find a man who plays every position perfectly, always gets a hit, never strikes out, and never makes a fielding error."

The other coach sighed in agreement and added, "Yeah, if we could just get him to lay down his hot dog and come down out of the stands."

Playing life's game to the fullest requires taking risks. Without risk, life has little emotion—little that can be counted as exhilarating or fulfilling.

To laugh is to risk appearing the fool.
To weep is to risk appearing sentimental.
To reach out to another is to risk
    involvement.
To expose feelings is to risk exposing
    one's true self.
To place ideas and dreams before a
    crowd is to risk ridicule.
To love is to risk not being loved in
    return.
To live is to risk dying.
To hope is to risk despair.
To try is to risk failure.

Yet the person who risks nothing does nothing, has nothing, and ultimately becomes nothing. Don't be afraid to go for it. Get down out of the stands, and play ball!

o o o o o

You cannot discover new oceans unless you have the courage to lose sight of the shore.

What risks do I need to be willing to take?

Peter got out of the boat, and walked on the water and came toward Jesus.

MATTHEW 14:29 NASB

Ask God to Open Your Eyes

What resources has God placed right in front of me?

_____

_____

_____

_____

_____

_____

_____

_____

_____

_____

_____

_____

_____

_____

_____

_____

_____

Many years ago in South Africa, a man sold his farm so that he might spend his days in search of diamonds. He was consumed with dreams of becoming wealthy. When he had finally exhausted his resources and his health and was no closer to his fortune than the day he sold his farm, he threw himself into a river and drowned.

One day, the man who had bought his farm spotted an unusual-looking stone in a creek bed. He placed it on his fireplace mantle as a conversation piece. A visitor noticed the stone and examined it closely. He then voiced his suspicion that the stone was actually a diamond. The discreet farmer had the stone analyzed, and sure enough, it was one of the largest and finest diamonds ever found.

Still operating with great secrecy, the farmer searched his stream, gathering similar stones. They were all diamonds. In fact, his farm was covered with diamonds just waiting to be picked up! The farm the diamond-seeker had sold turned out to be one of the richest diamond deposits in the world.

The lessons of wisdom can often be learned in the relationships and experiences we encounter every day. Ask God to reveal to you what you need to know in order to live the life He desires. The resources you need are probably right in front of you.

o o o o

I pray that your hearts will be flooded with light so that you can see something of the future he has called you to share.

EPHESIANS 1:18 TLB

As prayer is the voice of man to God, so revelation is the voice of God to man.

Hang in There

We all know the power of gravity. When we drop a hammer, it hits our toes; it never floats upward. We fall down, not up. But what many of us don't realize is that the gravitational *energy* of the whole earth has been estimated to amount to only a millionth of a horsepower! A toy magnet in the hands of a child probably has thousands of times more energy.

What gravity lacks in energy, however, it makes up in tenacity. Gravity simply refuses to let go.

Not only is gravity tenacious, but it has far-reaching effects. Gravitational pull appears to be virtually limitless, reaching across the universe with nearly unimaginable power. Gravitational pull is what keeps the moon orbiting the earth, the planets revolving around the sun, and the sun—along with a billion other stars—rotating around the center of our galaxy like a cosmic pinwheel.

You may not have a great deal of power or energy today, but as the popular phrase states, you can "hang in there."

Don't stop believing! Don't give up hope! Eventually the door will be opened.

o o o o o

Perseverance is a great element of success; if you only knock long enough and loud enough at the gate, you are sure to wake up somebody.

I refuse to let go of God's promise to . . .

_____ .
_____ .
_____ .
_____ .
_____ .
_____ .
_____ .
_____ .
_____ .
_____ .
_____ .
_____ .
_____ .
_____ .
_____ .
_____ .

"Everyone who asks and keeps on asking receives; and he who seeks and keeps on seeking finds; and to him who knocks and keeps on knocking, the door shall be opened."

LUKE 11:10 AMP

What can I do to stay focused on my goal?

. _____

. _____

. _____

. _____

. _____

. _____

. _____

. _____

. _____

. _____

. _____

. _____

. _____

. _____

. _____

In March of 1987, Eamon Coughlan was running in a qualifying heat at the World Indoor Track Championships in Indianapolis. The Irishman was the reigning world record-holder at fifteen hundred meters, and he was favored to win the race easily. Unfortunately, with two-and-a-half laps left to run, he was tripped and fell hard. Even so, he got up, and with great effort, he managed to catch the race leaders. With only twenty yards to go, he was in third place, which would have been good enough to qualify for the final race.

Then Couglan looked over his shoulder to the inside. Seeing no one there, he relaxed his effort slightly. What he hadn't noticed, however, was that a runner was charging hard on the outside. This runner passed Couglan just a yard before the finish line, thus eliminating him from the finals.

Coughlan's great comeback effort ended up being worthless for one and only one reason: he momentarily took his eyes off the finish line and focused on the would-be competitors instead.

One of the most important factors in reaching your goals in life is to have single-minded focus. Don't let yourself become distracted by what others do or say. Run your race to win!

o o o o

I press on toward the goal to win the prize for which God has called me heavenward in Christ Jesus.

PHILIPPIANS 3:14 NIV

Consider the postage stamp: its usefulness consists in the ability to stick to one thing till it gets there.

Down to Earth

What are some practical things I can do to serve others?

People often think of heart surgeons as being the arrogant prima donnas of the medical world. But those who know Dr. William DeVries, the surgeon who pioneered the artificial heart, couldn't disagree more. Coworkers at Humana Hospital Audubon in Louisville, Kentucky, describe DeVries as the kind of doctor who shows up on Sundays just to cheer up discouraged patients. He occasionally changes dressings—traditionally considered a nurse's job—and if a patient wants him to stick around and talk, he always does.

Friends say DeVries is an "old shoe" who fits in wherever he goes. He likes to wear cowboy boots with his surgical scrubs, and he often repairs hearts to the beat of Vivaldi or jazz. "He has always got a smile lurking," says Louisville cardiologist Dr. Robert Goodin, "and he's always looking for a way to let it out."

No matter how high you rise, never forget that you started out at ground zero. Even if you were born to great wealth and privilege, you still were born as a helpless babe. Real success comes, not in thinking you have arrived at a place where others should serve you, but in recognizing that in whatever place you are, you have arrived at a position where you can serve others.

○ ○ ○ ○ ○

He who takes his rank lightly raises his own dignity.

"He that is greatest among you shall be your servant."

MATTHEW 23:11

Only Speak Well of Others

I need to repent of being judgmental toward . . .

. _____
. _____
. _____
. _____
. _____
. _____
. _____
. _____
. _____
. _____
. _____
. _____
. _____
. _____

A fool's mouth is his destruction, and his lips are the snare of his soul.

PROVERBS 18:7

After several months of romance, Napoleon and Josephine decided to marry. The notary who made out the marriage contract was one of Josephine's friends. He secretly advised her against marrying "an obscure little officer who has nothing besides his uniform and sword and has no future." He thought she should find someone of greater worth. With her charms, he advised, she might attract a wealthy man, perhaps an army contractor or a business investor.

Napoleon was in the next room while the notary was giving this advice to his beloved. He could hear every word that was said. Still, he did not disclose he had overheard. Years later, however, he had his revenge.

After his coronation as Emperor, this same notary appeared before him on a matter of business. At the conclusion of their appointment, Napoleon smiled and observed that Madame de Beauharnais—now that she was queen of France—had done very well, after all, to have married that "obscure little officer who possessed nothing besides his uniform and sword and had no future."

The notary was forced to agree that Madame, indeed, had done well. As for himself, he was still a notary!

Be careful before you pass judgment on another. You're revealing something about yourself, and your words may come back to bite you.

○ ○ ○ ○ ○

A man never discloses his own character so clearly as when he describes another's.

What is the next level I want to strive for?

One day during the early 1960s, the University of Florida football team was in a practice session. They were running wind sprints for conditioning. One of the large linemen, Jack Katz, had proven himself to be the fastest lineman on the team.

Katz went to Coach Ray Graves and asked if he might be allowed to run sprints with the faster and smaller backfield players. Permission was granted.

For the next several days, Katz managed to finish last in every race with the backfield runners. Nobody was surprised. The coach went to Katz to ask if he wouldn't rather go back to winning against the other linemen, rather than losing every race against the backs.

Katz responded, "I'm not out here to outrun the linemen. I already know I can do that. I'm here to learn how to run faster; and if you've noticed, I'm losing by a little less every day."

Indeed, a lineman's job is not only to break through and scatter the line on the other team, but also to tackle its backfield players. Katz was preparing himself for his ultimate goal: real-game tackles.[10]

When you master one level, go on to the next. It is the only way to keep growing and developing your skills!

o o o o o

If you succeed in all you do, it's a sure sign you're not reaching high enough.

I do not mean that I am already as God wants me to be. I have not yet reached that goal, but I continue trying to reach it and to make it mine.

PHILIPPIANS 3:12 NCV

Let Your Work Reflect Who You Are

HOW do my actions correspond with who God created me to be?

_____
_____
_____
_____
_____
_____
_____
_____
_____
_____
_____
_____
_____
_____
_____
_____

A young man once made an appointment with a well-published author. The first question the author asked him was, "Why did you want to see me?"

The young man stammered, "Well, I'm a writer too. I was hoping you could share with me some of your secrets for successful writing."

The author asked a second question, "What have you written?"

"Nothing," the young man replied, "at least nothing that is finished yet."

The author asked a third question, "Well, if you haven't written, then tell me, what are you writing?"

The young man replied, "Well, I'm in school right now, so I'm not writing anything at present."

The author then asked a fourth question, "So why do you call yourself a writer?"

Writers write. Composers compose. Painters paint. Workmen work. What you do to a great extent defines who you are and what you become. What does your work say about you? When your work on the outside coincides with who you are on the inside, you have found your true purpose in life and will find ultimate fulfillment.

○ ○ ○ ○ ○

As in water face reflects face,
So the heart of man reflects man.

PROVERBS 27:19 NASB

Every man's work, whether it be literature, or music, or pictures, or architecture, or anything else, is always a portrait of himself.

Self-Discipline Can Help You Overcome

During a homecoming football game against rival Concordia, Augsburg College found itself losing miserably. But late in the fourth quarter, nose guard David Stevens came off the bench and sparked a fire. He initiated or assisted in two tackles, and when a Concordia player fumbled the ball, David fell on it. As he held the recovered ball high, the crowd roared. It was an unforgettable moment for Augsburg fans!

David Lee Stevens was born to a woman who had taken thalidomide, an anti-nausea drug given to many pregnant women in the early '60s that was quickly proven to cause severe birth defects. David's feet appeared where his legs should have started. Abandoned by his mother, David was adopted by a foster family. Bee and Bill Stevens imposed strict rules of behavior on David, nurtured him, and loved him. They insisted he learn to do things for himself, and they never put him in a wheel-chair. At age three, he was fitted with "legs."

In school, David became a student leader, made good grades, organized special events, and befriended new students. In high school, he not only played football but baseball, basketball, and hockey. He became a champion wrestler. When offered handicap license plates, he refused them stating simply, "Those are for people who need them. I am not 'disabled.'"

David was taught to discipline himself, and so he was able to perform, in spite of his apparent handicap. Whatever obstacle may be in your way, self-discipline can help you either rise above it or plow right through it.

o o o o o

What we do on some great occasion will probably depend on what we already are; and what we are will be the result of precious years of self-discipline.

What can I do to become more self-disciplined?

_____.
_____.
_____.
_____.
_____.
_____.
_____.
_____.
_____.
_____.
_____.
_____.
_____.
_____.

I keep under my body, and bring it into subjection.

I CORINTHIANS 9:27

Let Your Deeds Reflect Integrity

What do my actions reveal about my character?

_____

_____

_____

_____

_____

_____

_____

_____

_____

_____

_____

_____

_____

In the fourth round of a national spelling bee in Washington, eleven-year-old Rosalie Elliot, a champion from South Carolina, was asked to spell the word avowal. Her soft southern accent made it difficult for the judges to determine if she had used an a or an e as the next to last letter of the word. They deliberated for several minutes and also listened to tape-recorded playbacks, but they still couldn't determine which letter had been pronounced. Finally the chief judge, John Lloyd, put the question to the only person who knew the answer. He asked Rosalie, "Was the letter an a or an e?"

Rosalie, surrounded by whispering young spellers, knew by now the correct spelling of the word. But without hesitation, she replied that she had misspelled the word and had used an e.

As she walked from the stage, the entire audience stood and applauded her honesty and integrity, including dozens of newspaper reporters covering the event. While Rosalie had not won the contest, she had definitely come out a winner that day.

We often think that who we are determines what we do. Equally true, what you do today will determine, in part, who you become tomorrow.

○ ○ ○ ○

Even a child is known by his actions, by whether his conduct is pure and right.

PROVERBS 20:11 NIV

Our deeds determine us, as much as we determine our deeds.

Let Your Actions Reflect Your Beliefs

During the Korean War, a South Korean civilian was arrested by the communists and sentenced to execution. When the young communist leader learned that the prisoner in his charge was the head of an orphanage caring for young children, he decided to spare him. But he ordered that the man's son be executed in his place. The nineteen-year-old boy was shot in the presence of his father.

After the war, the United Nations captured the young communist leader. He was tried for his war crimes and condemned to death. But before the sentence could be carried out, the Christian whose son had been killed pleaded for the life of the killer. He argued that the communist had been young when he ordered the execution and that he really didn't know what he was doing. "Give him to me," the man requested, "and I will train him."

The United Nations forces granted the unusual request, and the father took the murderer of his son into his own home and cared for him. The young communist eventually became a Christian pastor.

For good or for bad, what we do speaks loudly.

o o o o o

What you do speaks so loud that
I cannot hear what you say.

What are my actions saying to those who have wronged me?

_____.
_____.
_____.
_____.
_____.
_____.
_____.
_____.
_____.
_____.
_____.
_____.
_____.
_____.
_____.

Show me your faith without deeds, and I will show you my faith by what I do.

JAMES 2:18 NIV

Walk Justly and Love Mercy

HOW can I treat others more justly today?

. _____
. _____
. _____
. _____
. _____
. _____
. _____
. _____
. _____
. _____
. _____
. _____
. _____
. _____
. _____
. _____
. _____

He hath showed thee, O man, what is good; and what doth the LORD require of thee, but to do justly, and to love mercy, and to walk humbly with thy God?

MICAH 6:8

To crack the lily-white system of higher education in Georgia in the 1960s, black leaders decided they needed to find only two "squeaky-clean" students who couldn't be challenged on moral, intellectual, or educational grounds. In a discussion about who might be chosen, Alfred Holmes immediately volunteered his son, Hamilton, the top black male senior in the city. Charlayne Hunter-Gault also stepped forward and expressed an interest in applying to the university. Georgia delayed admitting both boys on grounds it had no room in its dormitories, and the matter eventually ended up in federal court. Judge Bootle ordered the university to admit the two, who were qualified in every respect, and thus, segregation ended at the university level in that state and soon, the nation.

Attorney General Robert Kennedy declared in a speech not long after: "We know that it is the law which enables men to live together, that creates order out of chaos. . . . And we know that if one man's rights are denied, the rights of all are endangered."

Justice may be universal, but it always begins at the individual level.

o o o o o

All virtue is summed up in dealing justly.

Your Future Is Spotless

Willingway Hospital is one of the nation's top treatment centers for alcoholism and drug addiction. There would be no Willingway, however, if it weren't for Dot and John, who at one time seemed the least likely candidates to found such a hospital. Early in their courtship, Dot and John drank heavily, and after they married, they began taking amphetamines. John, a medical doctor, was arrested for writing himself narcotic prescriptions. He spent six months in prison, eventually falling on his knees and crying out to God for help in overcoming his addictions.

When John returned to medical practice drug-free and alcohol-free, he began to receive referrals from other doctors to treat their alcoholic patients. Dot and John set up three beds under the chandelier in their own dining room as a detox room. Among their patients have been three of their own four children, each of whom struggled with addictions.

As word of their compassion spread, they established a forty-bed hospital on eleven acres close to their home. The chandelier still hangs in the detox room as a symbol of hope. All four children have worked on the medical staff or administration of Willingway. With God's help, they truly became a family in "full recovery."

Regardless of our past, the future is a blank slate, waiting to be written upon.

o o o o

No matter what a man's past may have been, his future is spotless.

From what do I need to be set free?

I will do a new thing; now it shall spring forth; shall ye not know it? I will even make a way in the wilderness, and rivers in the desert.

ISAIAH 43:19

Be Wise with Your Seed

What are some ways I can be faithful over what God has given me?

_____
_____
_____
_____
_____
_____
_____
_____
_____
_____
_____
_____
_____
_____

"His lord said unto him, Well done, good and faithful servant; thou hast been faithful over a few things, I will make thee ruler over many things: enter thou into the joy of thy lord."

MATTHEW 25:23

Three young men were each given three kernels of corn by a wise old sage who admonished them to go out into the world and use the corn to bring themselves good fortune.

The first young man put his three kernels of corn into a bowl of hot broth and ate them. The second thought, _I can do better than that,_ and he planted his three kernels of corn. Within a few months, he had three stalks of corn. He took the ears of corn from the stalks, boiled them, and had enough corn for three meals.

The third man said to himself, _I can do better than that!_ He also planted his three kernels of corn, but when his three stalks of corn produced, he stripped one of the ears and replanted all of the seeds from it, gave the second ear of corn to a sweet maiden, and ate the third. His one-full-ear's worth of replanted corn kernels gave him two hundred stalks of corn! And the kernels of these he continued to replant, setting aside only a bare minimum to eat. He eventually planted a hundred acres of corn. With his fortune, he not only won the hand of the sweet maiden, but also purchased the land owned by the sweet maiden's father. He never hungered again.

If you want to receive in life, you must first learn to give.

o o o o o

Wisdom is the wealth of the wise.

Hustle While You Wait

In 1928, a happy, ambitious young nursing student was diagnosed with tuberculosis. Her family sent her to a nursing home in Saranac Lake for several months of "curing." She would remain in bed for twenty-one years! Most people might have given up but not Isabel Smith. She approached the threshold of death on several occasions, but she never ceased to pursue the art of living. She read voraciously, loved to write letters, studied geography, and taught other patients to read and write. From her bed, she studied atomic energy with a fellow patient, a young physicist, and organized a town hall on the topic.

While ill, she met a kind, gentle man, who was also a patient at the sanitarium. She dreamed of marrying him and having a little house "under the mountains." At her lowest ebb, her dream kept her going, and in 1948, they did marry. She then wrote a book about "all the good things life has brought me." *Wish I Might*, published in 1955, earned her enough in royalties to buy her mountain retreat.

A tragic life? Hardly! Isabel Smith achieved everything she set out to achieve, even when the odds against her were a thousand to one. Even flat on her back in bed, she never quit growing, learning, and giving.

o o o o

Everything comes to him who hustles while he waits.

What goals do I want to achieve despite the odds?

We do not want you to become lazy, but to imitate those who through faith and patience inherit what has been promised.

HEBREWS 6:12 NIV

What are some "pure things" I can think about?

._____

._____

._____

._____

._____

._____

._____

._____

._____

._____

._____

._____

._____

> "I tell you that if anyone looks at a woman and wants to sin sexually with her, in his mind he has already done that sin with the woman."
>
> MATTHEW 5:28 NCV

According to an old legend, two monks named Tanzan and Ekido were traveling together down a muddy road one day. Heavy monsoon rains had saturated the area, and they were grateful for a few moments of sunshine to make their journey. Before long, they came around a bend and encountered a lovely girl in a silk kimono. She looked extremely forlorn as she stared at the muddy road before her.

At once, Tanzan responded to her plight. "Come here, girl," he said. Then lifting her in his arms, he carried her over the slippery ooze and set her down on the other side of the road.

Ekido didn't speak again to Tanzan. It was apparent to Tanzan that something was bothering his fellow monk deeply, but try as he would, he couldn't get Ekido to talk to him. Then that night after they reached their intended lodging, Ekido could no longer restrain his anger and disappointment. "We monks don't go near females," he said to Tanzan in an accusing voice. "We especially don't go near young and lovely maidens. It is dangerous. Why did you do that?"

"I left the girl back there, Ekido," replied Tanzan. And then he asked the key question, "Are you still carrying her?"

Train your mind to think on pure things. Make a conscious decision to stop any thought that doesn't line up with the teachings of the Bible.

o o o o o

There is nothing either good or bad, but thinking makes it so.

There once was a young man who lived a most miserable life. Orphaned before he was three, he was taken in by strangers. He was kicked out of school, suffered from poverty, and as the result of inherited physical weaknesses, he developed serious heart trouble as a teenager. His beloved wife died early in their marriage. He lived as an invalid most of his adult life, and he eventually died at the young age of forty. By all outward appearances, he was defeated by life and doomed to be forgotten by history.

Even so, he never quit trying to express himself and to achieve success over the twenty years of his active work life. In that period, he produced some of the most brilliant articles, essays, and criticisms ever written. His poetry is still read widely and studied by virtually every high school student in the United States. His short stories and detective stories are famous. One of his poems, on display at the famous Huntington Library in California, has been valued at more than fifty thousand dollars, which is far more than the young man earned in his entire lifetime.

His name? Edgar Allan Poe.

Circumstances don't affect your chances for success nearly as much as your level of effort!

*Defeat is not the worst of failures.
Not to have tried is the true failure.*

Am I willing to put forth the necessary effort to achieve my success?

_____ .
_____ .
_____ .
_____ .
_____ .
_____ .
_____ .
_____ .
_____ .
_____ .
_____ .
_____ .
_____ .
_____ .
_____ .
_____ .

Be strong and of a good courage;
be not afraid, neither be thou dismayed:
for the LORD thy God is with thee
whithersoever thou goest.

JOSHUA 1:9

You Need Only Please One

Am I a people-pleaser or a God-pleaser?

A young man once studied violin under a world-renowned violinist and master teacher. He worked hard for several years at perfecting his talent, and the day finally came when he was called upon to give his first major public recital in the large city where both he and his teacher lived. Following each selection, which he performed with great skill and passion, the performer seemed uneasy about the great applause he received. Even though he knew that those in the audience were musically astute and not likely to give such applause to a less-than-superior performance, the young man acted almost as if he couldn't hear the appreciation that was being showered upon him.

At the close of the last number, the applause was thunderous, and numerous "Bravos" were shouted. But the talented young violinist had his eyes glued on one spot only. Finally, when an elderly man in the first row of the balcony smiled and nodded to him in approval, the young man relaxed and beamed with both relief and joy. His teacher had praised his work! The applause of thousands meant nothing until he had first won the approval of the master.

Whom are you trying to please today? You will never be able to please everyone, but you can please the One who matters most—your Father God. Keep your eyes on Him, and you can't fail.

Am I now trying to win the approval of men, or of God?

GALATIANS 1:10 NIV

I don't know the secret to success, but the key to failure is to try to please everyone.

Let God Take You to the Other Side

The engineers hired to build a suspension bridge across the Niagara River faced a serious problem: how to get the first cable from one side of the river to the next. The river was too wide to throw a cable across it and too swift to cross by boat.

An engineer finally came up with a solution! With a favoring stiff wind, a kite was lofted and allowed to drift over the river and land on the opposite shore. Attached to the kite was a very light string, which was threaded through the kite's tip so that both ends of the string were in the hands of the kite flyer. Once the kite was in the hand of engineers on the far side, they removed the kite from its string and set up a pulley. A small rope was attached to one end of the original kite string and pulled across the river. At the end of this string, a piece of rope was attached and pulled across and so on, until a cable strong enough to sustain the iron cable, which supported the bridge, could be drawn across the water.

Let your faith soar like that kite! Release it to God, believing that He can and will help you. When you link your released faith with patience and persistence, you will have what it takes to tackle virtually any problem.

○ ○ ○ ○ ○

*Kites rise highest against
the wind, not with it.*

I will allow my faith to soar,
believing God's promises to . . .

_____.
_____.
_____.
_____.
_____.
_____.
_____.
_____.
_____.
_____.
_____.
_____.
_____.
_____.
_____.

They that wait upon the LORD shall renew their strength; they shall mount up with wings as eagles; they shall run, and not be weary; and they shall walk, and not faint.

ISAIAH 40:31

Faith on the Inside, Works on the Outside

Do I have a good balance between faith and works in my life?

· _____
· _____
· _____
· _____
· _____
· _____
· _____
· _____
· _____
· _____
· _____
· _____
· _____
· _____

Wallace E. Johnson, president of Holiday Inns and one of America's most successful builders, once said:

> I always keep a card in my billfold with the following verses and refer to them frequently: "Ask and it shall be given you; seek and ye shall find; knock, and it shall be opened unto you: for everyone that asketh receiveth; and he that seeketh findeth; and to him that knocketh, it shall be opened" (Matthew 7:7-8). These verses are among God's greatest promises. Yet they are a little one-sided. They indicate a philosophy of receiving but not of giving. One day as my wife, Alma, and I were seeking God's guidance for a personal problem, I came across the following verse which has since been a daily reminder to me of what my responsibility as a businessman is to God: "Study to show thyself approved unto God, a workman that needeth not to be ashamed, rightly dividing the word of truth" (2 Timothy 2:15). Since then I have measured my actions against the phrase: *A workman that needeth not to be ashamed.*

Faith on the inside + works on the outside = a successful life!

o O o O o

As the body without the spirit is dead, so faith without works is dead also.

JAMES 2:26

Faith is the root of works. A root that produces nothing is dead.

A Cheerful Attitude Makes Everything Better

A little boy was once overheard talking to himself as he strutted out of his house into the backyard, carrying a baseball bat and ball. Once in the yard, he tipped his baseball cap to his eager puppy, and picking up the bat and ball, he announced with a loud voice, "I'm the greatest hitter in the world!"

He then proceeded to toss the ball into the air, swing at it, and miss. "Strike one!" he cried, as if playing the role of umpire.

He picked up the ball, threw it into the air, and said again, "I'm the greatest baseball hitter ever!" Again he swung at the ball and missed. "Strike two!" he announced to his dog and the yard.

Undaunted, he picked up the ball, examined his bat, and then just before tossing the ball into the air, announced once again, "I'm the greatest hitter who ever lived!" He swung the bat hard but missed the ball for the third time. "Strike three!" he cried. Then he added, "Wow! What a pitcher! I'm the greatest pitcher in all the world!"

A positive mental attitude goes a long way toward making a difficult job seem easier.

o o o o o

The cheerful man will do more in the same time, will do it better, will preserve it longer, than the sad or sullen.

When a man is gloomy, everything seems to go wrong; when he is cheerful, everything seems right!

PROVERBS 15:15 TLB

HOW can I involve God in the financial area of my life?

. _____

. _____

. _____

. _____

. _____

. _____

. _____

. _____

. _____

. _____

. _____

. _____

. _____

. _____

The rich ruleth over the poor, and the borrower is servant to the lender.

PROVERBS 22:7

At the age of twenty-four, financial advisor and author Ron Blue felt he had everything he needed to be successful—an MBA degree, a CPA certificate, and a prestigious position in the New York City office of the world's largest CPA firm. But then at the age of thirty-two, he committed his life to Jesus Christ and began to see life from a new perspective. When he decided to establish his own financial advisory firm, he used his skills to develop a business plan and arrange for a ten-thousand-dollar line of credit at a bank. Almost immediately, however, he felt convicted that God did not want him to borrow money to start his business. He canceled the credit line, not knowing what to do next, but knowing he was not to go into debt.

One day, while explaining his business idea to a friend, the friend said, "Would you consider designing a financial seminar for our executives who are getting ready to retire?" Ron jumped at the opportunity. His friend was the training director for a large company, and the company agreed to pay six thousand dollars in advance for development of the seminar, then one thousand dollars each for four seminars during the year. Ron had the ten thousand dollars he needed without borrowing a dime.

Do your best to stay out of debt. You'll feel much freer, and God will bless you for trusting in Him.

o o o o o

*Money is a good servant,
but a dangerous master.*

Do Your Part to Overcome

What price am I willing to pay to achieve my dream?

Nelson Diebel, a hyperactive and delinquent child, was enrolled in The Peddie School where he met swimming coach Chris Martin, who believed the more one practices, the better one performs. Within a month, he had Nelson swimming thirty to forty hours a week, even though Nelson could not sit still in a classroom for fifteen minutes. Martin saw potential in Nelson. He constantly put new goals in front of the boy, trying to get him to focus and turn his anger into strength. Nelson eventually qualified for the Junior Nationals, and his fast times qualified him for the Olympic Trials.

Then Nelson broke both hands and arms in a diving accident, and doctors warned he probably would never regain his winning form. Martin said to him, "You're coming all the way back. . . . If you're not committed to that, we're going to stop right now." Nelson agreed, and within weeks after his casts were off, he was swimming again.

In 1992, Nelson Diebel won an Olympic gold medal. As he accepted his medal, he recalls thinking: *I planned and dreamed and worked so hard, and I did it!* The kid who once couldn't sit still and who had no ambition had learned to make a plan, pursue it, and achieve it. He had become a winner in far more than swimming!

Let your plans motivate you to start working toward your goals. Dream big dreams!

○ ○ ○ ○ ○

No plan is worth the paper it is printed on unless it starts you doing something.

Be ye doers of the word, and not hearers only, deceiving your own selves.

JAMES 1:22

What gifts has God given me to use for His glory?

_____

_____

_____

_____

_____

_____

_____

_____

_____

_____

_____

_____

_____

_____

_____

The German sculptor Dannaker worked for two years on a statue of Christ until it looked perfect to him. He called a little girl into his studio, and pointing to the statue, he asked her, "Who is that?"

The little girl promptly replied, "A great man."

Dannaker was disheartened. He took his chisel and began anew. For six long years, he toiled. Again, he invited a little girl into his workshop, stood her before the figure, and asked, "Who is that?"

She looked up at it for a moment, and then tears welled up in her eyes as she folded her hands across her chest and said, "Suffer the little children to come unto me" (Mark 10:14). This time Dannaker knew he had succeeded.

The sculptor later confessed that during those six years, Christ had revealed himself to him in a vision, and he had only transferred to the marble what he had seen with his inner eyes.

Later, when Napoleon Bonaparte asked him to make a statue of Venus for the Louvre, Dannaker refused. "A man," he said, "who has seen Christ can never employ his gifts in carving a pagan goddess. My art is henceforth a consecrated thing."

The true value of a work comes not from effort, nor its completion, but from Christ who inspires it.

o o o o o

Whatsoever ye do, do all to the glory of God.

I CORINTHIANS 10:31

Only passions, great passions, can elevate the soul to great things.

Don't Let Excuses Slow You Down

Sadie Delaney's father taught her always to strive to do better than her competition. She proved the value of that lesson shortly before she received her teaching license. A supervisor came to watch her and two other student teachers. Their assignment was to teach a class to bake cookies. Since the supervisor didn't have time for each teacher to go through the entire lesson, she divided the lesson, and Sadie was assigned to teach the girls how to serve and clean up.

The first student teacher panicked and forgot to divide the recipe in half and preheat the oven. The second girl was so behind because of the first girl's errors that the students made a mess in forming and baking the cookies. Then it was Sadie's turn. She said to the girls, "Listen, we have to work together as a team." They quickly baked the remaining dough. Several girls were lined up to scrub pans as soon as the cookies came out of the oven. Within ten minutes, they had several dozen perfect cookies and a clean kitchen. The supervisor was so impressed, she offered Sadie a substitute teacher's license on the spot. Sadie soon became the first black person ever to teach domestic science in New York City's public high schools.

Even when you have every right to blame others who have gone before you, don't make excuses. Do what it takes to get the job done!

o o o o o

You may often make excuses for another, never for yourself.

What can I do to become more productive?

_____ .
_____ .
_____ .
_____ .
_____ .
_____ .
_____ .
_____ .
_____ .
_____ .
_____ .
_____ .
_____ .
_____ .
_____ .
_____ .

Don't point your finger at someone else, and try to pass the blame to him!

HOSEA 4:4 TLB

Only Speak Good Words

What is the quality of the words that I speak?

_____

_____

_____

_____

_____

_____

_____

_____

_____

_____

_____

_____

_____

_____

_____

A man once sat down to have dinner with his family. Before they began to eat, the family members joined hands around the table, and the man said a prayer, thanking God for the food, the hands that had prepared it, and for the Source of all life. During the meal, however, he complained at length about the staleness of the bread, the bitterness of the coffee, and a bit of mold he found on one edge of the brick of cheese.

His young daughter asked him, "Daddy, do you think God heard you say grace before the meal?"

"Of course, honey," he answered confidently.

Then she asked, "Do you think God heard everything that was said during dinner?"

The man answered, "Why, yes, I believe so. God hears everything."

She thought for a moment and then asked, "Daddy, which do you think God believed?"

The Lord hears everything we say during a day, not only those words that are addressed specifically to Him. Once you've said something, you can't take it back. Would you mind if God listened in on your conversations?

o o o o

Once a word has been allowed to escape, it cannot be recalled.

Let no corrupt communication proceed out of your mouth, but that which is good to the use of edifying, that it may minister grace unto the hearers.

EPHESIANS 4:29

Who Says It's Impossible?

Consider these examples of resistance to ideas and inventions that we now consider commonplace:

1. In Germany, "experts" proved that if trains went as fast as fifteen miles an hour—considered a frightful speed—blood would spurt from the travelers' noses, and passengers would suffocate when going through tunnels. In the United States, experts said the introduction of the railroad would require the building of many insane asylums since people would be driven mad with terror at the sight of the locomotives.

2. The New York YWCA announced typing lessons for women in 1881, and vigorous protest erupted on the grounds that the female constitution would break down under the strain.

3. When the idea of iron ships was proposed, experts insisted that they would not float, would damage more easily than wooden ships when grounding, that it would be difficult to preserve the iron bottom from rust, and that iron would play havoc with compass readings.

4. New Jersey farmers resisted the first successful cast-iron plow invented in 1797, claiming that the cast iron would poison the land and stimulate the growth of weeds.

Don't let the word "impossible" stop you. If inventors and visionaries left every "impossible" task undone, our lives would be considerably more difficult. Nothing worth doing is impossible with the help of God!

○ ○ ○ ○ ○

Most of the things worth doing in the world had been declared impossible before they were done.

What is to be my response to those who say I can't?

_____.
_____.
_____.
_____.
_____.
_____.
_____.
_____.
_____.
_____.
_____.
_____.
_____.
_____.
_____.
_____.
_____.

"With God all things are possible."

MATTHEW 19:26

What Bible promise can I focus on?

_____
_____
_____
_____
_____
_____
_____
_____
_____
_____
_____
_____
_____
_____
_____
_____

Peter . . . walked on the water toward Jesus. But when he looked around at the high waves, he was terrified and began to sink.

MATTHEW 14:29-30 TLB

During the darkest days of the Civil War, the hopes of the Union nearly died. When certain goals seemed unreachable, the leaders of the Union turned to President Abraham Lincoln for solace, guidance, and encouragement. Once when a delegation called at the White House and detailed a long list of crises facing the nation, Lincoln told this story:

"Years ago a young friend and I were out one night when a shower of meteors fell from the clear November sky. The young man was frightened, but I told him to look up in the sky past the shooting stars to the fixed stars beyond, shining serene in the firmament, and I said, 'Let us not mind the meteors, but let us keep our eyes on the stars.'"

When times are troubled or life seems to be changing too quickly, keep your inner eyes of faith and hope on those things that you know to be lasting and sure. Don't limit your gaze to what you know or whom you know, but focus instead on the One you know. God alone—and a relationship with Him that is eternal—is the Supreme Goal. He never changes, and He cannot be removed from His place as the King of Glory.

o o o o o

Obstacles are those frightful things you see when you take your eyes off the goal.

In *Up from Slavery*, Booker T. Washington describes meeting an ex-slave from Virginia:

I found that this man had made a contract with his master, two or three years previous to the Emancipation Proclamation, to the effect that the slave was to be permitted to buy himself, by paying so much per year for his body; and while he was paying for himself, he was to be permitted to labor where and for whom he pleased.

Finding that he could secure better wages in Ohio, he went there. When freedom came, he was still in debt to his master some 300 dollars. Notwithstanding that the Emancipation Proclamation freed him from any obligation to his master, this black man walked the greater portion of the distance back to where his old master lived in Virginia, and placed the last dollar, with interest, in his hands.

In talking to me about this, the man told me that he knew that he did not have to pay his debt, but that he had given his word to his master, and his word he had never broken. He felt that he could not enjoy his freedom till he had fulfilled his promise.

Your ability to keep your word, not your ability to acquire money, is your true measure as a person!

○ ○ ○ ○ ○

God looks with favor at pure, not full, hands.

IS there a vow I need to fulfill?

_____.
_____.
_____.
_____.
_____.
_____.
_____.
_____.
_____.
_____.
_____.
_____.
_____.
_____.

A GOOD name is rather to be chosen than great riches.

PROVERBS 22:1

Correct Your Mistakes

Is there a mistake that I need to correct today?

_____
_____
_____
_____
_____
_____
_____
_____
_____
_____
_____
_____
_____
_____
_____
_____

A janitor at the First Security Bank in Boise, Idaho, once accidentally put a box of eight thousand checks worth $840,000 on a trash table. That night, the operator of the paper shredder dutifully dumped the box of checks into his machine, which cut the checks into quarter-inch shreds. He then dumped the paper scraps into a garbage can outside the bank. When the bank supervisor realized what happened the next morning, he wanted to cry.

Most of the checks had been cashed at the bank and were awaiting shipment to a clearinghouse. Their loss represented a bookkeeping nightmare since most of the checks were still unrecorded, and as a result, the bankers could not know who paid what to whom.

What did the supervisor do? He ordered that the shredded pieces be reconstructed. So fifty employees worked in two shifts for six hours a day inside six rooms—shifting, matching, and pasting the pieces together as if they were jigsaw puzzles—until all eight thousand of the checks were put together again.

Humpty Dumpty may have fallen from the wall, but did the king's men do everything in their power to try to put him together again? If you make a mistake, work on a solution!

o o o o

A man who refuses to admit his mistakes can never be successful. But if he confesses and forsakes them, he gets another chance.

PROVERBS 28:13 TLB

An error doesn't become a mistake until you refuse to correct it.

A Fresh Perspective

After two years in the navy, Willard Scott returned to his old job with NBC radio, but to a new supervisor. Willard found himself at odds with his new boss at every turn, and he was furious when he rescheduled *Joy Boys,* a comedy show Willard did with Eddie Walker, for the worst slot on radio—eight to midnight. Willard was braced for a change-or-I'll-leave confrontation when he recalled Proverbs 19:11 NIV: *A man's wisdom gives him patience; it is to his glory to overlook an offense.* He and Eddie decided to work themselves to the bone, and within three years, they made *Joy Boys* the top-rated show in Washington.

Willard says, "I learned that I, too, had been wrong. In all my dealings with my boss, I had aggravated the problem. I knew he didn't like me, and in response I was barely civil to him and dodged him as much as I could. But one day he invited me to a station party I couldn't avoid. There I met his fiancée. She was bright, alive, and down-to-earth. *How could a woman like that care for anybody who didn't have something to recommend him?* I was able to get new insight into my boss's character. As time went on, my attitude changed, and so did his." Willard and his boss became friends, and he remained at NBC.

Is there someone with whom you are at odds? If you're looking for the negative qualities in a person, you're sure to find them. Try seeing that person with new eyes. A fresh perspective can change everything.

○ ○ ○ ○ ○

Hating people is like burning down your own house to get rid of a rat.

HOW can I change my attitude about the people I don't like?

If instead of showing love among yourselves you are always critical and catty, watch out! Beware of ruining each other.

GALATIANS 5:15 TLB

A Good Sense of Humor

Do I have a good sense of humor, or do I take life too seriously?

_____
_____
_____
_____
_____
_____
_____
_____
_____
_____
_____
_____
_____
_____

A missionary from Sweden was once urged by his friends to give up his idea of returning to India because it was so hot there. "Man," the fellow Swede urged, as if telling his friend something he didn't already know, "it's 120 degrees in the shade in that country!"

The Swedish missionary replied, "Well, we don't always have to stay in the shade do we?"

Humor is not a sin. It is a God-given escape hatch. Being able to see the lighter side of life is a virtue. Every vocation and circumstance of life has a lighter side if we are only willing to see it. Wholesome humor can do a great deal to help defuse a tense, heated situation. In developing a good sense of humor, we must be able to laugh at our own mistakes; accept justified criticism and recover from it; and learn to avoid using statements that are unsuitable, even though they may be funny.

James M. Gray and William Houghton—two Godly men—were praying together one day, and the elderly Dr. Gray concluded his prayer by saying, "Lord, keep me cheerful. Keep me from becoming a cranky, old man."

Keeping a sense of humor is a great way to become a sweet, patient, and encouraging person. Learn to laugh at yourself occasionally!

o o o o

Laughter is the sun that drives winter from the human face.

Be cheerful no matter what.
I THESSALONIANS 5:16 THE MESSAGE

Pass Out Some Smiles and Thoughtful Words

It has been estimated that more than 95 percent of all Americans receive at least one or more Christmas cards each year. The average is actually more than seventy cards per family! Millions of cards are mailed worldwide each holiday season. Have you ever wondered where this custom began?

A museum director in the mid-nineteenth century had a personal habit of sending notes to his friends at Christmastime each year, just to wish them a joyful holiday season. One year, he found he had little time to write, and yet he still wanted to send a message of good cheer. He asked his friend, John Horsely, to design a card that he might sign and send. Those who received the cards loved them so much they created cards of their own. Thus the Christmas card was born!

It's often the simple heartfelt gestures in life that speak most loudly of friendship. Ask yourself today, *What can I do to bring a smile to the face of a friend? What can I do to bring good cheer into the life of someone who is in need, trouble, sickness, or sorrow?* Follow through on your answer. It's not a gift you are giving as much as a friendship you are building!

o o o o o

Good nature begets smiles, smiles beget friends, and friends are better than a fortune.

What kind gesture can I cheer someone up with today?

My heart will thrill to your thoughtful, wise words.

PROVERBS 23:15 TLB

Find Ways to Benefit Others

What can I give to others today?

. _____

. _____

. _____

. _____

. _____

. _____

. _____

. _____

. _____

. _____

. _____

. _____

. _____

. _____

This American received a medical degree from New York University College of Medicine. He received an appointment to the Virus Research Laboratory at the University of Pittsburgh. He received an assignment from the army to develop a vaccine against influenza, and among the many honors he received was a Presidential Medal of Freedom.

However, Jonas Salk is not known for what he received but for what he gave. He and his team of researchers gave their efforts to prepare an inactivated polio virus that could serve as an immunizing agent against polio. By 1952, they had created a vaccine, and in 1955, the vaccine was released for widespread use in the United States, virtually ending the ravaging, crippling effects of polio.

You will receive many opportunities in your life and, most likely, a number of certificates, diplomas, and awards. But what ultimately will count is what you do with the training you receive and the skills and traits you develop.

Find a way to give, create, or generate something today that will benefit others. Then your actions will be not only a potential for fame and reward, but also great personal satisfaction—the reward of highest value.

○ ○ ○ ○

No person was ever honored for what he received. Honor has been the reward for what he gave.

The righteous give without sparing.

PROVERBS 21:26 NIV

Think Before You Speak

April 10

HOW can I make the things I say to others worth listening to?

Consider the infamous statements listed below, and notice as you read that they all could be corrected by changing or inserting only one word!

- "Everything that can be invented has been invented."—Charles H. Duell, U.S. Patent Office director, 1899
- "Who wants to hear actors talk?"—H.M. Warner, Warner Brothers Pictures, 1927
- "Sensible and responsible women do not want to vote."—President Grover Cleveland, 1905
- "There is no likelihood man can ever tap the power of the atom."—Robert Millikan, Nobel Prize winner in physics, 1923
- "Heavier-than-air flying machines are impossible."—Lord Kelvin, president, Royal Society, 1895
- "[Babe] Ruth made a big mistake when he gave up pitching."—Tris Speaker, 1927
- *Gone with the Wind* is going to be the biggest flop in Hollywood history."—Gary Cooper

Isn't it amazing what a difference a word or two can make! Choose your words carefully. Always think before you speak.

○ ○ ○ ○ ○

The difference between the right word and the almost right word is the difference between lightning and the lightning bug.

When a good man speaks, he is worth listening to, but the words of fools are a dime a dozen.
PROVERBS 10:20 TLB

April 10

Whom do I need to make things right with today?

_____

_____

_____

_____

_____

_____

_____

_____

_____

_____

_____

_____

_____

An evil man is stubborn, but a
godly man will reconsider.

PROVERBS 21:29 TLB

A feud developed between two families who lived side by side in the mountains of Kentucky. It started when Grandpa Smith's cow jumped a stone fence and ate Grandpa Brown's corn. Brown shot the cow. A Smith boy then shot two Brown boys. The Browns shot one Smith. Bill Brown planned to kill a second Smith, but before he could, he was called away to war. While he was away, Bill's mother had a hard time making ends meet for her family since Bill's father had been one of the feud victims.

At Christmas, the head of the Smith clan took his family to church. Usually he stayed outside, but this year it was so cold he went in to wait. The sermon was on Christ, the Prince of Peace, who died in _our_ place for _our_ sins. It struck him hard. He realized what a crime he had committed, repented, and then secretly hired a young boy to carry a basket of food to the Brown's home every day until Bill returned.

Once home, Bill set out to discover who had so generously helped his family. He followed the boy to the Smith's house, where Smith met him and said, "Shoot me, Bill, if you want to. But Christ has already died for my sins, and I hope you'll forgive me too." Bill did, and neighbors truly became neighbors again.

Never reach the point in life where you think you can't learn something new or change your opinion about something. You are never too old, or too young, to be forgiven.

o o o o o

_This world belongs to the man who is
wise enough to change his mind
in the presence of facts._

Words Make a Difference

One day, a young altar boy was serving the priest at a Sunday Mass being held in the country church of his small village. The boy, nervous in his new role at the altar, accidentally dropped the cruet of wine. The village priest immediately struck the boy sharply on the cheek and in a very gruff voice, shouted so that many people could hear, "Leave the altar and don't come back!" That boy became Tito, the communist leader who ruled Yugoslavia for many decades.

One day in a large city cathedral, a young boy was serving a bishop at a Sunday Mass. He, too, accidentally dropped the cruet of wine. The bishop turned to him, but rather than responding in anger, gently whispered with a warm twinkle in his eyes, "Someday you will be a priest." That boy grew up to become Archbishop Fulton Sheen.

Words have power. The childhood phrase, "Sticks and stones can break my bones, but words can never hurt me," simply isn't true. Words do hurt. They wound—sometimes deeply.

But words also can reward, build self-esteem, create friendships, give hope, and render a blessing. Words can heal and drive accomplishment. Watch what you say to a friend today!

○ ○ ○ ○ ○

Do not remove a fly from your friend's forehead with a hatchet.

HOW do I respond to the blunders of others?

_____ .
_____ .
_____ .
_____ .
_____ .
_____ .
_____ .
_____ .
_____ .
_____ .
_____ .
_____ .
_____ .
_____ .
_____ .
_____ .
_____ .
_____ .

It only takes a spark, remember, to set off a forest fire. A careless or wrongly placed word out of your mouth can do that. By our speech we can ruin the world.

JAMES 3:5-6 THE MESSAGE

Who do I believe God created me to be?

_____

_____

_____

_____

_____

_____

_____

_____

_____

_____

_____

_____

_____

A farmer once caught a young eagle in the forest, brought it home, and raised it among his ducks and turkeys. Five years later, a naturalist came to visit him and saw the bird. "That's an eagle, not a chicken!" he said.

"Yes," said the farmer, "but I've raised it to be a chicken."

"Still," said the naturalist, "it has a wingspan of fifteen feet. It's an eagle!"

"It will never fly," said the farmer. The naturalist disagreed, and they decided to put their argument to the test.

First, the naturalist picked up the eagle and said, "Eagle, thou art an eagle; thou dost belong to the sky and not to this earth; stretch forth thy wings and fly." The eagle saw the chickens and jumped down. The next day, the naturalist took the eagle to the top of the house and said the same thing before letting the eagle go. Again, it spotted the chickens below and fluttered down to join them in feeding.

"One more try," said the naturalist. He took the eagle up a mountain. The trembling bird looked around, and then the naturalist made it look into the sun. Suddenly, the eagle stretched out its wings, gave a mighty screech, and flew away, never to return.

People may say you are just a hunk of flesh—a chicken rather than an eagle. But deep inside, you have a spirit created in God's image, and you are destined to fly.

○ ○ ○ ○ ○

God said, Let us make man in our image, after our likeness.

GENESIS 1:26

Man is the miracle of miracles, the great inscrutable mystery of God.

Never Too Great to Serve

Shortly after Booker T. Washington became head of the Tuskegee Institute in Alabama, he was walking past the house of a wealthy family. The woman of the house, assuming Washington was one of the yard workers her husband had hired, asked him if he would chop some wood for her. Professor Washington smiled, nodded, took off his coat, and chopped the wood. When he carried the armload of wood into the woman's kitchen, a servant girl recognized him and rushed to her mistress to tell her of his identity.

The next morning, the woman appeared in Washington's office. Apologizing profusely, she said repeatedly, "I did not know it was you I put to work."

Washington replied with generosity, "It's entirely all right, madam. I like to work, and I'm delighted to do favors for my friends."

The woman was so taken with his manner and his willingness to forgive that she gave generous gifts to the institute and persuaded many of her wealthy acquaintances to do likewise. In the end, Washington raised as much money for the institute from this one act of chopping wood as he did from any other fund-raising event!

A great leader is never beyond hard work. The willingness to serve others is the essence of true leadership.

o o o o o

A great man is always willing to be little.

HOW willing am I to serve others?

_____.
_____.
_____.
_____.
_____.
_____.
_____.
_____.
_____.
_____.
_____.
_____.
_____.
_____.
_____.

The meek shall inherit the land, and delight themselves in abundant prosperity.

PSALM 37:11 NRSV

Real Friends Want What's Best for You

What changes do I need to make to my team roster?

. _____

. _____

. _____

. _____

. _____

. _____

. _____

. _____

. _____

. _____

. _____

. _____

. _____

. _____

Do not be misled: "Bad company corrupts good character."

I CORINTHIANS 15:33 NIV

Coach Gregory watched with pride as Rashaan Salaam accepted the Heisman Trophy. He recalled the hotshot eighteen-year-old who, finally free from his mother's tight discipline, had arrived in Colorado ready to devour the world. He said, "Rashaan was a gangster wannabe. He came here wearing all this red stuff, talking about gangs. He hadn't done it back home because his mother would never have tolerated it." And neither did Gregory. He never lectured or preached to Rashaan, but he did ask him questions. When Rashaan came to him, talking about his new friends, Gregory said, "Sure, they are your friends, but are you their friend? They know what you're trying to accomplish. They know the potential you have to do great things. If you are their friend, when they get ready to get into something, they'll say, 'Salaam, get out of here. Go home and study.'"

As a coach, Gregory wanted Salaam to "find daylight" and get into the end zone, but as his friend, he wanted him to live in the daylight and make it to life's goal line as a productive citizen. Winning a football game is never a one-man effort. It's a team effort. The same holds true for life, and the good news is you can choose the players on your team!

o o o o o

'Tis better to be alone, than in bad company.

Persuasion Is Better than Force

A fable is told about a dispute the North Wind had with the Sun over who was the more powerful of the two. They finally agreed to settle their argument with this wager: the first to cause a wayfaring man to strip away his clothing would be the victor.

The North Wind huffed and puffed and blew with all his might, but the more it blew, the closer the traveler wrapped his cloak around him. He finally gave up, and the Sun moved in to have a turn.

The Sun happily shone with all his warmth. As his rays warmed the traveler, he took off first one garment and then the next. At last, nearly overcome by the radiant heat, he undressed completely and plunged himself into a stream for a cool and soothing swim.

The Sun turned to the North Wind and said, "Persuasion is better than force."

Criticism and harsh demands can turn a warm heart cold. Rebellion is more likely to be the result than improved performance. In contrast, praise and encouragement warm the heart. The person who feels appreciated not only follows the leader who gives such applause, but turns in a better performance. Whether the people over which you have influence are siblings, friends, or teammates, God has given you that position for a reason. Use it wisely.

o o o o o

You do not lead by hitting people over the head—that's assault, not leadership.

HOW do I handle the leadership role God has given me?

The servant of the Lord must not strive; but be gentle unto all men, apt to teach, patient.

2 TIMOTHY 2:24

Let Your Patience Work for You

HOW can I exercise my patience as I pursue my goal?

. _____

. _____

. _____

. _____

. _____

. _____

. _____

. _____

. _____

. _____

. _____

. _____

. _____

We often think of great artists and musicians as having "bursts" of genius. More often, they are models of painstaking patience. Their greatest works tend to have been accomplished over long periods and in the midst of extreme hardships.

Beethoven is said to have rewritten each bar of his music at least a dozen times.

Joseph Haydn produced more than eight hundred musical compositions before writing *The Creation*, the oratorio for which he is most famous.

Michelangelo's *Last Judgment* is considered one of the twelve master paintings of the ages. It took him eight years to complete. He produced more than two thousand sketches and renderings in the process.

Leonardo da Vinci worked on *The Last Supper* for ten years, often working so diligently that he forgot to eat.

When he was quite elderly, the pianist Ignacy Paderewski was asked by an admirer, "Is it true that you still practice every day?"

He replied, "Yes, at least six hours a day."

The admirer said in awe, "You must have a world of patience."

Paderewski said, "I have no more patience than the next fellow. I just use mine."

Put your patience to use in the pursuit of your dreams.

o o o o o

Ye have need of patience, that, after ye have done the will of God, ye might receive the promise.

HEBREWS 10:36

Patience is bitter, but its fruit is sweet.

Three things I want to accomplish are . . .

In 1972, *Life* magazine published a story about the amazing adventures of John Goddard. When he was fifteen, John's grandmother said, "If only I had done that when I was young. . . ." Determined not to make that statement at the end of his life, John wrote out 127 goals for his life.

He named ten rivers he wanted to explore and seventeen mountains he wanted to climb. He set goals of becoming an Eagle Scout, a world traveler, and a pilot. Also on his list were the following: ride a horse in the Rose Bowl parade, dive in a submarine, retrace the travels of Marco Polo, read the Bible from cover to cover, and read the entire *Encyclopedia Britannica*.

He also planned to read the entire works of Shakespeare, Plato, Dickens, Socrates, Aristotle, and several other classic authors. He desired to learn to play the flute and violin, marry, have children (he had five), pursue a career in medicine, and serve as a missionary for his church.

Sound impossible? At the age of forty-seven, John Goddard had accomplished 103 of his goals!

Your list of goals may not be as extensive as John Goddard's, but if you don't have *some* goals in life, you'll find that you have little motivation to get up in the morning and little satisfaction as your head hits the pillow each night.

o o o o

Motivation is when your dreams put on work clothes.

Whatever you do, work at it with all your heart, as working for the Lord, not for men.
COLOSSIANS 3:23 NIV

Can You Control Your Tongue?

HOW can I do a better job of controling my tongue?

_____

_____

_____

_____

_____

_____

_____

_____

_____

_____

_____

_____

_____

_____

_____

William Penn, founding leader of the colony that became Pennsylvania, had these rules for conversation:

- Avoid company where it is not profitable or necessary, and in those occasions, speak little, and last.
- Silence is wisdom where speaking is folly, and always safe.
- Some are so foolish as to interrupt and anticipate those that speak instead of hearing and thinking before they answer, which is uncivil, as well as silly.
- If thou thinkest twice before thou speakest once, thou wilt speak twice the better for it.
- Better to say nothing than not to the purpose. And to speak pertinently, consider both what is fit and when it is fit to speak.
- In all debates, let truth be thy aim, not victory or an unjust interest; and endeavor to gain, rather than to expose, thy antagonist.

Though few achieve it, one of the greatest skills you can develop in life is the ability to control your tongue! It is an invaluable asset in every area of life. Yet many people never appreciate its worth. How about you?

o o o o o

Self-control means controlling the tongue! A quick retort can ruin everything.

PROVERBS 13:3 TLB

The great test of a man's character is his tongue.

Pass the Test

The Koh-in-noor diamond is among the world's most spectacular. It is part of the British crown jewels, presented to Queen Victoria by a maharaja in India when the maharaja was only a young boy.

Years later, when he was a grown man, the maharaja visited Queen Victoria in England. He asked that the stone be brought from the Tower of London, where it was kept in safety, to Buckingham Palace. The queen did as he requested.

Taking the diamond in his hand, he knelt before the queen and presented it back to her, saying, "Your Majesty, I gave this jewel when I was a child, too young to know what I was doing. I want to give it to you again in the fullness of my strength, with all of my heart and affection, and gratitude, now and forever, fully realizing all that I do."

A day will come when you likely will look back and say, "I'm grateful for my teachers and the lessons they taught me about discipline, concentration, hard work, cooperation, and the right and wrong ways to compete." Even more valuable will be the day when you look in a mirror and say, "Knowing what I now know about life, I see value in continuing to teach these lessons to myself."

o o o o o

School seeks to get you ready for examination; life gives the finals.

What life lessons am I learning?

Examine yourselves to see whether you are in the faith; test yourselves.

2 CORINTHIANS 13:5 NIV

Success Doesn't Come by Chance

In what areas do I need to become more diligent?

. _____
. _____
. _____
. _____
. _____
. _____
. _____
. _____
. _____
. _____
. _____
. _____
. _____
. _____

The Sixty-Four Thousand-Dollar Question was the hottest show on television in 1955. The more Joyce watched the program, the more she thought, *I could do that.* At the time, Joyce had quit her teaching job to raise her daughter, and she and her husband were living on fifty dollars a month. She never dreamed of winning the top prize—*any* prize at that point would have helped greatly.

As a psychologist by training, Joyce analyzed the show. She saw that each contestant had a built-in incongruity—the marine who was a gourmet cook, the shoemaker who knew about opera. She looked at herself. She was a short, blond psychologist and mother with no incongruity. After some thought, she decided to become an expert in boxing! She ate, drank, and slept boxing, studying its statistics, personalities, and history. When she felt she was ready, she applied as a contestant for the show, was accepted, won, and won again, until she eventually won the sixty-four-thousand-dollar prize.

That experience led her to dream of a career as a television journalist who might translate the results of psychological research into terms that people could use in their everyday lives. Once she saw that possibility, there was no stopping Dr. Joyce Brothers.

True success never comes by chance. Diligently apply yourself to your goals, and your dreams will come true.

o o o o o

The plans of the diligent lead to profit.

PROVERBS 21:5 NIV

Diligence is the mother of good fortune.

The first thing to emerge at a baby giraffe's birth is its front hooves and head. Minutes later, the newborn is hurled from its mother's body, falls ten feet, and lands on its back. Within seconds, it rolls to an upright position with its legs tucked under its body. From this position, it views the world for the first time and shakes off any remaining birthing fluid.

The mother giraffe lowers her head just long enough to take a quick look at her calf, and then she does what seems to be a very unreasonable thing—she kicks her baby, sending it sprawling head over heels. If it doesn't get up, she kicks it again and again until the calf finally stands on its wobbly legs. Then what does the mother giraffe do? She kicks it off its feet! Why? She wants it to remember how to get up.

In the wild, baby giraffes must be able to get up as quickly as possible to stay with the herd and avoid becoming a meal for lions, hyenas, leopards, or wild hunting dogs. The best way a mother giraffe has of ensuring that her calf lives is for her to teach it to get up quickly and get with it.

Don't complain if those who love you push you into action when you'd rather be in "park." They are doing you a favor.

o o o o o

The road to success is dotted with many tempting parking places.

What is my attitude toward those who try to motivate me?

_____.
_____.
_____.
_____.
_____.
_____.
_____.
_____.
_____.
_____.
_____.
_____.
_____.
_____.
_____.
_____.

Let us lay aside every weight, and the sin which doth so easily beset us, and let us run with patience the race that is set before us.

HEBREWS 12:1

HOW enthusiastic am I in serving others?

_____

_____

_____

_____

_____

_____

_____

_____

_____

_____

_____

_____

_____

_____

_____

_____

On May 21, 1946, a scientist at Los Alamos was carrying out a necessary experiment in preparation for an atomic test to be conducted in the waters of the South Pacific. He had successfully performed this experiment many times before. It involved pushing two hemispheres of uranium together to determine the amount of U-235 needed for a chain reaction—the amount scientists call "critical mass." Just as the mass became critical, he would push the hemispheres apart with his screwdriver, instantly stopping the chain reaction.

That day, however, just as the material became critical, the screwdriver slipped. The hemispheres of uranium came too close together, and instantly, the room was filled with a dazzling bluish haze. Young Louis Soltin, instead of ducking and thereby possibly saving himself, tore the two hemispheres apart with his hands, thus interrupting the chain reaction.

In this instant, self-forgetful act, he saved the lives of seven other people who were in the room. He, however, died in agony nine days later.

Today, do something for someone else with the same energy you would use if you were doing it for yourself.

o o o o

Each of you should look not only to your own interests, but also to the interests of others.

PHILIPPIANS 2:4 NIV

When you are laboring for others, let it be with the same zeal as if it were for yourself.

Make Your Work Enjoyable

When David was twelve, he convinced a restaurant manager that he was actually sixteen and was hired as a lunch-counter waiter for twenty-five cents an hour. The place was owned by two Greek immigrant brothers, Frank and George, who had started their lives in America as a dishwasher and hot-dog seller. David remembers that they set high standards and never asked anything of their employees that they wouldn't do themselves. Frank once told David, "As long as you try, you can always work for me. But when you don't try, you can't work for me." Trying meant everything from working hard to treating customers politely. Once when Frank noticed a waitress giving a customer a rough time, he fired her on the spot and waited on the table himself. David determined that would never happen to him.

The usual tip for waiters in those days was a dime, but David discovered that if he brought the food out quickly and was especially polite, he sometimes got a quarter as a tip. He set a goal for himself to see how many customers he could wait on in one night. His record was one hundred!

Today, R. David Thomas is better known as "Dave," the founder and senior chairman of Wendy's International, Inc., a chain of forty-three hundred restaurants.

No matter what job you do, do it well.

o o o o

The Bible knows nothing of a hierarchy of labor. No work is degrading. It if ought to be done, then it is good work.

How can I make my chores or job more enjoyable?

_____ .
_____ .
_____ .
_____ .
_____ .
_____ .
_____ .
_____ .
_____ .
_____ .
_____ .
_____ .
_____ .
_____ .

To rejoice in his labour;
this is the gift of God.
ECCLESIASTES 5:19

Keep Reaching

What things do I allow to hinder me from pursuing my dream?

_____

_____

_____

_____

_____

_____

_____

_____

_____

_____

_____

_____

_____

_____

McCormick's father was what many might call a "tinkerer." A mechanical genius, he invented many farm devices. Sadly, however, he became the laughingstock of his community for attempting to make a grain-cutting device. For years, he worked on the project but never succeeded in getting it to operate reliably.

In spite of the discouragement his father experienced and the continuing ridicule of neighbors, young McCormick took up the old machine as his own project. He also experienced years of experimentation and failure. Then one day, he succeeded in constructing a reaper that would harvest grain.

Even so, jealous opposition prevented the invention from being used for a number of years. McCormick was able to make sales only after he gave a personal guarantee to each purchaser that the reaper would do the job he claimed it could do. Finally, after decades of trial and error, hoping and waiting, a firm in Cincinnati agreed to manufacture one hundred machines, and the famous McCormick reaper was "born."

To get to the ripest peach on the highest branch, you need to climb one limb at a time and not be defeated by the scrape of bark, the occasional fall, and the frequent feeling of being left dangling!

o o o o

Don't get discouraged and give up, for we will reap a harvest of blessing at the appropriate time.

GALATIANS 6:9 NLT

The ripest peach is highest on the tree.

Hard Work Pays Rich Dividends

The bee is often described as being "busy." It deserves this adjective! To produce one pound of honey, a bee must visit 56,000 clover heads. Since each head has sixty flower tubes, a bee must make a total of 3,360,000 visits. In the process, the average bee would travel the equivalent of three times around the world.

To make just one *tablespoon* of honey, the amount that might go on a biscuit, a little bee must make 4,200 trips to the flowers, averaging about ten trips a day, each trip lasting approximately twenty minutes. It visits 400 different flowers.

Day in, day out, the work of a bee is fairly unglamorous. It flies, it takes in nectar, it flies some more, and it deposits nectar. But in the process, it produces, and what it produces creates a place for it in the hive.

You may think your daily chores are a waste of time. But in fact, your completion of those chores is "making" *you*. One day, you won't even have to think: *I must get disciplined. I must get to work. I must stick with it.* If you have done your chores faithfully and to the best of your ability, the chores will have become a part of the way you tackle every challenge the rest of your life.

o o o o o

When you do the things you have to do when you have to do them, the day will come when you can do the things you want to do when you want to do them.

HOW can I improve my attitude toward my daily responsibilities?

_____.
_____.
_____.
_____.
_____.
_____.
_____.
_____.
_____.
_____.
_____.
_____.
_____.
_____.
_____.

We want each of you to go on with the same hard work all your lives so you will surely get what you hope for.

HEBREWS 6:11 NCV

Don't Worry; Be Happy

Nothing can get me down because . . .

_____

_____

_____

_____

_____

_____

_____

_____

_____

_____

_____

_____

_____

_____

_____

_____

Dr. Ashley Montagu met two young men shortly after the end of World War II. They had spent two years in Auschwitz—the cruel death camp operated by the Nazis. Prior to Auschwitz, they had lived in Vienna in a cellar, where they had been kept hidden by Christian friends. All of the others housed with them in the cellar had been exterminated solely because they were Jews. After the war ended, these two men had walked from Vienna to Berlin, hoping to find relatives. There, they were picked up by an American Jewish soldier who brought them to America. Both of them wanted to become physicians, and that's how Dr. Montagu, a professor in a medical school, came to meet them. Noting that they "didn't exhibit any of the scars that one might have expected from their unhappy existence," he asked them how they came to be such cheerful people.

They replied, "A group of us decided that no matter what happened, it wouldn't get us down." They told him they had attempted to be cheerful regardless of their circumstances, never yielding for a moment to the idea that they were either inferior or doomed.

They were living proof to Dr. Montagu that even under impossible conditions, it's possible to be happy!

o o o o

He that is of a merry heart hath a continual feast.

PROVERBS 15:15

A man without mirth is like a wagon without springs; he is jolted disagreeably by every pebble in the road.

Small Courtesies Speak Volumes

There's an old saying that goes, "It needs more skill than I can tell, to play the second fiddle well."

Along that line, Leonard Bernstein was once asked which instrument was the most difficult to play. He thought for a moment and said, "The second fiddle. I can get plenty of first violinists, but to find someone who can play the second fiddle with enthusiasm—that's a problem. And if we have no second fiddle, we have no harmony."

General Robert E. Lee was a man who knew the value of playing second fiddle. This great general never stopped being a true Southern gentleman. Once, while riding on a train to Richmond, he was seated at the rear of the car. All the other places were filled with officers and soldiers. A poorly dressed, elderly woman boarded the coach at a rural station, and finding no seat offered to her, she trudged down the aisle toward the back of the car. Immediately, Lee stood up and offered her his place. One after another of the men then arose and offered the general his seat. "No, gentlemen," he replied, "if there is none for this lady, there can be none for me!"

Genuine humility is what prompts us to offer a heartfelt thank you and to favor others over ourselves.

o o o o o

The two most important words: "Thank you." The most important word: "We." The least important word: "I."

HOW well do I play second fiddle to others?

Don't be selfish. . . . Be humble, thinking of others as better than yourself.

PHILIPPIANS 2:3 TLB

See the Possibilities

I can stimulate the creativity God has placed inside me by . . .

· _____

· _____

· _____

· _____

· _____

· _____

· _____

· _____

· _____

· _____

· _____

· _____

· _____

· _____

A number of years ago, the John Hancock Mutual Life Insurance Company ran an ad that read:

There was once a man who loved nature with such a deep and moving love that she told him one of her secrets. She gave him the power to create new plants. The man, whose name was Luther Burbank . . . saw that every plant was a child. It had its own face, own promise, its unique touch of genius or character. And if that promise were tended and encouraged, the plant would grow more useful and beautiful each year. Luther Burbank . . . made potatoes grow larger, whiter, more delicious than they had ever been. He taught the cactus of the desert to throw away its spines, so that cattle could fatten upon it, and made the blackberry shed its thorns, so it would not cut the fingers of the pickers. For him, the plum grew without pits, and strawberries ripened all year . . . he left the earth covered with flowers and fruits that no one had ever attempted to grow before. And all because he knew a secret. He knew that everything that lives has the power to become greater.

Choose to see new possibilities. Put your mind to them. Let them be the focus of your thoughts and then pursue them! You will become greater for it.

○ ○ ○ ○

Make a careful exploration of who you are and the work you have been given, and then sink yourself into that.

GALATIANS 6:4 THE MESSAGE

Somebody is always doing what somebody else said couldn't be done.

Resolve to Succeed

Famous stage and film actress Helen Hayes believed her "resoluteness" about her own potential for success played an important role at the beginning of her career. She once told the story of a particular audition:

Before the authors gave me the script, they observed, in a matter-of-course manner, "Of course you play piano? You'll have to sing to your own accompaniment in the piece." As these alarming tidings were in the course of being made, I caught a bewildered look in my mother's eyes, and so I spoke up before she could. "Certainly I play piano," I answered.

As we left the theater, my mother sighed, "I hate to see you start under a handicap," she said. "What made you say you could play piano?"

"The feeling that I will play before rehearsals begin," I said. We went at once to try to rent a piano and ended by buying one. I began lessons at once, practiced finger exercises till I could no longer see the notes—and began rehearsals with the ability to accompany myself. Since then, I have never lived too far from a piano.

What you believe about your own potential for success counts far more than what any other person may believe. Believe what God believes about you—you were created for success.

○ ○ ○ ○ ○

Always bear in mind that your own resolution to succeed is more important than any other one thing.

What does God believe about me?

_____ .

_____ .

_____ .

_____ .

_____ .

_____ .

_____ .

_____ .

_____ .

_____ .

_____ .

_____ .

_____ .

_____ .

_____ .

_____ .

_____ .

The Lord God will help me; therefore shall I not be confounded: therefore have I set my face like a flint, and I know that I shall not be ashamed.

ISAIAH 50:7

You Can Triumph

Which of my dreams are important enough to me to keep me trying?

_____

_____

_____

_____

_____

_____

_____

_____

_____

_____

_____

_____

_____

_____

_____

_____

Many years ago in England, a small boy grew up speaking with a lisp. He was never a scholar in school. When war broke out involving his nation, he was rejected from service, told that "we need *men*." He once rose to address the House of Commons, and all present walked out of the room. In fact, he often spoke to empty chairs and echoes. But one day, he became Prime Minister of Great Britain, and with stirring speeches and bold decisions, he led his nation to victory. His name was Sir Winston Churchill.

Many years ago in Illinois, a man with only a few years of formal education failed in business in '31, was defeated in a run for the state legislature in '32, again failed in business in '33, was elected to the legislature in '34, but defeated for speaker in '38. He was defeated for elector in '40, defeated for Congress in '43, elected to Congress in '46, but defeated in '48. He was defeated for Senate in '55, defeated for the vice-presidential nomination in '56, and defeated for the Senate in '58. But in 1860, he was elected president. His name was Abraham Lincoln.

No one is defeated until he gives up trying.

o o o o o

Triumph is just "umph" added to try.

Thanks be unto God, which always causeth us to triumph in Christ.

2 CORINTHIANS 2:14

Persistence Pays Off

A young man in need of work once saw this advertisement in a Boston newspaper: "Wanted: young man as an understudy to a financial statistician, P.O. Box 1720." The young man decided this was just the kind of job he wanted, so he replied to the ad but received no answer. He wrote again and even a third time with no reply. Next, he went to the Boston post office and asked the name of the holder of Box 1720, but the clerk refused to give it, as did the postmaster.

Early one morning, an idea came to the young man. He rose early, took the first train to Boston, went to the post office, and stood watch near Box 1720. After a while, a man appeared, opened the box, and took out the mail. The young man followed him as he returned to the office of a stock brokerage firm. The young man entered and asked for the manager.

In the interview, the manager asked, "How did you find out that I was the advertiser?" The young man told about his detective work, to which the manager replied, "Young man, you are just the kind of persistent fellow I want. You are employed!"

If a goal is worthy, there's no good reason to stop pursuing it! Find something you truly want to do, then go for it with all your heart, mind, and strength.

o o o o o

The heights by great men reached and kept were not attained by sudden flight, But they, while their companions slept, Were toiling upward in the night.

In my situation, to be persistant means I will . . .

_____ .
_____ .
_____ .
_____ .
_____ .
_____ .
_____ .
_____ .
_____ .
_____ .
_____ .
_____ .
_____ .
_____ .
_____ .

"If you keep knocking long enough he will get up and give you everything you want—just because of your persistence."

LUKE 11:8 TLB

Pay Attention

If I would pay attention more often, I would . . .

_____

_____

_____

_____

_____

_____

_____

_____

_____

_____

_____

_____

_____

_____

"Pick strong, healthy, good-looking lads," he said; "those who have read widely in many fields, are well informed, alert and sensible, and have enough poise to look good around the palace."

DANIEL 1:4 TLB

Henry P. Davison was a prominent American financier and one-time head of the American Red Cross. He worked his way up from being a poor boy to become president of a large New York City bank.

While he was a cashier of that bank, a would-be robber came to his window, pointed a revolver at him, and passed a check across his window counter. The check was for one million dollars, payable to the Almighty. Davison remained calm, even though he realized the gravity of the situation. In a loud voice, he repeated the words on the check back to the person standing in front of him, emphasizing the "million dollars." Then he graciously asked the would-be robber how he would like to have the "million dollars" for the Almighty. He then proceeded to count out small bills. In the meantime, the suspicion of a guard had been aroused by the strange request he had overheard. He disarmed the robber and prevented the theft.

In later years, Davison was often asked to give his wisdom to others seeking success. He often advised that courtesy, readiness, willingness, and alertness do more for a person than just being smart.

It has been said that one of the skills of a good communicator is the ability to listen. Paying attention to the words and actions of those around you may be the best schooling you'll ever receive.

o o o o o

I think the one lesson I have learned is that there is no substitute for paying attention.

Listen Up

An American Indian was once visiting New York City, and as he walked the busy Manhattan streets with a friend from the city, he suddenly stopped, tilted his head to one side, and said, "I hear a cricket."

"You're crazy," his friend said.

The Cherokee answered, "No, I hear a cricket. I do! I'm sure of it."

The friend replied, "It's the noon hour. People are jammed on the sidewalks, cars are honking, taxis are whizzing by, the city is full of noise. And you think you can hear a cricket?"

"I'm sure I do," said the visitor. He listened even more closely and then walked to the corner, spotted a shrub in a large cement planter, dug into the leaves underneath it, and pulled out a cricket. His friend was astounded. The man said, "The fact is, my friend, that my ears are different than yours. It all depends on what your ears have been tuned to hear. Let me show you." At that, he reached into his pocket, pulled out a handful of loose change, and dropped the coins on the pavement. Every head within a half block turned. "See what I mean?" he said, picking up the coins. "It all depends on what you are listening for."

Listen today to those things that will make you wise. Don't neglect those things that will prepare you for eternity.

o o o o o

A good listener is not only popular everywhere, but after a while he knows something.

What would God have me listen for?

Listen to your father and mother. What you learn from them will stand you in good stead; it will gain you many honors.

PROVERBS 1:8-9 TLB

What are the things that keep me from making decisions?

_____

_____

_____

_____

_____

_____

_____

_____

_____

_____

_____

_____

_____

_____

Former President Ronald Reagan enjoyed telling the following story about himself. He claimed it was how he learned, early in life, to make firm and resolute decisions.

According to the story, a kindly aunt once took him to a cobbler to have a pair of shoes custom made for him. The shoemaker asked, "Do you want a square toe or a round one?" The young Reagan hemmed and hawed, so the cobbler said, "Come back in a day or two and tell me what you want."

A few days later the cobbler saw Reagan on the street and asked what he had decided about the shoes. "I haven't made up my mind," Reagan answered.

"Very well," the cobbler said, and then he announced to his customer, "Your shoes will be ready tomorrow." When Reagan got the shoes, one had a round toe and the other a square toe!

Reagan concluded, "Looking at those shoes every day taught me a lesson. If you don't make your own decisions, somebody else will make them for you."

Remember always that no decision, is a decision!

o o o o o

Indecision is often worse than the wrong action.

They can't make up their minds.
They waver back and forth in
everything they do.

JAMES 1:8 NLT

Be Strong and of Good Courage

In *The Seven Habits of Highly Effective People*, Stephen R. Covey writes the following:

One of the most inspiring times Sandra and I have ever had took place over a four-year period with a dear friend of ours named Carol who had a wasting cancer disease. She had been one of Sandra's bridesmaids, and they had been best friends for over twenty-five years.

When Carol was in the very last stages of the disease, Sandra spent time at her bedside helping her write her personal history. She returned from those protracted and difficult sessions almost transfixed by admiration for her friend's courage and her desire to write special messages to be given to her children at different stages in their lives.

Carol would take as little pain-killing medication as possible, so that she had full access to her mental and emotional faculties. Then she would whisper into a tape recorder or to Sandra directly as she took notes. Carol was so proactive, so brave, and so concerned about others that she became an enormous source of inspiration to many people around her.

In today's world, perhaps one trait is needed desperately. Seek to develop it. It's called *courage*.

HOW can I develop more courage?

The coward seeks release from pressure. The courageous pray for strength.

Be of good courage, and he shall strengthen your heart, all ye that hope in the LORD.

PSALM 31:24

Faithfulness

HOW can I be more faithful in my position?

A quiet forest dweller who lived high above an Austrian village in the Alps was hired by a town council to keep the pristine mountain springs—the source of the town's water supply—clear of debris. With faithful regularity, the old man patrolled the hills, clearing away silt and removing leaves and branches from the springs. Over time, the village became prosperous. Mill wheels turned, farms were irrigated, and tourists came. Years passed. Then at a council meeting about the city budget, a member noticed the salary figure for the old man. He asked, "Who is he, and why do we keep him on the payroll? Has anybody seen him? For all we know, he might be dead." The council voted to dispense with his services.

For several weeks nothing changed. Then the trees began to shed their leaves. One afternoon, a town citizen noticed a brown tint to the water. Within another week, a slick covered sections of the canals, and a foul odor was detected. Sickness broke out.

The town council called a special meeting, and reversing their error in judgment, they rehired the old man. Renewed life soon returned to the village as the sparkling waters returned.

Not everyone's job will make the six o'clock news everyday, but no matter where God places you, do your work unto Him, and He will reward you for your faithfulness.

o o o o

A faithful employee is as refreshing as a cool day in the hot summertime.

PROVERBS 25:13 TLB

Is your place a small place? Tend it with care!—He set you there.

One of the great disasters of history took place in 1271. In that year, Niccolo and Matteo Polo, the father and uncle of Marco Polo, visited Kubla Khan who was considered the world ruler, with authority over all of China, India, and the East.

The Kubla Khan was attracted to the story of Christianity as Niccolo and Matteo told it to him. He said to them, "You shall go to your high priest and tell him on my behalf to send me a hundred men skilled in your religion, and I shall be baptized, and when I am baptized, all my barons and great men will be baptized, and their subjects will receive baptism, too, and so there will be more Christians here than there are in your parts."

Nothing was done, however, in response to what the Kubla Khan had requested. After thirty years, only a handful of missionaries was sent. It was too few, too late.

The West apparently did not have the vision to see the East won to Christ. The mind boggles at the possible ways the world might be different today if thirteenth-century China, India, and the other areas of the Orient had been converted to Christianity.

If you lack vision today, ask God for it. He has wonders to reveal to you that you can't yet imagine!

o o o o o

In spite of all appearances to the contrary, God has a plan for this bankrupt world. He still has something in store for it.

What do I sense God calling me to do?

_____ .
_____ .
_____ .
_____ .
_____ .
_____ .
_____ .
_____ .
_____ .
_____ .
_____ .
_____ .
_____ .
_____ .
_____ .

I ask—ask the God of our Master, Jesus Christ, the God of glory—to make you intelligent and discerning in knowing him personally, your eyes focused and clear, so that you can see exactly what it is he is calling you to do.
EPHESIANS 1:17-18 THE MESSAGE

Don't Just Hope for Change

IS there a cause about which I
feel I should take action?

. _____

. _____

. _____

. _____

. _____

. _____

. _____

. _____

. _____

. _____

. _____

. _____

. _____

Many people remember President
Theodore Roosevelt as an avid hunter and
sportsman. Few, however, know of his efforts
for conservation, which is a far greater legacy.

After a hunting trip to the Dakota region
in 1887—years before he was president—
Roosevelt returned to his East Coast home,
reporting that trees were being cut down
carelessly, animals were being slaughtered by
"swinish game-butchers," and that wilderness
was in danger. He expressed great shock at
how quickly this region that he loved was
being stripped of its glory—the big game gone,
the ponds drying up, the beavers disappearing,
the grasslands becoming desert.

But Roosevelt did more than talk. He
founded the Boone & Crockett Club,
dedicated to the preservation of wilderness in
America. Largely through that club's influence,
legislation was passed to care for Yellowstone
National Park, to protect sequoia trees in
California, to set aside nature reserves for bird
and sea life, and to limit the shooting of big
game. Laws were also passed to regulate
hunting practices.

Hoping for change rarely brings about
change. Work, however, generally does!

o o o o o

*People who are waiting for something
to turn up might start with their own
shirt sleeves.*

Let them shout for joy, and be glad, that
favour my righteous cause.

PSALM 35:27

Sweet Release

Lloyd John Ogilvie wrote the following in *Let God Love You:*

The hardest time to be gentle is when we know we are right and someone else is obviously dead wrong.... But the greatest temptation for most of us is when someone has failed us and has admitted it, and their destiny or happiness is in our hands. We hold the power to give or refuse a blessing.

Recently, a dear friend hurt me in both word and action. Each time we met ... I almost began to enjoy the leverage of being the offended one. His first overtures of restitution were resisted because of the gravity of the judgment I had made. He had taken a key idea I had shared with him in confidence and had developed it as his own before I had a chance to use it. The plagiarism of ideas had been coupled with the use of some of my written material, reproduced under his name.... The most difficult thing was to surrender my indignation and work through my hurt....

Finally, the Lord got me where he wanted me.... His word to me was clear and undeniable, "Lloyd, why is it so important to you who gets the credit, just so my work gets done?" I gave up my right to be what only God could be as this man's judge and savior. The gentle attitude began to flow.

When we withhold forgiveness, it not only hurts the person we don't want to forgive, it hurts us. Our creativity and joy in life are stifled. When we forgive, we release peace and restoration to the forgiven and to ourselves.¹¹

o o o o o

Forgiveness means giving up your right to punish another.

Am I willing to give up my right to punish those who've hurt me?

_____ .
_____ .
_____ .
_____ .
_____ .
_____ .
_____ .
_____ .
_____ .
_____ .
_____ .
_____ .
_____ .
_____ .
_____ .

"When you stand praying, if you hold anything against anyone, forgive him, so that your Father in heaven may forgive you your sins."

MARK 11:25 NIV

A Lesson from the Bee

What lesson can I learn from the bee today?

_____

_____

_____

_____

_____

_____

_____

_____

_____

_____

_____

_____

_____

_____

Many people today seem to go through their day with their "stingers out," ready to attack others or to defend their position at the slightest provocation. We all do well, however, to consider the full nature of the bees we sometimes seem to emulate.

Bees readily feed each other, sometimes even a bee of a different colony. The worker bees feed the queen bee, who cannot feed herself. They feed the drones during their period of usefulness in the hive. They feed the young. They seem to enjoy this social act of mutual feeding.

Bees cluster together for warmth in cold weather and fan their wings to cool the hive in hot weather, thus working for one another's comfort.

When the time comes for bees to move to new quarters, scouts report back to the group, doing a dance very similar to the one used to report a find of honey. When enough scouts have confirmed the suitability of the new location, the bees appear to make a common decision, take wing, and migrate together—all at the same time—in what we call a swarm.

Only as a last-resort measure of self-defense do bees engage their stingers, and then, never against their fellow bees. We would do well to learn from them!

o o o o o

See that no one pays back evil for evil, but always try to do good to each other and to everyone else.

I THESSALONIANS 5:15 TLB

The most important single ingredient in the formula of success is knowing how to get along with people.

Grow into Your Full Potential

Andrew Carnegie, considered to be one of the first to emphasize self-esteem and the potential for inner greatness, was famous for his ability to produce millionaires from among his employees. One day a reporter asked him, "How do you account for the fact you have forty-three millionaires working for you?"

Carnegie replied, "They weren't rich when they came. We work with people the same way you mine gold. You have to remove a lot of dirt before you find a small amount of gold."

Andrew Carnegie knew how to bring about change in people. He helped them realize their hidden treasure within, inspired them to develop it, and then watched with encouragement as their lives were transformed.

The philosopher and psychologist William James once said, "Compared to what we ought to be, we are only half awake. We are making use of only a small part of our physical and mental resources. Stating the thing broadly, the human individual thus lives far within his limits. He possesses powers of various sorts which he habitually fails to use."

In other words, most people only develop a fraction of their abilities. Go for a bigger percentage in *your* life. Find the gold within!

o o o o o

Everyone thinks of changing the world, but no one thinks of changing himself.

Is there any dirt covering the gold within me?

We are to grow up in all aspects into Him, who is the head, even Christ.

EPHESIANS 4:15 NASB

Which of God's promises could I speak to the tigers in my life?

_____

_____

_____

_____

_____

_____

_____

_____

_____

_____

_____

_____

_____

_____

_____

_____

Several years ago, a well-known television circus developed an act involving Bengal tigers. The act was performed live before a large audience. One night, the tiger trainer went into the cage with several tigers, and the door was routinely locked behind him. Spotlights flooded the cage, and television cameras moved in close, so the audience could see every detail as he skillfully put the tigers through their paces.

In the middle of the performance, the worst happened: the lights went out. For nearly thirty long seconds, the trainer was locked in with the tigers in the darkness. With their superb night vision, the tigers could see him, but he could not see them. Still, he survived. When the lights came back on, he calmly finished his performance.

When the trainer was asked how he felt, he admitted to feeling chilling fear at first, but then, he said, he realized that even though he couldn't see the big cats, they didn't know he couldn't see them. He said, "I just kept cracking my whip and talking to them until the lights came on. They never knew I couldn't see them as well as they could see me."

Keep talking back to the tigers of fear that seem to be stalking you. They will obey your voice of faith!

o o o o o

The devil, your enemy, goes around like a roaring lion looking for someone to eat. Refuse to give in to him, by standing strong in your faith.

I PETER 5:8-9 NCV

The triumphant Christian does not fight for victory; he celebrates a victory already won. The victorious life is Christ's business, not yours.

He Hears Every Prayer

Both a major thoroughfare in Tel Aviv and a bridge that spans the Jordan River are named in honor of Viscount Edmund Henry Hynman Allenby, a British solider. As commander of the Egyptian Expeditionary Forces, he outwitted and defeated the Turks in Palestine in 1917 and 1918, conquering Jerusalem without ever firing a single gun.

As a British solider, Allenby was noncommittal about the official British policies concerning the establishment of a Jewish national home, but he did have a deep understanding of the Jews' desire to dwell in Palestine. At a reception in London, he once told how as a little boy, he had knelt to say his evening prayers, repeating with his child-hood lisp the words his mother prayed: "And, O Lord, we would not forget Thine ancient people, Israel; hasten the day when Israel shall again be Thy people and shall be restored to Thy favor and to their land."

Allenby concluded, "I never knew then that God would give me the privilege of helping to answer my own childhood prayers."

What you pray today may well be part of tomorrow's work. The world you envision in prayer may well be the world in which you one day will live!

o o o o

Prayer is an invisible tool which is wielded in a visible world.

What prayer rises up within me most often?

_____ .
_____ .
_____ .
_____ .
_____ .
_____ .
_____ .
_____ .
_____ .
_____ .
_____ .
_____ .
_____ .
_____ .

The weapons of our warfare are not carnal, but mighty through God to the pulling down of strong holds.

2 CORINTHIANS 10:4

Be a Giver

What can I give to benefit another today?

. _____

. _____

. _____

. _____

. _____

. _____

. _____

. _____

. _____

. _____

. _____

. _____

A strange memorial can be found in the Mount Hope Cemetery of Hiawatha, Kansas. John M. Davis, an orphan, developed a strong dislike for his wife's family and insisted that none of his fortune go to them. He also refused requests that he eventually bequeath his estate for a hospital desperately needed in the area. Instead, after his wife died in 1930, Mr. Davis chose to invest in an elaborate tomb for himself and his wife. The tomb includes a number of statues depicting the couple at various stages of their lives. One statue is of Mr. Davis as a lonely man seated beside an empty chair. It is titled *The Vacant Chair*. Another shows him placing a wreath in front of his wife's tombstone. Many of the statues are made of Kansas granite. No money was left for the memorial's upkeep.

Today, largely because of its weight, this costly memorial is slowly sinking into the ground. It has become weathered and worn from the strong winds in this plains state. The townspeople regard the Davis tomb as an "old man's folly," and many predict that within the next fifty years, the memorial will have become obliterated beyond recognition and will need to be demolished. What could have been a living legacy will eventually become granite dust.

The Bible encourages us many times not to hoard up money to be used for our own selfish desires but to be kind to the poor. When we do so, God blesses us with more. The more we give, the more we receive, and our legacy will last well into the future instead of sinking into oblivion.

o o o o o

Money is like an arm or leg:
use it or lose it.

"If you give, you will receive. Your gift will return to you in full measure, pressed down, shaken together to make room for more, and running over. Whatever measure you use in giving—large or small—it will be used to measure what is given back to you."
LUKE 6:38 NLT

In 1894, a sixteen-year-old found this note from his rhetoric teacher at Harrow, in England, attached to his report card: "A conspicuous lack of success." The young man kept on trying and went on to become one of the most famous speakers of the twentieth century. His name was Winston Churchill.

In 1902, an aspiring twenty-eight-year-old writer received a rejection letter from the poetry editor of the *Atlantic Monthly*. Returned, with a batch of poems he had sent, was this curt note: "Our magazine has no room for your vigorous verse." He kept on trying, however, and went on to see his work published. The poet's name was Robert Frost.

In 1905, the University of Bern turned down a Ph.D. dissertation as being fanciful and irrelevant. The young physics student, who wrote the dissertation, kept on trying and went on to develop some of his ideas into widely accepted theories. His name was Albert Einstein.

When rejection shakes your resolve and dims your goals, keep on trying. If you do not quit, one day, you will be living out your dreams!

o o o o

In trying times, don't quit trying.

HOW do these people's lives inspire me?

———————————————— .
———————————————— .
———————————————— .
———————————————— .
———————————————— .
———————————————— .
———————————————— .
———————————————— .
———————————————— .
———————————————— .
———————————————— .
———————————————— .
———————————————— .
———————————————— .

The righteous will move onward and forward, and those with pure hearts will become stronger and stronger.

JOB 17:9 NLT

Let Your Character Shine

HOW do I respond to those who are different from me?

———————————————
———————————————
———————————————
———————————————
———————————————
———————————————
———————————————
———————————————
———————————————
———————————————
———————————————
———————————————
———————————————
———————————————
———————————————

When Chief Justice Charles Evans Hughes moved to Washington, DC, to take up his duties on the Supreme Court, he transferred his church membership letter to a Baptist church in the area.

It was customary for all new members in this church to come to the front of the sanctuary at the close of the worship service, so they might be officially introduced and welcomed. The first person to be called forward that morning was Ah Sing, a Chinese laundryman who had moved to Washington from the West Coast. He took his place at the far side of the church. As the dozen or so others were called forward that day, they came forward and stood on the opposite side of the church, leaving Ah Sing standing alone.

Finally Chief Justice Hughes was called forward, and he immediately made his way to the front and proceeded to stand next to Ah Sing. The minister who welcomed the group into the church fellowship said, "I do not want this congregation to miss this remarkable illustration of the fact that at the cross of Jesus Christ, the ground is level."

Your character is shown in many ways, but one of the most obvious is the way you treat people. You will grow in character and reputation if you treat others with kindness.

o o o o

Those members of the body, which we think to be less honourable, upon these we bestow more abundant honour.

I CORINTHIANS 12:23

Let us not say, "Every man is the architect of his own fortune"; but let us say, "Every man is the architect of his own character."

Jesus Is Your Path

E. Stanley Jones tells the story of a missionary who became lost in an African jungle. Looking around, he saw nothing but bush and a few clearings. He stumbled about until he finally came across a native hut. He asked one of the natives if he could lead him out of the jungle and back to the mission station. The native agreed to help him.

"Thank you!" exclaimed the missionary. "Which way do I go?"

The native replied, "Walk." And so they did, hacking their way through the unmarked jungle for more than an hour.

In pausing to rest, the missionary looked around and had the same overwhelming sense that he was lost. Again, all he could see was bush and a few clearings. "Are you quite sure this is the way?" he asked. "I don't see any path."

The native looked at him and replied, "Bwana, in this place there is no path. I am the path."

When we have no clue as to which direction we're going, we must remember that God who guides us is omniscient—all-wise. When we run out of time, we must remember that God is omnipresent—all time is in His hand. When we are weak, we must remember that God is omnipotent—all-powerful. He is everything we need.

o o o o o

It is impossible for that man to despair who remembers that his Helper is omnipotent.

Since Jesus is the way for me, I can . . .

—————————————— .
—————————————— .
—————————————— .
—————————————— .
—————————————— .
—————————————— .
—————————————— .
—————————————— .
—————————————— .
—————————————— .
—————————————— .
—————————————— .
—————————————— .
—————————————— .

Jesus told him, "I am the Way."

JOHN 14:6 TLB

Today I will read . . .

. _____
. _____
. _____
. _____
. _____
. _____
. _____
. _____
. _____
. _____
. _____
. _____
. _____
. _____

After experiencing numerous failures in business and politics, Abraham Lincoln still maintained his daily habit of reading. A critic scoffed, "What good is all that education? It has never earned you a decent living."

Lincoln replied, "Education is not given for the purpose of earning a living; it's learning what to do with a living after you earn it that counts."

One of America's greatest reading advocates is Jim Trelease. He has devoted nearly two decades to promoting what he considers the most important social factor in our lives today. "The more you read," he says, "the smarter you grow. The smarter you grow, the longer you stay in school. The longer you stay in school, the more money you earn. The more you earn, the better your children will do in school. So if you hook a child with reading, you influence not only his future, but also that of the next generation."

Reading researchers agree. They have long seen a correlation between the time a person spends reading and the number of innovative ideas and creative solutions a person has. Reading affects a person's ability to reason and to communicate, by providing an extended and accurate vocabulary.

Spend some time reading today. It will be time well spent because investing in your personal growth affects your future success. As the poster often seen hanging in libraries and classrooms says, "Succeed . . . Read!"

o o o o o

A man who does not read good books has no advantage over the man who can't read them.

Apply thine heart unto instruction, and thine ears to the words of knowledge.

PROVERBS 23:12

In the 1700s, an English cobbler kept a map of the world on his workshop wall so that he might be reminded to pray for the nations of the world. As the result of such prayer, he became especially burdened for a specific missionary outreach. He shared this burden at a meeting of ministers but was told by a senior minister, "Young man, sit down. When God wants to convert the heathen, He will do it without your help or mine."

The cobbler, William Carey, did not let this man's remarks put out the flame of his concern. When he couldn't find others to support the missionary cause that had burdened his soul, he became a missionary himself. His pioneering efforts in India are legendary; his mighty exploits for God are recorded by many church historians.

Be careful how you respond to the enthusiasm of others. Don't dampen someone's zeal for God. Be cautious in how you respond to the new ideas of another so that you don't squelch their God-given creativity.

Be generous and kind in evaluating the work of others so that you might encourage those things which are worthy. Be slow to judge and quick to praise. Then pray for the same in your own life!

o o o o o

Those that have done nothing in life are not qualified to judge those that have done little.

Don't suppress the Spirit, and don't stifle those who have a word from the Master.

I THESSALONIANS 5:19-20 THE MESSAGE

The Source of Fulfillment

What can I give away to bless another person?

A young man once came to Jesus, asking Him what he needed to do to have eternal life. Jesus replied that he should keep the commandments. The young man then claimed that he had always kept them. Jesus advised, "If you would be perfect, sell everything you have, give the money to the poor, and come and follow me." (See Matthew 19:21.)

The Scriptures tell us that the young man "went away sorrowful: for he had great possessions" (v. 22). The young man not only had great possessions, but apparently those possessions had him! He couldn't bear to part with earthly, temporary goods in order to obtain heavenly, eternal goods. Jesus also taught, of course, that Heaven's "wealth" can be ours now. This young man didn't have to wait until he died to attain the benefits of eternal life. If he had been willing to give up his hold on his "stuff," he could have enjoyed great joy, peace, and fulfillment in life—things he was apparently lacking, or he wouldn't have asked Jesus the question.

Take a look at your possessions today. Are there books, tapes, CDs, or clothes you could give away to someone in need of learning, inspiration, or clothing? Discover how rewarding giving can be!

o   o   o   o

"I am come that they might have life, and that they might have it more abundantly."

JOHN 10:10

People, places, and things were never meant to give us life. God alone is the Author of a fulfilling life.

The Most Important Person in Your Life

When Ruth Bell was a teenager, she was sent from her childhood home in China to school in Korea. At the time, she fully intended to follow in her parents' footsteps and become a missionary. She envisioned herself a confirmed "old maid," ministering to the people of Tibet. While at school, however, Ruth did give some serious thought to the kind of husband that she *might* consider. As she tells in her book *A Time for Remembering*, she listed these particulars:

If I marry: He must be so tall that when he is on his knees, as one has said, he reaches all the way to heaven. His shoulders must be broad enough to bear the burden of a family. His lips must be strong enough to smile, firm enough to say no, and tender enough to kiss. Love must be so deep that it takes its stand in Christ and so wide that it takes the whole lost world in. He must be active enough to save souls. He must be big enough to be gentle and great enough to be thoughtful. His arms must be strong enough to carry a little child.

Ruth Bell never did become a full-time missionary in Tibet. However, she did find a man worth marrying—Billy Graham. As his wife, Ruth Bell Graham became a missionary to the whole world!

Your spouse will be the most important person in your life. It's crucial to marry the right person. Think about the qualities that you would like to have in a mate. If you haven't already, begin to pray for the person you will eventually marry. Even if you haven't met him or her yet, God knows who it is.

o o o o o

You will never make a more important decision than the person you marry.

What are the most important traits I desire in a mate?

_____ .
_____ .
_____ .
_____ .
_____ .
_____ .
_____ .
_____ .
_____ .
_____ .
_____ .
_____ .
_____ .
_____ .

A man shall leave his father and mother and be joined to his wife, and they shall become one flesh.

GENESIS 2:24 NKJV

Safe Sex

HOW do I feel about following God's plan for sex?

_____

_____

_____

_____

_____

_____

_____

_____

_____

_____

_____

_____

_____

_____

_____

_____

Marriage should be honored by all, and the marriage bed kept pure, for God will judge the adulterer and all the sexually immoral.

HEBREWS 13:4 NIV

The 1960s were known for many rebellions, among them the sexual revolution. "Free love" spilled from the hippie movement into the mainstream American culture. Premarital sexual relations sanctioned by the "new morality" became openly flaunted.

One of the unexpected results of this trend, however, received little publicity. As reported by Dr. Francis Braceland, past president of the American Psychiatric Association and editor of the _American Journal of Psychiatry_, an increasing number of young people were admitted to mental hospitals during that time. In discussing this finding at a National Methodist Convocation of Medicine and Theology, Braceland concluded, "A more lenient attitude on campus about premarital sexual experience has imposed stresses on some college women severe enough to cause emotional breakdown."

Looking back over the years since the "new morality" was sanctioned by a high percentage of the American culture, one finds a rising number of rapes, abortions, divorces, premarital pregnancies, single-family homes, and cases of sexually transmitted diseases, including herpes and HIV.

The evidence is compelling: the old morality produced safer, healthier, and happier people! Even if you have slipped, it's never too late to start over. Be courageous enough to ask for God's forgiveness and the grace to hold out for His best. You'll be glad you did.

o o o o o

The Bible has a word to describe "safe" sex: it's called marriage.

Good Manners Matter

We often refer to courtesy as "common courtesy," but it is far from common these days. In fact, it is pretty rare.

A father once remarked about his three children: "My children may not be the brightest children in their class. They may not be the most talented or the most skilled. They may not achieve great fame or earn millions of dollars. But by my insisting that they have good manners, I know they will be welcome in all places and by all people." How true!

Good manners—exhibiting common courtesies—are like a calling card. They open doors that are otherwise shut to those who are rude, crude, or unmannerly. They bring welcome invitations and, quite often, return engagements. They cover a multitude of weaknesses and flaws. They make other people feel good about themselves, and they, in turn, extend kindness and generosity they might not otherwise exhibit. Good manners are a prerequisite for good friendships, good family relations, good business associations, and good marriages. It is a key to success!

○ ○ ○ ○ ○

Nothing is ever lost by courtesy. . . .
It pleases him who gives and him
who receives, and thus, like mercy,
it is twice blessed.

How courteous am I toward my family and others?

_____ .
_____ .
_____ .
_____ .
_____ .
_____ .
_____ .
_____ .
_____ .
_____ .
_____ .
_____ .
_____ .
_____ .

The wisdom that comes from heaven is first
of all pure and full of quiet gentleness.
Then it is peace-loving and courteous.

JAMES 3:17 TLB

Problems Can Work in Your Favor

DO I trust God to show me a solution to my problems?

_____

_____

_____

_____

_____

_____

_____

_____

_____

_____

_____

_____

_____

For years, farmers in southern Alabama had one mainstay crop: cotton. They plowed as much ground as they could each year to plant their big cash crop, and year after year, they lived by their cotton production. Then one year, the dreaded boll weevil devastated the entire area's crops. Optimistic that the tragedy was an isolated event, the farmers mortgaged their homes and planted cotton again the next year, hoping for a big harvest to help them recoup their losses. But once again, the insect destroyed the crop, and as a result, most of the farmers were wiped out.

The few farmers who were able to survive two years of boll weevil infestation decided to do something the third year that they had never done before—plant peanuts. The peanuts proved to be resistant to insects, and the market was strong. Most of those who planted peanuts were able to reap enough profit that third year to pay off all their debts. They chose to plant peanuts from that point on, and they greatly prospered.

In the following years, the farmers actually erected a monument to their old enemy—the boll weevil. They concluded that if it hadn't been for the boll weevil, they never would have discovered peanuts.[12]

If a problem forces you to take a detour, don't be discouraged. You may find it is a better road!

○ ○ ○ ○

A sensible man watches for problems ahead and prepares to meet them. The simpleton never looks, and suffers the consequences.

PROVERBS 27:12 TLB

Problems are opportunities in work clothes.

Bless Your Parents

A mother watched with raised eyebrows as her two sons took a hammer and a few nails from the kitchen utility drawer and scurried to one of the boys' rooms, giggling and talking in low voices. When she didn't hear any hammering, she continued with her chores. Then from the kitchen window, she saw one of the boys take a stepladder from the garage. He disappeared from sight before she could call to him. A few minutes later her other son came into the kitchen to ask if she had any rope. "No," Mom said. "What's going on?"

Her son said, "Nothin'."

Mom pressed, "Are you sure?" But her son was out of sight. Highly suspicious, she went to her son's room and found the door closed and locked. She knocked. "What are you boys doing in there?" she asked.

One son replied, "Nothin'."

Suspecting great mischief, she demanded entrance. "I want you to open this door right now!" she said.

A few seconds later, the door popped open, and her son shouted, "Surprise!" as he handed her a rather crudely wrapped present.

"Happy birthday, Mom!" the other boy added.

Truly surprised, the mother stammered, "But what about the hammer, nails, ladder, and rope?"

The boys grinned, "Those were just decoys, Mom."

o o o o o

Children who bring honor to their parents reap blessings from their God.

I will bless my parents today by . . .

_____ .
_____ .
_____ .
_____ .
_____ .
_____ .
_____ .
_____ .
_____ .
_____ .
_____ .
_____ .
_____ .

Honor your father and your mother, so that you may live long in the land the LORD your God is giving you.

EXODUS 20:12 NIV

HOW good am I at yielding to others?

_____

_____

_____

_____

_____

_____

_____

_____

_____

_____

_____

_____

_____

_____

_____

_____

While driving down a country road, a man came to a very narrow bridge. In front of the bridge, there was a sign that read, "Yield." Seeing no oncoming cars, the man continued across the bridge and to his destination. On his way back using this same route, he came to the same one-lane bridge, now from the opposite direction. To his surprise, he saw another "Yield" sign posted there.

Curious, he thought, _I'm sure there was one positioned on the other side._ Sure enough, when he reached the other side of the bridge and looked back, he saw the sign. Yield signs had been placed at both ends of the bridge, obviously with the intent that drivers from both directions were requested to give each other the right-of-way. It was a reasonable and doubly sure way to prevent a head-on collision.

If you find yourself in a combative situation with someone who has more authority than you—or equal authority—it is always wise to yield to him or her. If that person does have more authority, a lack of submission will put you into a position to be punished or reprimanded. If you are of equal authority, an exercise of your power will only build resentment in a person better kept as an ally. As the Bible says, we are to "prefer one another" (Romans 12:10).

o o o o o

Show respect for everyone. Love Christians everywhere. Fear God and honor the government.

I PETER 2:17 TLB

Those who desire to lead must first learn to respect authority and obey.

Jesus Will Help You Overcome

Ray Charles has been able to do what few musicians can—create music that appeals to young and old, black and white, rich and poor. He successfully crosses major boundaries.

Charles lost both parents and a brother before he was grown. He grew up in a school for the blind, where he learned to play piano and sing. By his late teens, he was a hit in central and north Florida. His friends believed in his talent, and Charles believed in them. In 1946, when Lucky Millinder's band arrived in Orlando, Charles managed to get an audition. It was his first chance at the big time.

Charles sang and played with all his might. Millinder listened quietly. At the end of the audition, as Charles expected to hear praise, all he heard was silence and then finally these devastating words, "Ain't good enough, kid." Charles thought he had heard incorrectly and asked Millinder to repeat what he had said. "You heard me. You don't got what it takes." Charles later said of the incident, "I went back to my room and cried for days."

In retrospect, Charles considers that blow to be the "best thing that ever happened to me. After I got over feeling sorry for myself, I went back and started practicing, so nobody would ever say that about me again."[13]

Everybody takes a hit sometime. The successful bounce back.

○ ○ ○ ○ ○

Success consists of getting up more times than you fall.

Do I have the courage to rise above pity and go on?

_____.
_____.
_____.
_____.
_____.
_____.
_____.
_____.
_____.
_____.
_____.
_____.
_____.
_____.
_____.

"Here on earth you will have many trials and sorrows; but cheer up, for I have overcome the world."
JOHN 16:33 TLB

Be Creative

HOW can I tap the creativity inside me?

_____

_____

_____

_____

_____

_____

_____

_____

_____

_____

_____

_____

_____

_____

Shortly after moving into a new home a number of years ago, a family was besieged by salesmen offering everything from laundry service to life insurance. One busy day a dairyman came to their door. "No," the woman of the house said firmly, "my husband and I don't drink milk."

"I'd be glad to deliver a quart every morning for cooking," the salesman said.

"That's more than I need," she replied, starting to close the door.

"Well, ma'am, how about some cream? Berries comin' in now, and . . ."

She said curtly, "No, we never use cream."

The dairyman slowly retreated, and the woman congratulated herself on her sales resistance. The fact was, she had already ordered from another dairy and had simply taken the easy way out. The next morning, however, the same dairyman appeared at her door, a bowl of dewy ripe strawberries held carefully in one hand and a half-pint bottle of cream in the other. "Lady," he said, as he poured the cream over the berries and handed them to her, "I got to thinkin'—you sure have missed a lot!" Needless to say, she switched dairies.[8]

You haven't exhausted all of your opportunities until you've tapped all your creativity—and creativity is an inexhaustible resource![14]

o o o o o

The intelligent man is always open to new ideas. In fact, he looks for them.

PROVERBS 18:15 TLB

Imagination is more important than knowledge.

Always Leave Them Wanting More

Mr. Brown was in his final year of seminary, preparing to become a pastor. The policy of his school called for him to be available at a moment's notice to fill in for local churches that might need a preacher. Mr. Brown eagerly awaited such an opportunity, and at long last, his moment arrived. The pastor of a country church was called away on an emergency, and Mr. Brown was asked to fill the pulpit.

Having waited so long for the opportunity, and having so much to say, Mr. Brown soon became completely immersed in his own words. The more he preached, the more he became inspired to preach. When he glanced at his watch, he was shocked to see that he had preached for a full hour. He was truly embarrassed since he had been allotted only thirty minutes to preach. Knowing that he had preached well into the lunch hour, he made a heartfelt apology to the congregation and sat down.

A young woman hurried to him after the service ended. Obviously more impressed with his personality and appearance—and perhaps his availability—than she was with his message, she gushed, "Oh, Brother Brown, you needn't have apologized. You really didn't talk long—it just seemed long."

The old rule of thumb is, "Always leave them wanting more."

o o o o o

God has given man one tongue but two ears that we may hear twice as much as we speak.

Do I leave people wanting more from me?

Do not keep talking so proudly or let your mouth speak such arrogance.

I SAMUEL 2:3 NIV

No Turning Back

What things in my life keep me looking back?

_____

_____

_____

_____

_____

_____

_____

_____

_____

_____

_____

_____

_____

_____

Most baseball fans know that from 1960 to 1966, the record for the most stolen bases was held by Maury Wills of the Los Angeles Dodgers. In 1962, Wills seemed to set fire to the path between first and second, stealing 104 bases in one season.

Maury Wills set another record during those same years—a rather dubious one. In 1965, a year in which he held the top honors for the most stolen bases, he also held the record for being thrown out the most times while attempting to steal a base! He was caught trying to steal thirty-one times that year.

We don't really remember the bases Wills didn't steal, only the ones he did. But the fact is, had Maury Wills allowed himself to become discouraged at being thrown out, he never would have set the records he did. He was a man determined to "go for it," to do his best, to take the risk of trying, to push the envelope a little in the lead he took off first base, to get a jump on the pitch and fly to second base in a race against the catcher. Once Wills set out to steal a base, there was no turning back.

Whatever it is you desire to do today, do it with your whole heart and all your determination—no looking back.

o o o o

You cannot steal second base while keeping one foot on first base.

Lot's wife looked back as she was following along behind him, and became a pillar of salt.

GENESIS 19:26 TLB

What Kind of Memories Are You Leaving?

A painting in an ancient temple depicts a king forging a chain from his crown, while nearby, another scene shows a slave converting his chain into a crown. Underneath the painting is this inscription: "Life is what one makes it, no matter of what it is made."

You may have been born with certain "ingredients," just as a baker may find the staples of flour, sugar, and oil in his kitchen, but what you create from the talents and abilities God has given you is up to you! Live your life so that it might be measured according to these words of an anonymous poet:

Not—How did he die? But—How did
he live?
Not—What did he gain? But—What did
he give?
These are the units to measure the
worth
Of a man as a man, regardless of birth.
Not—What was his station? But—Had
he a heart?
And—How did he play his God-given
part?
Was he ever ready with a word of good
cheer,
To bring back a smile, to banish a tear?
Not—What was his shrine? Nor—What
was his creed?
But—Had he befriended those really in
need?
Not—What did the sketch in the
newspaper say?
But—How many were sorry when he
passed away?

○ ○ ○ ○ ○

When you were born, you cried, and the world rejoiced. Live your life in such a manner that when you die, the world cries, and you rejoice.

If I were to die today, what would people say about me?

_____ .

_____ .

_____ .

_____ .

_____ .

_____ .

_____ .

_____ .

_____ .

_____ .

_____ .

_____ .

_____ .

_____ .

_____ .

The memory of the righteous
will be a blessing.

PROVERBS 10:7 NIV

Consider Advice

What advice have I come across that I should heed?

._____

._____

._____

._____

._____

._____

._____

._____

._____

._____

._____

._____

._____

After arguing heatedly for several hours about which type of water main to purchase for their city, the town council of Pacific Vista was still deadlocked. One member suggested, "Let's appoint a committee to confer with the city engineer in Los Angeles about this matter. If we can profit by another city's experience and learn from their mistakes, I think we should do so."

At that point, an angry councilman—obviously full of civic pride but little discretion—pounded his fist on the table and replied, "Why should we have to learn from the mistakes Los Angeles has made? Gentlemen, I contend that Pacific Vista is a big enough town to make its own mistakes!"

Most of us are surrounded by good advice at any given time.

- The books in our libraries are full of it.
- Pastors proclaim it weekly.
- People with highly varied experiences and backgrounds abound with it.
- Schools give access to it.
- Labs report it.
- Commentators and columnists gush with it.

But all the good advice in the world is worth very little if it is ignored. Be one of the wise—value and apply the advice you receive.

o o o o o

Pride only breeds quarrels, but wisdom is found in those who take advice.

PROVERBS 13:10 NIV

Many receive advice; only the wise profit by it.

HOW can I become a better friend?

Mary Lennox "was not an affectionate child and had never cared much for anyone." And that was not so difficult to understand. Ignored by her parents and raised by servants, she had no concept of what life was like outside of India. Other children called her "Mistress Mary Quite Contrary" because she didn't like to share and always insisted on having her own way.

When Mary was nine years old, her parents died of cholera, and she was sent to live at her uncle's home in England. The move did nothing to improve her disposition. She expected anyone and everyone to jump when she snapped her fingers.

Gradually, however, Mary began to change. Realizing how lonely she was, she asked a robin in the garden to be her friend. She also began treating her maid with more respect. Won over by the guilelessness of her maid's little brother, Dickon, and craving his approval, Mary found herself seeking his advice. She even revealed to him the location of her secret garden. Eventually, Mary convinced her crippled cousin, Colin, to grab hold of life with both hands. By the last page of *The Secret Garden,* Mary's transformation is complete. She is happy with herself and surrounded by friends.

To make a friend, you first must make a decision to be a friend.

o o o o

The only way to have a friend is to be one.

A man that hath friends must shew himself friendly.
PROVERBS 18:24

HOW would God want me to channel my passion?

_____

_____

_____

_____

_____

_____

_____

_____

_____

_____

_____

_____

_____

_____

_____

In *The Great Divorce*, C.S. Lewis tells the story of a ghost who carries a little red lizard on his shoulder. The lizard constantly twitches its tail and whispers to the ghost, who all the while urges it to be quiet. When a bright and shining presence appears and offers to rid the ghost of his troublesome "baggage," the ghost refuses. He realizes that to quiet the beast, it is necessary to kill it.

A series of rationalizations begins. The ghost reasons that perhaps the lizard need not die but instead might be trained, suppressed, put to sleep, or gradually removed. The shining presence responds that the only recourse is all or nothing.

Finally, the ghost gives permission for the presence to twist the lizard away from him. The presence breaks the lizard's back as he flings it to the ground. In that moment, the ghost becomes a flesh and blood man, and the lizard becomes a beautiful gold and silver stallion, a creature of power and beauty. The man leaps onto the great horse, and they ride into the sunrise as one.

Lewis concludes by saying, "What is a lizard compared with a stallion? Lust is a poor, weak, whimpering, whispering thing compared with that richness and energy of desire which will arise when lust has been killed."

When you give God your all, you put yourself in a position to receive His all.

o o o o

Don't spend your time in wild parties and getting drunk or in adultery and lust, or fighting, or jealousy. But ask the Lord Jesus Christ to help you live as you should.

ROMANS 13:13-14 TLB

We use for passions the stuff that has been given to us for happiness.

One Day at a Time

Warmiwañusca, aptly translated "Dead Woman's Pass," loomed in front of Debra like an impenetrable fortress. The pass rose 13,750 feet—seemingly straight up. Debra longed for a switchback, or better yet, a 7-11. Halfway up, she had her first bout with altitude sickness. But there was no way she'd turn back.

Her guide suggested she try the Peruvian "Walk of the Patient One." "Take one step only one inch ahead of your last," he explained. "Don't try to keep up with the others. Go at the pace God designed you for."

Debra not only reached the top, but finished the four-day trek over Peru's Inca Trail. The forty-year-old mother of two fulfilled a dream she'd had since she was twelve. "If I'd known what the path was going to be like, I never would have gone," she said. "I would've thought I'd never make it. And I would have missed the greatest adventure of my life."

Graduation is a time of great expectations and adventures. But in His wisdom, God only let's you see as far ahead as today. When life's rough mountain peaks and deep valleys stand in the way of your goals, don't be discouraged. Take your eyes off those around you. Take a fresh look at the person God designed you to be. Then, continue toward your destination, one step at a time.

o o o o o

The best thing about the future is that it comes only one day at a time.

What step am I to take today toward my final destination?

_____ .
_____ .
_____ .
_____ .
_____ .
_____ .
_____ .
_____ .
_____ .
_____ .
_____ .
_____ .
_____ .
_____ .
_____ .
_____ .

"Don't be anxious about tomorrow. God will take care of your tomorrow too. Live one day at a time."

MATTHEW 6:34 TLB

Willing to Change the Agenda

I will practice hearing
God's prompting by . . .

_____

_____

_____

_____

_____

_____

_____

_____

_____

_____

_____

_____

_____

"Okay, God," prayed Becky. "This afternoon is set aside for You. I'm taking the next two hours just to pray." Becky had never talked to God that long before. Feeling that it might become difficult to stay with it, she wrote out an extensive list of people and problems she felt she needed to pray about.

Soon after she started, Becky felt that she should give her friend Teri a call. She'd wanted to invite Teri and her family over to lunch but had never quite gotten around to asking them. Fearing that her mind was starting to wander, Becky tried to go back to her list. But Teri kept coming to mind. After several attempts to get her mind back on what she was doing, Becky gave up and picked up the phone to give Teri a call.

As Becky began to voice her invitation, Teri started laughing. Taken aback, Becky wondered what great social blunder she had just committed. But Teri explained, "Just five minutes ago, I was having a regular pity party, crying because no one at our church ever invites us over. I had just said those very words to my husband when the phone rang."

Are you willing to let God change your agenda? His timing is always perfect. Today when you pray, be sure to listen for God's voice speaking to your heart even as you verbalize your concerns to Him. Why settle for a monologue when you can enjoy a two-way conversation?

o o o o o

If you go the wrong way—to the right or to the left—you will hear a voice behind you saying, "This is the right way. You should go this way."

ISAIAH 30:21 NCV

Blessed is the one who finds out which way God is moving and then gets going in the same direction.

Theodor was an artist, of sorts. He drew cartoons for a "creature-of-the-month" ad campaign for a popular insecticide called "Flit." But Theodor wanted to expand the scope of his commercial illustrating. Unfortunately, his advertising contract wouldn't allow it. So instead, he decided to try his hand at writing and illustrating children's books.

After twenty-seven rejections of his first attempt, *A Story No One Can Beat*, Theodor was ready to give up. On his way home to burn his manuscript, Theodor ran into an old schoolmate who had just been hired as a children's book editor at Vanguard Press. With a change of the title to *And To Think It Began on Mulberry Street*, Theodor's first book finally made it to press.

Thus began the career of the best-selling children's author of all time, Theodor Seuss Geisel. In addition to winning the Pulitzer Prize for fiction in 1984, "Dr. Seuss" was also awarded eight honorary degrees. When he died at the age of eighty-seven, Theodor's books had sold more than two hundred million copies, and he was receiving nearly fifteen hundred fan letters a week.[15]

How soon is too soon to give up? Any time before you're absolutely certain God wants you to head in a new direction. After all, who knows what unexpected rewards the second try, the tenth, or the twenty-seventh will hold?

○ ○ ○ ○ ○

Never think that God's delays are God's denials. Hold on; hold fast; hold out. Patience is genius.

Am I too quick to give up?

—————————————————— .
—————————————————— .
—————————————————— .
—————————————————— .
—————————————————— .
—————————————————— .
—————————————————— .
—————————————————— .
—————————————————— .
—————————————————— .
—————————————————— .
—————————————————— .
—————————————————— .
—————————————————— .
—————————————————— .
—————————————————— .

Whenever you face trials of any kind, consider it nothing but joy, because you know that the testing of your faith produces endurance.

JAMES 1:2-3 NRSV

Perspective

What do I need to see from a fresh perspective?

_____
_____
_____
_____
_____
_____
_____
_____
_____
_____
_____
_____
_____
_____
_____

A story is told about the chance meeting of Pablo Picasso and an American soldier. The two of them were seated at a Parisian café and decided to share a drink or two. It wasn't surprising that their conversation soon turned to art. So, Picasso tried to explain to the soldier the style of art for which he was known.

"I just don't like modern art," remarked the soldier.

When Picasso asked him why not, the soldier said that modern art was not realistic. He said that he preferred paintings that actually looked like the things they were supposed to be paintings of.

Picasso said nothing. To break the uncomfortable silence, the soldier decided to share a few photos from his wallet of his girlfriend back in the States. Picasso looked at each of the photos politely. Then holding one of the photos in his hand, he commented to the soldier, "Goodness! Is she really this small?"[16]

Every situation in your life can be seen from a variety of angles, each presenting a different point of view. But, there is only one true reality—life seen from God's point of view. There is a bigger picture, an eternal one, hidden behind the canvas of every ordinary day. Even though you can't always see it, it is there.

o o o o o

Now we see through a glass, darkly; but then face to face: now I know in part; but then shall I know even as also I am known.

I CORINTHIANS 13:12

The world is governed more by appearances than realities.

Honoring Elders

The restaurant was almost empty. Still, the waiter seated Lisa and her grandmother right next to a single businessman, who was enjoying his newspaper and a leisurely lunch. Lisa began to panic. She was accustomed to her grandmother's idiosyncrasies since the onset of Alzheimer's, but she wasn't sure the businessman would be as understanding.

As soon as they were seated, the questions began. "How am I going to pay for this food? I don't have any money. Who's paying my bills? I shouldn't have moved here. I'm just a burden. Why don't you leave me in the gutter to die?"

Patiently, Lisa tried to calm her grandmother's fears, answering the same questions she answered week after week. Forty minutes passed. Lisa couldn't stop worrying about the man sitting next to them. *He's trying to relax,* she thought. *My grandmother's probably driving him crazy.*

Lisa was relieved when the man finally folded his paper and prepared to leave. Then to her surprise, he headed straight for their table. Lisa prepared to apologize for any aggravation her grandmother might have caused him. Instead, he looked at Lisa with a smile and whispered, "When I get older, I hope I have a granddaughter just like you."

Even the smallest gesture of kindness can make a big difference in someone's life. Keep your eyes and heart open for the opportunities today brings.

o o o o o

Do all the good you can to all the people you can, in all the ways you can, as often as ever you can, as long as you can.

HOW can I show respect for my elders?

_____.
_____.
_____.
_____.
_____.
_____.
_____.
_____.
_____.
_____.
_____.
_____.
_____.
_____.
_____.

Reverently honor an older woman as you would your mother. . . . If a widow has family members to take care of her, let them learn that religion begins at their own doorstep and that they should pay back with gratitude some of what they have received.

I TIMOTHY 5:2,4 THE MESSAGE

Do Something Creative with Your Circumstances

HOW can I respond more positively to difficult circumstances?

_____
_____
_____
_____
_____
_____
_____
_____
_____
_____
_____
_____
_____
_____

None of the kids on the block knew why Mrs. Greer was so mean. All they knew for sure was that she hated kids. If a ball rolled into her yard, they forgot it. After knocking on her door once, no one ever tried it again. One day, out of spite, the elderly woman turned on her sprinkler. Instead of watering her front lawn, it was set to water the sidewalk, preventing the children from even riding their bikes in front of her house.

Since the children were not old enough to cross the street on their own, one of their favorite pastimes came to a standstill. Then a smile spread across one child's face, and as he whispered his idea to the others, smiles spread throughout the group. Each kid ran home with a mission. On that sunny, cloudless day, the children returned with their bikes—and their raincoats. Their bike ride became a wet and wild adventure as they rode through the sprinklers, laughing harder than they had with their original game.

When it comes to difficult circumstances, the choice is yours. You can let a seed of bitterness rob you of joy, like it did the old woman. Or you can let circumstances stretch your creativity and lead you in a new direction. Who knows, you may find yourself somewhere you never expected, just grateful for the opportunity to be there.

○ ○ ○ ○ ○

We know that in all things God works for the good of those who love him, who have been called according to his purpose.

ROMANS 8:28 NIV

If you can't change your circumstances, change the way you respond to them.

Are You Making a Mountain Out of a Molehill?

Trevor knew he was supposed to sit quietly in church and pay attention. But the gurgling and rumbling in his stomach had captured his full attention. He tried holding his breath, closing his eyes, even humming quietly to himself. But, suddenly, what he feared most seemed inevitable. Noticing the panicked look on his face, his mother whispered, "Trevor, what's the matter?"

Trevor quickly whispered back, "I think I'm gonna be sick!" His mother told him that the restroom was at the back of the church. With that, Trevor darted up from the pew.

He returned so quickly, that his mother was a little worried. "Trevor, did you make it to the bathroom?"

Trevor replied with a smile, "I didn't have to Mom. In the back of the church, they had a nice little box right by the door that says, 'For the Sick.'"[17]

What did you worry about when you were a kid? Monsters under your bed? Being the shortest kid in the class? The tallest? Taking like what seemed forever to master riding a bike? As we grow older, childhood fears seem almost ridiculously small. But as a child, they seemed monumental.

Let hindsight teach you something about the problems that may be overwhelming you today. A molehill right in front of you can loom larger than the mountain on the horizon, merely because of where you're standing.

o o o o

You may laugh out loud in the future at something you're eating your heart out over today.

What mountain do I need to see from God's perspective?

_____ .

_____ .

_____ .

_____ .

_____ .

_____ .

_____ .

_____ .

_____ .

_____ .

_____ .

_____ .

_____ .

_____ .

_____ .

I lift up my eyes to the hills—from where will my help come? My help comes from the LORD, who made heaven and earth.

PSALM 121:1-2 NRSV

God's Magnificent Creation

What are some of the details God created in me?

_____

_____

_____

_____

_____

_____

_____

_____

_____

_____

_____

_____

_____

_____

Beth focused her camera on the field of wildflowers. From a distance, it looked like a uniform blanket of purple. Closer inspection revealed individual flowers, similar in composition yet each bearing a unique combination of leaves and petals. She finished the roll of film and called it a day.

It wasn't until she enlarged the wildflower photos that she noticed it. Within each of the tiny purple flowers, which themselves were no larger than the eraser of a pencil, there was a ring of white. The enlargements revealed that the ring itself was made of a tiny circle of perfectly formed white flowers, each no bigger than the size of a pencil point. Without magnification, the intricate beauty these common wildflowers contained would have gone unnoticed.

God weaves hidden beauty into places too small to be seen by the human eye—distant planets, blood cells, DNA strands. But why the extravagance? Why go to the extra work, even if you are the Creator of the universe?

During the Renaissance period, artists carefully finished the backs of statues fashioned for churches. They did this even though they knew only the eyes of God would ever enjoy them. In the same way, God must take delight in the act of creation, as well as its outcome. As God's most precious creation, He takes delight in every detail that makes you who you are.

o o o o o

I will praise thee; for I am fearfully and wonderfully made: marvellous are thy works; and that my soul knoweth right well.

PSALM 139:14

The more we learn about the wonders of our universe, the more clearly we are going to perceive the hand of God.

God Makes Heroes Out of Ordinary People

Raoul Wallenberg was a Swedish diplomat in the 1940s. Though the Holocaust of World War II threatened many lives, Wallenberg's wasn't one of them. His work for the Swedish government put him in a safe and privileged position. Yet, Wallenberg worked to help save the lives of Hungarian Jews.

Having business connections in Hungary, Wallenberg set up an office issuing fake passports. But he didn't stop there. He set up safe housing, soup kitchens, and hospitals for those to whom he was extending bogus passports. On one occasion, he saw Jews being loaded onto a train destined for the death camps. He demanded that all of the prisoners with passports get off the train. Prisoners waved at him any piece of paper they could find—eyeglass prescriptions, driver's licenses, even deportation papers. He honored them all as passports, saving three hundred lives. It is estimated that during the war, Wallenberg offered diplomatic protection to approximately two hundred thousand Hungarian Jews—just because he felt it was the right thing to do.[18]

God chooses unlikely heroes. Take David, facing Goliath with nothing but a handful of stones; or Moses, raised in the privileged safety of Pharaoh's house, yet leading the Israelites, simply because God asked him to. Doing the right thing, even when it doesn't seem very dramatic or noteworthy, takes courage. Has God hidden a hero inside of you?

○ ○ ○ ○ ○

The test of courage comes when we are in the minority; the test of tolerance when we are in the majority.

How can I be a hero in my situation?

_____ .
_____ .
_____ .
_____ .
_____ .
_____ .
_____ .
_____ .
_____ .
_____ .
_____ .
_____ .
_____ .
_____ .
_____ .
_____ .

Be on your guard; stand firm in the faith; be men of courage; be strong. Do everything in love.

1 CORINTHIANS 16:13-14 NIV

HOW do I handle my freedom and responsibility?

_____

_____

_____

_____

_____

_____

_____

_____

_____

_____

_____

_____

_____

The mind controlled by the
Spirit is life and peace.

ROMANS 8:6 NIV

What do the books and authors listed below have in common?

Tarzan by Edgar Rice Burroughs
Alice's Adventures in Wonderland by Lewis Carroll
The Divine Comedy by Dante
Grimm's Fairy Tales by the Brothers Grimm
The Merchant of Venice by William Shakespeare
Works by Francis Bacon, Miguel de Cervantes, Socrates, John Calvin, Martin Luther, and Homer
The American Heritage Dictionary
Mother Goose
The Bible

The answer is that at some time in history, each of these books and authors was banned. Those who chose to read these words, if they could even obtain a copy in the first place, did so at their own risk. Today things have changed, at least in the United States. Here, individuals decide for themselves what they will read, watch, listen to, stand up for, and stand against.

Yet that parental admonition still rings true: With greater freedom, comes greater responsibility. What weighs heaviest when you form an opinion or make a decision? Your gut reaction? The general consensus? The way you were raised? And how do you respond when someone's opinion differs from your own? Do you jump on your soapbox? Feel threatened? Or do you listen with love? Giving careful consideration to what you believe and why gives you the strength you need to stand in support of the crowd or alone against it.[19]

o o o o o

The mind grows by what it feeds on.

What is my source of joy?

Kara pressed her face against the window of her train compartment. Even though the sun had set long ago, she didn't want to miss a thing. It was her first trip to Egypt, and everything seemed so different from her home in California. That morning, an exodus of angry cockroaches had greeted her when she turned on the hotel shower. And one quick surge from her blow-dryer was enough to black out the power on the entire floor. Egypt didn't feel like another country; it felt like another world.

After miles of dimly lit desert, her eyes were drawn to a flicker of light. As the train approached, she saw it was a fire, surrounded by tents. A group of men were nearby, laughing animatedly. A young boy was reading a book by firelight, a camel enjoying the blaze by his side. Kara immediately felt sorry for the boy. *Probably a student like me,* she thought. Only here he was trying to do his homework by firelight and would sleep in a makeshift tent. But something about the boy's expression made her reconsider. Who was she to argue with such a contented smile?

Circumstances change daily. If your happiness depends solely on what's going on around you, it cannot last. But if your joy comes from what is going on inside you, you can carry it with you wherever you go.

o o o o o

The greater part of our happiness depends on our disposition and not our circumstances.

I know how to live on almost nothing or with everything. I have learned the secret of contentment in every situation.

PHILIPPIANS 4:12 TLB

Surprises

HOW do I handle unexpected circumstances?

Trina and Heather carefully placed their beach chairs by the edge of the water—close enough to get their feet wet but not so close that a wave would splash salt water on their books. By the third day of their family vacation, the sisters had it down to an exact science. Or so they thought.

One moment, Heather was seated next to Trina, reading. The next, Trina looked over, and Heather was gone. Rolled up in her beach chair, Heather was tumbling end over end toward the ocean as the rogue wave receded. After the salt water was coughed up, the mountain of sand dislodged from her suit, and the convulsive laughter calmed to a controlled giggle, Heather turned to Trina and said, "You didn't even get wet! No fair!"

Sometimes, life just doesn't look fair. One person sits relaxing on the beach. The one right next to her faces her own mini-tidal-wave trauma. One person wins the lottery while another faces financial ruin. One person gets engaged while another contemplates the future as a single. One person's medical test results come back negative, another's positive.

But God is there with you in the face of every surprise, both welcome or not. It is your heart and not your circumstances that will determine whether each "surprise" will draw you away from Him or even closer to His side.

o o o o o

The Lord watches over all the plans and paths of godly men, but the paths of the godless lead to doom.

PSALM 1:6 TLB

To believe in God is to know that the rules will be fair—and that there will be many surprises!

As long as he could remember, Jason had wanted to be a police officer. It wasn't just the fact that he loved playing cops and robbers. More importantly, he wanted to do something with his life that mattered.

After graduation, he had the chance to apply for a spot at the police academy. But first came the interview. When the veteran officer pulled up a chair in front of him, Jason realized his childhood dream could rest upon that very moment. As he confidently answered each question, he felt the officer's approval. Jason knew he was doing well.

"One last question," the officer said. "Suppose you're called to help at the site of an explosion. There are numerous casualties. Nearby, you notice a woman has gone into labor. At the same time, you see a car, whose driver is obviously intoxicated, weaving down the road toward an elementary school. Then, you hear a cry from someone drowning in a nearby river, while a fight erupts next to you that could result in both injury and property damage. What do you do?"

Jason thought a moment, then replied, "Try and hide my uniform and mingle with the crowd?"

Some situations in life take more than just a cool head. They need a miracle. While praying for an answer, remember to also pray for courage so that you can do what God instructs.

o o o o

Take time to deliberate; but when the time for action arrives, stop thinking and go on.

How can I more effectively hear God's voice and obey it?

_____ .
_____ .
_____ .
_____ .
_____ .
_____ .
_____ .
_____ .
_____ .
_____ .
_____ .
_____ .
_____ .
_____ .
_____ .
_____ .

Rise up; this matter is in your hands. We will support you, so take courage and do it.

EZRA 10:4 NIV

What do I do when I know I need to speak up?

According to an old fable, three men once decided to engage in the religious practice of absolute silence. They mutually agreed to keep a "day of quiet" from dawn until the stroke of midnight, at which time a full moon was expected to rise from the horizon. They sat cross-legged for hours, concentrating on the distant horizon, eager for darkness to envelop them.

One of them unwittingly noted, "It's difficult not to say anything at all."

The second one replied, "Quiet. You're speaking during the time of silence!"

The third man sighed and then boasted, "Now I'm the only one who hasn't spoken yet."

A rap singer has updated some of the advice given by the book of Ecclesiastes:

There's a time to speak up and a time to shut up.

There's a time to hunker down and a time to go downtown.

There's a time to talk and a time to walk.

There's a time to be mellow and a time not to be yellow.

Silence can be good but never if it's the result of raw fear or lack of moral fiber.

○ ○ ○ ○

There are times when silence is golden; other times it is just plain yellow.

There's an opportune time to do things, a right time for everything on the earth . . . A right time to shut up and another to speak up.

ECCLESIASTES 3:1,7 THE MESSAGE

He Guides Us through the Maze

Up in the choir loft of the old church on Main Street, there was an organ. In between holiday celebrations, it sat idle collecting dust—and mice. The mice that were born inside the organ considered their home a kind of quiet maze, filled with hammers, wires, and chimes—until Christmas Eve.

As the first notes from the slightly off-tune instrument filled the home of the mice with music, they were awestruck. How their home moved and roared! What talent and timbre it possessed! But one small mouse wondered if there were more to the mystery. As he strained to pull himself through a small opening near the floorboards, he saw a woman carefully placing her fingers on the yellowed keys. The mouse realized it was the woman, not the organ itself, who possessed this wonderful gift of music. He ran back to tell everyone there was someone greater than the organ itself. Someone who was making it sing!

The other mice laughed and laughed. W___ould believe such a preposterous tale? A___, hadn't they seen the hammers move ___selves with their own eyes?

___ere's more to life—and truth—than ___ the eye. So, when someone tells you ___ is believing," remember, "Faith is being ___f what we hope for and certain of what ___ not see" (Hebrews 11:1 NIV).

o o o o

Without God, the world would be a maze without a clue.

Am I able to trust God when I can't see the whole picture?

_____

_____

_____

_____

_____

_____

_____

_____

_____

_____

_____

_____

_____

_____

This God is our God for ever and ever; he will be our guide even to the end.

PSALM 48:14 NIV

Moved with Compassion

HOW can I reach out to the underdogs in my life?

. _____

. _____

. _____

. _____

. _____

. _____

. _____

. _____

. _____

. _____

. _____

. _____

. _____

When Ryan found out his dog, Mulder, was going to have puppies, every morning was a race to the laundry room to see if the miracle had occurred while he slept. Finally one morning, Ryan was rewarded by the sight of nine squirming balls of fur. Knowing that his parents had said he could keep only one, Ryan made the difficult choice of deciding which one would stay and which ones would be given away.

Six weeks later, Ryan made a cardboard sign that he carefully attached to the mailbox in front of his house. It read, "Cute puppies. FREE!" After several weeks, only two of the puppies had been given away, so Ryan decided to try a new approach. His new sign read, "Five cute puppies and only one really ugly one. Free to a good home!" The puppies were gone within the day. Every person who knocked on the door wanted to come to the rescue of that one poor, ugly pup.

Plenty of people want to help the underdog. Too often they're just not sure of how to go about it. Whom has God put in your life that could use your help today? It could be a gift of time, finances, elbow grease, or maybe just friendship. But reaching out to help someone doesn't deplete your resources. It enlarges your capacity to care.

o o o o

> Seeing the multitudes, He felt compassion for them, because they were distressed and downcast like sheep without a shepherd.
>
> MATTHEW 9:36 NASB

The capacity to care gives life its deepest significance.

Do I humbly obey without question?

businessmen went to a
rem   n retreat for a weekend of
lea   ing. Expecting graphs, statis-
tic   ks, they were more than a
litt   n they were asked to trade
th   s in for shovels. Next, their
bo   son, gave them their assign-
m   weekend. "I want you to dig a
d   wide and ten inches deep
a   rimeter of the cabin." With
t   Mr. Clarkson walked back to the
                appeared inside.

                the group was silent, stunned by
                s task that lay ahead. But soon
                urned into questioning the
                the exercise, arguing if nine inches
                nough to ten, and complaining
                risen to the top of the corpo-
                only to be forced to do manual
                y, Bill, a newcomer to the group,
                the others and said, "Who cares
                ve to do this. Let's just do it, and
                with!"

                those words, the cabin door
                nd Mr. Clarkson reappeared.
                en," he said as he grabbed Bill's hand,
                ou to meet your new vice-president."

                whys of what you have to do in life
                ways be clear. But as long as you
                and the hows, the best thing to do is
                vork.

o o o o o

e easiest way to dignity is humility.

> God sets himself against the proud,
> but he shows favor to the humble.
>
> JAMES 4:6 NLT

Pierce the Darkness

Do I have any muddy layers to be washed away by the blood of Jesus?

Have you ever watched an icicle form one drop at a time? If the water is clean, the icicle remains clear and sparkles brightly in the sun; but if the water is slightly muddy, the icicle looks cloudy, its beauty spoiled.

Character is formed in the same way. Each thought and feeling, every decision—about matters both great and small—adds a layer. Every outside influence that touches our minds and souls—impressions, experiences, visual images, the words of others—helps to define our character.

We must remain concerned at all times about the "droplets" that we allow to drip into our lives. Just as habits born of hate, falsehood, and evil intent mar and eventually destroy us, acts that develop habits of love, truth, and goodness silently mold and fashion us into the image of God.

When you build a clear, sparkling character, the light reflected through you will pierce the darkness around you.

○ ○ ○ ○

Character is what you are in the dark.

The integrity of the upright shall guide them.

PROVERBS 11:3

Being Known for Your Inner Qualities

What inner qualities can I accentuate and develop?

[Abraham] Lincoln had a disarming and engaging [ability] to laugh at himself, especially his own [physical] appearance. When Senator Stephen A. Douglas once called him a "two-faced [man,] Lincoln responded, "I leave it to my audience. If I had another face, do you think I would wear this one?"

[On one time] he told a group of editors about [a] woman riding on horseback in [the woods. She] "looked at me intently, and said, 'I believe you are the ugliest man I ever [saw.' I said,] 'Madam, you are probably right, [but I can't] help it.' 'No,' she said, 'you can['t,] but you might stay at home.'"

[Although] his likeness is widely recognized, [Lincoln is] not known primarily for his appearance [but] for his courageous stance for [preserving] the Union and the abolition of slavery. [He is] often held up as an example of remarkable [pat]ience, determination, dedication, [integrity,] compassion, thoughtfulness, and [selflessness.] These inner qualities are [what] mark Lincoln as one of America's greatest [leaders.]

[Much comment] is made in our culture today on [our] appearance and material possessions. [We do] well to remember that it is only [our] inner qualities that create a lasting [impression.]

○ ○ ○ ○ ○

[When] God measures a person, [He] puts the tape around the [hea]rt instead of the head.

Don't judge by a man's face or height. . . .
I don't make decisions the way you do!
Men judge by outward appearance, but I
look at a man's thoughts and intentions.

I SAMUEL 16:7 TLB

Leave a Lasting Mark

What can I do that will long outlive my physical life on earth?

. _____

. _____

. _____

. _____

. _____

. _____

. _____

. _____

. _____

. _____

. _____

. _____

. _____

Although we do not have the original manuscripts of the New Testament, we do have more than 99.9 percent of the original text because of the faithful work of manuscript copyists over the centuries.

Copying was a long, arduous process. In ancient days, copyists did not sit at desks while writing but rather stood or made copies while sitting on benches or stools, holding a scroll on their knees. Notes at the end of some scrolls tell of the drudgery of the work:

"He who does not know how to write supposes it to be no labor; but though only three fingers write, the whole body labors."

"Writing bows one's back, thrusts the ribs into one's stomach, and fosters a general debility."

"As travelers rejoice to see their home country, so also is the end of a book to those who toil."

Even so, without the work of faithful copyists, we would not have the Christian Scriptures today. As one scribe aptly noted: "There is no scribe who will not pass away, but what his hands have written will remain forever."

When you are choosing what you will do as your life's work, there are many things to consider. Don't underestimate the satisfaction that comes from knowing what you do today will touch lives long after you are gone.

o o o o o

"Store up for yourselves treasures in heaven, where moth and rust do not destroy, and where thieves do not break in and steal."

MATTHEW 6:20 NIV

The greatest use of life is to spend it for something that will outlast it.

Quiet the Kitty

... n, a Tony-award-winning actr... ... a memorable acting lesson that ... ... relating to those who que... ... ...out stage fright:

... ...n Broadway, I became aware of ... ...udience. Suddenly, I saw it! A str... ...nchalantly crossing the stage. Th... ...d and turned toward the da... ... audience and seemed startled to ... ...t the darkness was alive. She ha... ...ence, as though there were a th... ... of eyes out there, which, of c... ... ...ere. That realization stopped th... ... her tracks. Then she fled into th... ...member thinking, *I know just h...*

... ... told this story to young a... ...e I think it shows that the job c... ...s to make contact with the kitty i... ...f us—the one that wants to ... ... when it feels those thousand ... ... on it. And to find the way to ... ...ty and just go on doing what we ...

... ...frightened or nervous is not a ... ...nding failure. It is a sign that you ... ...e performance ahead to be worth ... ...oing well! Keep your eyes on your ... ...member those who will benefit ... ...work. This focus will calm your ... ...l you with purpose.

○ ○ ○ ○ ○

...ecret of success is to be like a ...—smooth and unruffled on top, ...addling furiously underneath.

What steps can I take to tap into God's peace?

_____ .
_____ .
_____ .
_____ .
_____ .
_____ .
_____ .
_____ .
_____ .
_____ .
_____ .
_____ .
_____ .
_____ .
_____ .
_____ .
_____ .

His peace will keep your thoughts and your hearts quiet and at rest as you trust in Christ Jesus.

PHILIPPIANS 4:7 TLB

Flattery Will Get You Somewhere

Am I honest, or do I try to manipulate others with false compliments?

· _____

· _____

· _____

· _____

· _____

· _____

· _____

· _____

· _____

· _____

· _____

· _____

· _____

· _____

In ancient Greece, the philosopher Aristippus—considered by all who knew him to be the master of political craftiness—learned to get along well in royal circles by flattering the tyrant Denys. Not only did he flatter Denys, but he was proud that he did. In fact, Aristippus disdained less prosperous fellow philosophers and wise men who refused to stoop that low.

One day Aristippus saw his colleague Diogenes washing vegetables and said to him, "If you would only learn to flatter King Denys, you would not have to be washing lentils."

Diogenes looked up slowly and replied, "And you, if you had only learned to live on lentils, would not have to flatter King Denys."

Another way to regard flattery is this:

F—foolish
L—laughable
A—accolades
T—to
T—tell
E—everyone
R—'round
Y—you

Speak the truth sincerely. When the truth is painful, consider the option of remaining silent!

○ ○ ○ ○ ○

In the end, people appreciate frankness more than flattery.

PROVERBS 28:23 TLB

Really great men and women are those who are natural, frank, and honest with everyone with whom they come into contact.

Is the Grass Really Greener on the Other Side?

...ter once delivered a slab of
sto... ...hant. Seeing all his wonderful
goo... ...I wish I was a merchant and
had... ..." In the twinkling of an eye,
his... ...anted. Then one day, he saw a
pa... ...store window. He saw a
pr... ...in splendor, and he said, "I wish
I... ..." And immediately he became a
p... ...l the day the hot sun beat down
u... ...he said, "I wish I was the sun,
...any man." And he became the
...happy . . . until a cloud came
...and the earth. He said, "That
...adows me. I wish I was a cloud."
...sh was granted. He rained down
...h to his heart's content until he
...mountain, which wouldn't let him
...id, "That mountain is greater than
...vas a mountain." Instantly, he
...mountain, and he said, "Now I am
...st of all."

...one day a little man climbed up the
...and with a hammer and chisel
...tap away at it. The mountain, unable
...him, said, "That little man is greater
...wish I was a man who cut stone."
...gain his wish was granted, and he
...a stonecutter. He lived a long and
...ife, and everyone marveled at how
...he was.

○ ○ ○ ○ ○

*...grass may look greener on the other
side, but it still has to be mowed.*

Have I learned to be thankful for what I have?

_____ .
_____ .
_____ .
_____ .
_____ .
_____ .
_____ .
_____ .
_____ .
_____ .
_____ .
_____ .
_____ .
_____ .
_____ .

PRAISE ye the LORD. O give thanks
unto the LORD; for he is good:
for his mercy endureth for ever.

PSALM 106:1

June 27

His Rewards Are Better than Gold

What qualities must I exhibit in order to always do my best?

_____

_____

_____

_____

_____

_____

_____

_____

_____

_____

_____

_____

_____

_____

_____

These words were spelled out in lights at the eighteenth Olympics in Tokyo: "The most important thing in the Olympic Games is not to win but to take part; just as the most important thing in life is not the triumph but the struggle. The essential thing is to have fought well."

The athletes who make it to the Olympic Games are already the best of the best from each nation. Each athlete has excelled in ways few of his or her peers will ever reach. Yet only one will wear a gold medal, one a silver, and one a bronze.

Those who are so accustomed to winning face the devastating possibility of losing before not only their teammates, but also their countrymen, and in this age of worldwide television, before the entire world. How vital it is for these athletes to keep their perspective—that the important issue at the Olympics is not winning but rather the opportunity to compete, to try, and to give one's best effort.

Regardless of the arena in which you compete, winning is not what is truly important. Trying and giving your best effort is what molds within you the lasting character traits that are "better than gold."

o o o o o

You may be disappointed if you fail, but you are doomed if you don't try.

The sluggard craves and gets nothing, but the desires of the diligent are fully satisfied.

PROVERBS 13:4 NIV

pots and pans and things,
o time to be
doing lovely things,
ng late with Thee,
ing in the dawnlight,
ing heaven's gates,
a saint by getting meals,
hing up the plates.
I have Martha's hands,
Mary's mind;
en I black the boots and shoes,
dals, Lord, I find.
of how they trod the earth,
me I scrub the floor.
t this meditation, Lord,
n't time for more.
all the kitchen with Thy love,
light it with Thy peace;
ive me all my worrying,
make all grumbling cease.
u who didst love to give men food,
room or by the sea,
ept this service that I do—
o it unto Thee.

—Unknown

o o o o

Service is nothing
but love in work clothes.

Acts of service I can do for others include . . .

_____ .

_____ .

_____ .

_____ .

_____ .

_____ .

_____ .

_____ .

_____ .

_____ .

_____ .

_____ .

_____ .

_____ .

"The more lowly your service to others,
the greater you are. To be the
greatest, be a servant."
MATTHEW 23:11 TLB

June 29

Courtesy Makes Everything Sweeter

HOW can I improve my manners?

Which virtuous behaviors on earth will still be required in Heaven?

Courage? No. There will be nothing to fear in Heaven.

Hope? No. We will have all that we desire.

Faith? No. We will be in the presence of the Source of our faith, and all those things for which we have believed will have their fulfillment in Him and by His hand.

Acts of charity toward those in need? No. There will be no hunger, thirst, nakedness, or homelessness in Heaven. All needs will be supplied.

Sympathy? No. There will be no more tears and no more pain.

Courtesy? Yes! There will still be room for the exercise of courtesy—the kind greeting, the simple manners that offend no one but ease the way of all.

Good manners are important. They put people at ease, which in turn makes them more cooperative and happy.

Immanuel Kant once said, "Always treat a human being as a person, that is, as an end in himself, and not merely as a means to your end." Strive to impart dignity and self-worth to all you meet. Consider it dress rehearsal for your future life in Heaven!

o o o o

As we have opportunity,
let us do good to all people.

GALATIANS 6:10 NIV

Say "thank you" when you receive a favor and "excuse me" or "pardon me" when you need to interrupt a discussion.

When I can't RSVP right away, what can I do to ensure I don't forget?

_____.
_____.
_____.
_____.
_____.
_____.
_____.
_____.
_____.
_____.
_____.
_____.
_____.
_____.
_____.
_____.
_____.
_____.
_____.

RSVP stand for the French phra____ s_____ s'il vous plaît, which means "plea____ ____" This phrase on an invitation ____ ____ u let the host or hostess kno____ ____ ou plan to attend the func____ ____ nvitation marked with RSVP requ____ ____ u call or write the host to let ther____ ____ you either will or will not be t____.

____ ____ y, a handwritten invitation will rea____ ____ rets only." In this case, you are ____ ____ notify the host only if you will _not_ ____ ____ . However, a truly thoughtful gue____ ____ s to attend will call or mail a not____ ____ st to express thanks for the inv____ ____ confirm that he or she will be ____ e.

____ ____ at you planned a catered party for ____ ____ and you were paying twenty-fiv____ ____ guest. Then imagine that half yo____ ____ led to respond, and ten of th____ ____ show up. You would be spending $2____ ____ le who simply were not consid-e____ ____ to let you know that they could n____ ____ t. Would you consider those p____ ____ thoughtful friends?

____ ____ nd of guest that you would like t____ ____ d your own fanciest party!

o o o o o

____ VP _promptly when you receive an invitation._

Let everyone see that you are unselfish and considerate in all you do.

PHILIPPIANS 4:5 TLB

Treat It as Though It Were Yours

Do I need to return or replace something I've borrowed?

_____
_____
_____
_____
_____
_____
_____
_____
_____
_____
_____
_____
_____
_____

A store once had the following layaway policy: "We hold it in the store while you pay for it. You're mad. You take it from the store, and you don't pay for it. We're mad. Better that you're mad."

Mark Twain's neighbor may have had this policy in mind when Twain asked to borrow a certain book he had spotted in his neighbor's library. "Why, yes, Mr. Clemens, you're more than welcome to it," the neighbor said. "But I must ask you to read it here. You know I make it a rule never to let any book go out of my library."

Several days later, the neighbor came to Twain's house and asked if he could borrow his lawn mower since his had been taken to the repair shop. "Why, certainly," the humorist replied. "You're more than welcome to it. But I must ask you to use it only in my yard. You know I make it a rule."

Treat what you borrow as if it were a prized possession, returning it promptly. If something happens to it while it is in your possession, make repairs or replace it, not to your satisfaction, but to the satisfaction of the owner. Always remember, while the item is in your hands, it is not yours. It still belongs to the other person.

o o o o o

Don't act thoughtlessly,
but try to understand what
the Lord wants you to do.

EPHESIANS 5:17 NLT

Return what you borrow, on time and in good condition.

t's Not Wise to Tell All

HOW can I develop more common sense regarding what I say?

ng college graduate, spent a
sum   g at a small publishing
com   he end of the summer, the
pres   company told Stacy he
wan   o her about a full-time job.
Stac   old one of the editors about
her   eeting with the president to
disc

ground," came the reply.
"Do   o low."

er, Stacy burst into the
edit   Guess what I'll be making?"
she

y blurted out the amount, the
edit   ocked. "That's more than I
mak   quietly. "And I've been here
five

ay, the president summoned
Stac   e. "I have something of a
rev   nds," he told her evenly. "It
see   broadcast your salary, and
quit   ur coworkers are bitter
abo   as confidential information.
No   that we won't be able to
brir   ard. There would be too
mu   nt."

a few things you should never
disc   orkers: your love life, your
me   and your salary.

◦ ◦ ◦ ◦ ◦

D   leaving a few things unsaid.

A fool uttereth all his mind.
PROVERBS 29:11

You Are God's Masterpiece

Do I have the confidence to be who God made me?

_____

_____

_____

_____

_____

_____

_____

_____

_____

_____

_____

_____

_____

_____

_____

A man with what he thought was an amazing replica of a Leonardo da Vinci painting took his work of art to a museum. He showed the copied painting to the curator to get his reaction. The curator immediately identified the painting as a forgery—and also the forger, his nationality, and when the copy was made.

Then the curator turned the painting over. The information on the back confirmed that he was right on all three counts. "How did you know it was a fake?" the man asked. "It looks like an amazing likeness to me."

"People who make a living copying the masters have little imagination of their own," the curator explained. "And this person's choice of subject, brush strokes, and areas of emphasis practically scream 'Fake!' Think about those celebrity impersonators, how they overemphasize a certain vocal inflection or gesture. It's the same thing here."

If you truly want to distinguish yourself, be an innovator not an imitator. God has given you unique skills, ideas, and experiences. It's okay to be inspired by role models, but use that inspiration to develop your own distinctive style. The world doesn't need a clone of someone else. It needs the one and only you!

o o o o

If you want to be original, be yourself.

We are God's masterpiece.
He has created us anew in
Christ Jesus, so that we can do the
good things he planned for us long ago.

EPHESIANS 2:10 NLT

faithful and Consistent

...n never led major league
bas... ...ng average or home runs
du... ...e season. And he struck out
m... ...n almost any other batter.
H... ...it came to sheer persistence
a... ...nsistency, he was unmatched.
H... ...e Ruth's monumental record of
7... ...me runs—and kept right on
h... ...ut of the park. In fact, many
... ...rts wonder if his final total of
... ...be equaled.

...ter what kind of job you hold,
...consistency, and faithfulness will
...ild a solid reputation as a person
...counted on to deliver the goods.
...y, by its nature, isn't something
...oticed immediately; and it's not
...y to remain focused in today's
...shifting work environments. But
..., persistence and consistency
...nd shine.

...may see some flash-in-the-pan types
...all the attention, but keep hammer-
..., just as Hank Aaron did. When these
...e gone and forgotten, you will be
...bered—and valued.

o o o o o

*Consistency: It's the jewel worth
wearing . . . the anchor worth
weighing . . . the thread worth
weaving . . . the battle worth winning.*

Today I will work at being
faithful and consistent by . . .

_____.

_____.

_____.

_____.

_____.

_____.

_____.

_____.

_____.

_____.

_____.

_____.

_____.

To the holy and faithful brothers and
sisters in Christ . . . Grace and peace
to you from God our Father.

COLOSSIANS 1:2 NCV

Too Much of a Good Thing

HOW can I become more attuned to what my needs are?

_____

_____

_____

_____

_____

_____

_____

_____

_____

_____

_____

_____

_____

Japan's snow monkeys work hard just to stay alive in their frigid habitat. They must climb high mountains continuously as they search for food. Interestingly, however, they take frequent breaks to rest, renew themselves, even monkey around a little. They seem to have an innate understanding that all work and no play leads to exhaustion—and maybe extinction.

Contrast the monkeys to many of Japan's human workers who have literally worked themselves to death. The drive for performance—exemplified not only by output, but by hours put in—permeates their culture. This tragic syndrome has become so prevalent that it's been given its own name: _karoshi._

It's sad that those in the monkey business seem to have more sense than those in everyday human business. Like the monkeys, we humans have been instilled with certain instincts that tell us what our bodies, minds, and spirits need. Eat when your blood sugar drops, sleep when you're fatigued, seek quiet when the noise of the world sets you on edge, and so on.

Don't kill yourself trying to be top banana at school or work. Take the time to relax, and eat a banana instead.

○ ○ ○ ○

"Come to Me, all you who labor and are heavy laden, and I will give you rest. . . . My yoke is easy and My burden is light."

MATTHEW 11:28,30 NKJV

Rest and motion, unrelieved and unchecked, are equally destructive.

...ughter Is a Gift of God

... to nutritionist Pamela Smith,
on... ...ughs a day provide a cardio-
vas... ...ut equal to ten minutes of
ro... ...ng. Additionally, laughter stimu-
lat... ...ease the same way exercise
d... ...also helps fight infection by
s... ...ones into your bloodstream
t... ...mmune-weakening effects of
s... ...bs 14:30 NIV puts it this way: "A
... ...e gives life to the body."

...oday, with all its demands and
... ...s, can be like a giant pressure
... ...aughter is the safety valve that
... ...team escape before there's an
... ...n. Lighten up, and loosen up
... ...ssible. Laugh at the absurdities
... ...your school and friends will no
... ...rovide an almost endless supply
... ...rial.

... ...e to be a source of laughter at
... ...ome, and wherever you go. Not only
... ...enjoy your day more, but those
... ...ou will enjoy it too.

o o o o o

The place to be happy is here.
The time to be happy is now.

Today I will look for humor by . . .

_____ .
_____ .
_____ .
_____ .
_____ .
_____ .
_____ .
_____ .
_____ .
_____ .
_____ .
_____ .
_____ .
_____ .
_____ .
_____ .
_____ .

The light in the eyes [of him whose heart is joyful] rejoices the hearts of others.

PROVERBS 15:30 AMP

Resourcefulness Pays Off

I need to apply my can-do spirit to . . .

. _____
. _____
. _____
. _____
. _____
. _____
. _____
. _____
. _____
. _____
. _____
. _____
. _____
. _____
. _____

Each of you must take responsibility for doing the creative best you can with your own life.
GALATIANS 6:5 THE MESSAGE

In the late 1950s, the owner of a small chain of general merchandise stores in the South noticed that he couldn't keep the popular hula hoops in stock. This craze swept the country like wildfire, and not even the manufacturer could keep up with the demand.

"We're sorry," the manufacturer told the owner. "This product has become a nationwide craze, and we simply aren't able to produce our product quickly enough to keep up. You will have to wait quite awhile, we're afraid, before you will have more hula hoops."

The owner could have told his managers to apologize to customers, then explain that the popular item simply wasn't available. Instead, this man ordered some plastic tubing and began making his own hoops—at the astonishing rate of three thousand a night!

This resourceful, proactive store owner brought the same sense of resourcefulness and can-do attitude to everything he did. He was willing to jump through whatever hoops necessary to satisfy his customers. Eventually, his chain of stores grew to national prominence, and the man became a billionaire. His name? Sam Walton.

o o o o

No limits but the sky.

...ying Out of the Pigpen

What is my plan of escape when temptation comes?

... ...e a saying that goes, "Once
you'... ...n the pigpen, it's a little too
late ... ...out soiling your Sunday
clot... ...at sound piece of advice
carr... ...he farm. The key to avoiding
wro... ...compromise in life is to
dec... ...e to stay as far away from it
as p...

...y has a way of revealing itself
a li... ...e. Once we begin thinking
tha... ...of wrongdoing is "not so
ba... ...just a few more steps to the
pig... ...tle hope of escaping without
ge...

...God and yourself right now that
yo... ...even the appearance of wrong
w... ...encounter it. Decide ahead of
ti... ...will handle hypothetical situa-
ti... ...ou lie to a teacher? Copy
a... ...paper? Fudge on your tests?

...e what the "pigpens" are in
y... ...don't go near them. Remember
t... ...of prevention can be worth ten
p... ...rity.

○ ○ ○ ○ ○

*...character is revealed by what
...hen no one is watching you.*

_____.
_____.
_____.
_____.
_____.
_____.
_____.
_____.
_____.
_____.
_____.
_____.
_____.
_____.
_____.

I have hidden your word in my heart
that I might not sin against you.

PSALM 119:11 NIV

Our Real Home

When I realize that Heaven is my true home, I . . .

· _____

· _____

· _____

· _____

· _____

· _____

· _____

· _____

· _____

· _____

· _____

· _____

· _____

· _____

A young man completing a job application came to the line asking for his permanent address. He began to list his street address, but he paused for a moment. Then, with a small smile, he wrote, "Heaven." He understood that Heaven is a real place—and the ultimate home of all God's children.

We spend a lot of time at school. Sometimes it seems like way too much time. You may have found yourself uttering, "I practically live here!"

But school is not your true home. In fact, even the earth is not your true home. The time you spend at school is like one tiny dot on a continuous, unending line. Think about that the next time you need to regain perspective.

We will be more conscious of God in our everyday lives if we remember—like the young man—that He is the Landlord of our permanent home. Someday we will actually meet God. How we will feel about that experience depends on how we spend our time at our temporary home, this earth.

o o o o o

God is the author; men are only the players. These grand pieces which are played upon earth have been composed in heaven.

Godliness with contentment is great gain.
For we brought nothing into this world,
and it is certain we can carry nothing out.
I TIMOTHY 6:6-7

...ned guest, a king or queen or prin... ...live with you, what accommodati... ...you provide? Would you make you... ...ean, inviting, and pleasant as pos...? ...ould you let garbage accumulate... ...se go to ruin?

...you knew that the president of ...tates or some foreign dignitar... ...g to visit your home? If such a pe... ...you a surprise visit to your room to... ...uld you feel? Embarrassed? Pr... ...ed? Disgraced?

...Bible teaches that our bodies are th... ...God's Spirit. Is your temple an ap... ...velling place for God? Sadly, so... rooms are in a lot better sh... ...eir own bodies.

...have to be a hard-bodied m... ...Olympic athlete, but your body is ...God, and you are to honor Him ...are unsure about the state of y... ...ake this quick self-test: Which ...to take two at a time—candy ...? Vegetables or cigarettes? ...drugs?

o o o o o

...ody is matter, but it is God's ...n. . . . when it is neglected or ...at, God himself is insulted.

How am I treating my body?

_____.

_____.

_____.

_____.

_____.

_____.

_____.

_____.

_____.

_____.

_____.

_____.

_____.

_____.

_____.

Do you not know that your body is a temple
of the Holy Spirit, who is in you? . . .
Therefore honor God with your body.

1 CORINTHIANS 6:19 NIV

Am I faithful in the things no one sees but God?

_____

_____

_____

_____

_____

_____

_____

_____

_____

_____

_____

_____

_____

_____

Our world loves "bigness." Huge-screen Imax theaters. Super-sized value meals. Big-screen TVs. Warehouse-size stores to buy clothes, electronics, and music.

The bigger-is-better phenomenon affects our personal lives too. Brothers and sisters vie for the biggest bedroom. Students compete for the coolest clothes, best grades, or for a spot on the cheerleading squad. About the only thing we want to be small is maybe a cell phone, and even then we want to make sure we can get clear connections at all times to talk to our friends.

Our God is certainly capable of big feats. He parted the Red Sea. He created the universe in less than a week. But it's better not to measure our personal value by who our boyfriend or girlfriend is or our place on the football team. God isn't interested in whether you are class president or not. He's interested in your life and the small but faithful steps you take toward Him. Remember, a little obedience and faithfulness make a big difference to God.

○ ○ ○ ○ ○

Faithfulness in little things is a big thing.

"Well done, thou good and faithful servant: thou hast been faithful over a few things, I will make thee ruler over many things: enter thou into the joy of thy lord."

MATTHEW 25:21

What do I do when no one is looking?

[professio]nal carpet layer stepped back to s[ee]... [ne]w carpet he had just installed in a... [was] proud of his work and hur[ried]... [th]e effort. He reached into his jac[ket]... [f]or the Twinkie he had been sav[ing]... [snac]k time and found his pocket em[pty]. He [look]ed across the home's vast liv[ing]... [th]ere, in the middle of his ex[pensive] carpet, he noticed a lump—a T[winkie]... lump.

[The carp]et layer's heart sank as he r[ealized] [t]here was no way to retrieve his s[nack without] tearing up his work and begin-n[ing] a[gain]. [H]e thought for a few moments, [then grabbed] his hammer and beat the lump [down, destroyin]g any evidence of his embarrass-[ment]. Then he exited the home as if it [were nothing].

[As the] man climbed into his truck a [few momen]ts later, he saw his Twinkie lying [on the sea]t. Puzzled, he unwrapped his treat [and wolfe]d it down. Just as he was about [to start hi]s truck, the homeowner hurried [from the] house, frantic. "Excuse me," he [asked th]e carpet layer, "but while you were [laying th]e carpet, did you notice my son's [gerbil? It] seems to have escaped, and we [can't find] it anywhere!"

o o o o o

*My worth to God in public
is what I am in private.*

_____ .

_____ .

_____ .

_____ .

_____ .

_____ .

_____ .

_____ .

_____ .

_____ .

_____ .

_____ .

_____ .

_____ .

May integrity and uprightness protect me,
because my hope is in you.
PSALM 25:21 NIV

Don't Give Up

I will never give up regarding . . .

. _____
. _____
. _____
. _____
. _____
. _____
. _____
. _____
. _____
. _____
. _____
. _____
. _____

Wayne Dyer wrote a book that he believed was important and much needed by a lot of people. Upon completing his opus, he began to search for a publisher. All his search brought him were rejection slips. Not one publisher saw any market for Dyer's work.

Discouraged but undaunted, he dipped into his own pocket and published the book himself. Then, he took to the roads to peddle it. He'd book an appearance on local talk shows around the country, stuff his car full of books, and tell area booksellers he was going to be on the radio or TV the next day. Then he'd provide the booksellers books to meet the demand created by his appearance. He did this for two years, selling a few books at a time.

One night he taped a show in San Francisco—at 3 A.M. About seventeen people were tuned in. But, one of the people was Johnny Carson. Carson loved Dyer's stuff. Soon, Dyer appeared on *The Tonight Show,* and sales of his book *Your Erroneous Zones* skyrocketed. Dyer became a best-selling author and didn't have to do any more 3 A.M. tapings.

The lesson here: Always do your best and never, never give up. You never know who may be listening, or watching, or reading.

o o o o o

Work hard so God can say to you, "Well done."

2 TIMOTHY 2:15 TLB

Difficulty in achieving your goals will reveal one of two things: what you are made of—or what you are full of.

Teamwork

What can I contribute to my family team and other teams I'm on?

[...]or penguins of Antarctica
kno[...] [...]tance of teamwork. They
hud[...] [...] by the thousands, providing
enc[...] [...] to survive the brutal, freezing
we[...] [...] can make a hunk of steel as
bri[...] [...] to chip.

[...]ins take turns monitoring the
ou[...] giant huddle, on the lookout
for [...]od. After one of the birds has
fin[...] [...]ter duty," it moves to the
ins[...] [...]oup, so it can get warm and
sle[...] [...] penguins stand on their
m[...] [...]ds' feet to protect themselves
fr[...] [...]urfaces. If a penguin, big or
sn[...] [...] make it on its own, it wouldn't
su[...] [...]ozen winter night.

[...]ll learn from penguins.
T[...] [...]uals survival. And the tougher
t[...] [...]s, the more important it is for
w[...] [...]nd together. You may not ever
n[...] [...] physical warmth—unless the
h[...] [...]ut—but you can share encour-
a[...] [...]pathy, and ideas. You can share
t[...] [...] in times of crisis, and you can
s[...] [...]dit when success is achieved.

○ ○ ○ ○ ○

[...]ay a team plays as a whole
[...]s its success. You may have the
[...]unch of individual stars in the
[...] if they don't play together, the
[...] won't be worth a dime.

> Two can accomplish more than twice as much as one, for the results can be much better.
>
> ECCLESIASTES 4:9 TLB

Do What's Right

HOW strong is my conviction to always do what's right?

_____

_____

_____

_____

_____

_____

_____

_____

_____

_____

_____

_____

_____

_____

_____

James Burke, CEO of Johnson & Johnson, was facing a crisis. Someone had tampered with a few bottles of his Tylenol pain relievers, and Burke needed to respond to the public. He wanted to recall the product—remove it from the shelves completely until the source and scope of the tampering could be determined. His lawyers, financial advisors, and high-priced business consultants advised him that such a move was unnecessary—not to mention difficult to undertake and brutally expensive.

Despite the pressure, Burke removed every bottle of Tylenol from shelves across the country. He said that putting himself in a customer's shoes led him to the right decision. "If I'm a mother and use Tylenol," he said, "am I ever going to buy it again if there's the slightest chance of playing Russian roulette with my child's well-being?"

Today, Tylenol fills the shelves of supermarkets nationwide—featuring safety caps pioneered by Burke. People felt they could trust a man who was willing to sustain a great financial loss rather than jeopardize the safety of their children. Burke survived a potential crisis by acting on the strength of his convictions—not the misguided, panicky opinions of others.

o o o o

Don't worry about doing what is profitable, prudent, or politically correct. Do what's right.

Act with courage, and may the LORD be with those who do well.

2 CHRONICLES 19:11 NIV

Encourage One Another's Dreams

boy in Naples, Italy, he toiled
long ... factory. All the while, he
drea... a great singer. At age ten he
took ... ce lesson. After hearing his
voic... said bluntly, "You can't sing.
You ... voice at all. Your voice sounds
like ... the shutters." Not exactly the
foo... eeds to grow.

... mother, however, heard
son... in her son's voice—potential
gre... elieved in him. Even though
the ... oor, she assured her son, "My
bo... to make every sacrifice to pay
for ... essons."

... er's confidence and constant
en... paid off. The boy became one
of ... ved and critically acclaimed
op... n the world: Enrico Caruso.

... ent, what are your special
ta... reams? What can you do to
nu... ifts—and the gifts of your
fa... s and schoolmates? Do you
k... e who is ready to give up on a
d... can you do to help that person
k... m alive?

... God gives must be developed,
s... can open these gifts and enjoy
t...

o o o o

... est glory is not in never falling,
... rising every time we fall.

I can inspire the people I love by . . .

_____ .
_____ .
_____ .
_____ .
_____ .
_____ .
_____ .
_____ .
_____ .
_____ .
_____ .
_____ .
_____ .
_____ .
_____ .
_____ .
_____ .

Encourage one another daily, as long
as it is called Today.

HEBREWS 3:13 NIV

Set an Example

HOW can I lead by example?

_____

_____

_____

_____

_____

_____

_____

_____

_____

_____

_____

_____

_____

Ben Franklin wanted Philadelphia to lighten up. He believed that lighting the city's streets would not only improve it aesthetically, but also make it safer. But he didn't try to persuade Philly's citizens by talking to them. Instead, he hung a beautiful lantern near his front door. He kept the lantern brightly polished and carefully and faithfully lit the wick each evening just before dusk.

People strolling the dark street saw Franklin's light from a long way off. They found its glow to be friendly and beautiful—and a helpful, guiding landmark. Soon, Franklin's neighbors began placing lanterns in front of their own homes. Before long, the whole city was dotted with light, and more and more people began to appreciate the beauty and value of Franklin's bright idea.

Lighting the streets became a citywide—and city-sponsored—endeavor.

Just as Franklin's home became a point of light for his city, our actions can become beacons for our friends and peers. What they see, they copy. And when they see the light, they may be inspired to illuminate a candle of their own.

o O o O o

An ounce of leading by example is worth a pound of pressure.

"I have set you an example that you should do as I have done for you."

JOHN 13:15 NIV

July

How committed am I to the truth?

...n of a prominent family
won... ...to give their father as a gift.
Fina... ...ded to commission a profession... ...r to write a book chronicling
the... ...ry. The children met with the
wri... ...ided many documents and
ane... ...eave into his story—along
wit... ...photos.

...children pointed out, "We
ha... ...matter we need to discuss with
yo... ...y's wayward sheep." Then, in
hu... ...e told the biographer about an
ur... ...been convicted of first-degree
m... ...ecuted in the electric chair.

..."...blem," the biographer assured
t... ...I can handle this information in
a... ...avoid embarrassment."

..."...n't want to lie," said one of the
c...

..."...oblem," the biographer repeated.
..."...hat your Uncle Samuel occupied
...plied electronics at an important
...institution. He was attached to
...by the strongest of ties, and his
...as a real shock."

...bout your written and spoken
...tion at school. It can be technically
...thout being true. Pursue truth.

○ ○ ○ ○ ○

...is the cornerstone of all success.

Truthful lips endure forever.
PROVERBS 12:19 NIV

Bringing Out the Best in Each Other

Is there an issue I need to lovingly address with someone?

_____

_____

_____

_____

_____

_____

_____

_____

_____

_____

_____

_____

_____

_____

_____

A group of parents watched from the stands as their local high school's marching band performed on the field. The band was doing well, executing its formations with perfect precision. Almost.

One band member, a trumpet player, was noticeably out of synch. He veered right when his band-mates veered left. He was always a second late getting his instrument to his mouth. And when he marched along, he placed down his right foot when everyone else was landing on the left foot.

From the stands, the trumpeter's mother looked on. With exultant pride, she turned to her husband and exclaimed, "Will you look at that? The whole band is out of step—except for Jimmy!"

Unlike this mother, we can't always gloss over our family's or our friends' mistakes and weaknesses. But addressing such issues gently, tactfully, and privately is the best way to help others improve and become stronger, more confident individuals. We can choose to care about those around us in spite of their mistakes. And we can choose, too, to focus on the traits that make our friends and family members special, valuable, and likable.

o o o o o

Be patient with each other, making allowance for each other's faults because of your love.

EPHESIANS 4:2 NLT

I have yet to find the man, however exalted in his station, who did not do better work and put forth greater effort under a spirit of approval than under a spirit of criticism.

No One Likes a Snob

What masks do I try to hide behind?

_____ .
_____ .
_____ .
_____ .
_____ .
_____ .
_____ .
_____ .
_____ .
_____ .
_____ .
_____ .
_____ .
_____ .
_____ .
_____ .
_____ .
_____ .
_____ .

ed French poodles strolled thro   heir ebony noses high in the air. F   orner, they encountered a scru   a bad case of mange—and a wor   alitosis. They tried to sidestep this   ey hound, but he was eager to r   and trotted along beside the   ppily.

uld excuse us, please," one of the   ped icily, "we have items we mu

the mutt replied, "but at least tel   mes, so I know what to call yo   cross again."

st know," the poodle an   name is Yvette, spelled Y-V-E-T-T-   lleague here is Charlemagne, sp   R-L-E-M-A-G-N-E."

to meet you!" the mutt said. T   g the poodle's tone, he noted, "   ido—P-H-Y-D-E-A-U-X. Now, if   me, I have some garbage to r

e, there is really no place for p   les. Respect and dignity, yes. But h   ance born of popularity, p   loodline? That is barking up the   Ultimately, our world should be   qual-opportunity caring—a place   dog can have its day.

o o o o o

ceit is a strange disease:
akes everyone sick except
the person who has it.

Pride lands you flat on your face;
humility prepares you for honors.

PROVERBS 29:23 THE MESSAGE

Allow for Delays

I can allow for delays by . . .

_____

_____

_____

_____

_____

_____

_____

_____

_____

_____

_____

_____

_____

An old train on a branch line was puffing and creaking slowly through the countryside when suddenly it lurched to a stop. The only passenger in the three-car train rose quickly to his feet and hurried to find the conductor. "Why have we stopped?" he demanded. "I'm a salesman, and I have an appointment in less than an hour in the next town. Surely this old train can make it through a pasture!"

The conductor smiled, "Nothing to worry about, sir. Just a cow on the tracks. Gotta wait her out." The salesman returned to his seat, fuming and fidgeting until the train began to creep forward again about ten minutes later. It chugged along for a mile or two and then ground to a halt once again.

This time the conductor found the salesman. "Don't worry," he said. "We'll be on our way shortly. It's just a temporary delay."

The exasperated salesman asked, "What now? Did we catch up to the cow again?"

What this salesman didn't know was that the schedule for this particular train had been made so as to allow for temporary delays and cows on the track! The salesman made his appointment, but arrived worn to a frazzle by his own frustration and concern.

Allow for delays. You'll enjoy life's journey more.

o o o o o

WE CAN MAKE our plans, but the final outcome is in God's hands.

PROVERBS 16:1 TLB

Patience is the ability to keep your motor idling when you feel like stripping your gears.

...ght D. Eisenhower led the
Alli... ...f Europe during World War
II, h... ...responsibility of making one of
the ... ...lt and far-reaching decisions
eve... ...a single person. He made the
de... ...nge the date of the D-Day
inv... ...last moment. The potential
co... ...were so overwhelming that Ike
fel... ...shed by their weight. Still, he
w... ...me Commander and the only
o... ...make a choice that would
in... ...es of millions.

...about the pressure, Eisenhower
... ...I did not have the required
... ...turned to God. I asked God to
... ...wisdom. I yielded myself to Him. I
... ...myself. And He gave me clear
... ...gave me insight to see what was
... ...endowed me with courage to
... ...cision. And finally, He gave me
... ...d in the knowledge that, having
... ...by God to the decision, I could
... ...sults to Him."

...ecisions you make in your life
... ...pproach the magnitude of General
... ...'s. But whatever the size of the
... ...od wants you to trust Him and let
... ...you through it.

o o o o o

...ver *meant that man should scale*
...vens by strides of human wisdom.

About what decisions do I need to seek God's wisdom?

———————————————— .
———————————————— .
———————————————— .
———————————————— .
———————————————— .
———————————————— .
———————————————— .
———————————————— .
———————————————— .
———————————————— .
———————————————— .
———————————————— .
———————————————— .
———————————————— .
———————————————— .
———————————————— .
———————————————— .
———————————————— .

> If you need wisdom—if you want to
> know what God wants you to do—
> ask him, and he will gladly tell you.
> He will not resent your asking.
>
> JAMES 1:5 NLT

Don't Believe Everything You Hear

HOW can I help bring out the gifts in others?

_____

_____

_____

_____

_____

_____

_____

_____

_____

_____

_____

_____

_____

_____

A partially deaf boy trudged into his home one day after school. In his hand, he carried a note. It was a note from school officials, suggesting that his parents remove him from school. According to those wise officials, this boy was "too stupid to learn."

Upon reading the note, the boy's mother vowed, "My son Tom isn't too stupid to learn. I'll teach him myself." And that is exactly what she did.

Many years later when Tom died, many Americans paid tribute to him by turning off their lights for one full minute. This was a fitting tribute, for Tom Edison invented the light bulb—along with motion pictures and the phonograph. In all, he was credited with more than a thousand patents. He also had a gift for powerful, motivating words. You will read several of his quotes in this book.

Neither you nor anyone you go to school with is beyond learning. No one is beyond discovering new ways to express talent, enthusiasm, creativity, and love. No one is beyond receiving affection and encouragement.

Never give up on yourself, no matter what anyone else says. Stand up for others, and encourage them to stay the course as well. Your Heavenly Father hasn't given up on any of us. And He never will.

o o o o o

I cannot understand how you can bother with mere puny man, to pay any attention to him! And yet you have made him only a little lower than the angels, and placed a crown of glory and honor upon his head.

PSALM 8:4-5 TLB

The difference between genius and stupidity is that genius has its limits.

Gratitude

...hen, Mrs. March tells this stor... ...ghters: Once upon a time, ther... ...girls who had enough to eat and ... ...ear, a good many comforts and ... ...ind friends and parents—and yet ... ...ot content, always wishing for som... ...e. Finally they asked an old wo... ...ice. "When you feel disconten... ...ld them, "think over your ble... ...e grateful."

...ded to try her advice and were su... ...ee how well off they were. One gi... ...money couldn't keep shame a... ...ut of rich people's houses. A... ...ed she was a great deal happier ... ...h, health, and good spirits than a ... ...feeble old lady, who couldn't e... ...mforts. The third found that, ...as it was to help get dinner, it ... ...till to have to go begging for it. ... ...irl learned that even carnelian ... ...ot so valuable as good behavior. ... ...ed to stop complaining and enjoy ... ...s they already possessed.

...g something does not mean it's ... ...If you want to be content, learn ... ...ful for what you have.

o o o o o

...ented mind is a continual feast.

I am grateful for . . .

_____ .
_____ .
_____ .
_____ .
_____ .
_____ .
_____ .
_____ .
_____ .
_____ .
_____ .
_____ .
_____ .
_____ .

Oh, how grateful and thankful I am to the Lord because he is so good. I will sing praise to the name of the Lord who is above all lords.

PSALM 7:17 TLB

The Best Translation

HOW can I ensure that my life is a convincing translation?

_____

_____

_____

_____

_____

_____

_____

_____

_____

_____

_____

_____

_____

_____

Four men stood in a church lobby. They were arguing over which Bible translation was the best. One argued for the *King James Version,* citing its beautiful, eloquent old English.

The second man advocated the *American Standard Version,* noting its literalism and the confidence he felt in its commitment to accurately representing the message of the original texts. The third man praised *The Living Bible* for its conversational, easy-to-understand prose.

After giving thought to each of his friends' impassioned arguments, the fourth man said with certainty, "Frankly, I prefer my boss's translation."

"What do you mean?" the first man asked incredulously. "Your boss is just a shop foreman. He doesn't even have a college degree."

"I stand by my claim," the fourth man said. "My boss has translated the pages of the Bible into his life. He has lived the Message. And it has been the most convincing translation I have ever witnessed."

All the scholarly theological pursuits can't match the life lived through love and marked by kindness, truthfulness, and humility. That, in fact, is the way of living that is taught in every translation of the Scriptures.

o o o o o

Whatever you have learned or received or heard from me, or seen in me—put it into practice. And the God of peace will be with you.

PHILIPPIANS 4:9 NIV

A good example is the best sermon.

...s, two powerful men vied for
lead... ...eat Britain's government:
Wil... ...ne and Benjamin Disraeli.
The... ...se rivals. Disraeli once said of
his ... The difference between a
mis... ...a calamity [is this]: If
Gla... ...to the Thames [River], it
wo... ...ortune. But if someone
dra... ...t again, it would be a
cal...

...proved to be successful
lea... ...sraeli was seen as a man of
m... ...—and that edge was due to
so... ...er than his razor-sharp wit. The
ke... ...'s charismatic edge was best
ex... ...woman who dined with the
tw... ...on consecutive evenings.

...ed about her impressions of
th... ..."When I left the dining room
af... ...xt to Mister Gladstone, I thought
h... ...verest man in England. But after
si... ...Mister Disraeli, I thought I was
t... ...woman in England."

...to being an inspiring leader is
n... ...prove how important and smart
y... ...israeli knew, the true secret lies
i... ...y to make others feel important
a...

o o o o o

...est good you can do for others
...st to share your riches, but to
...veal to them their own.

I can make others feel important and valued by . . .

_____.

_____.

_____.

_____.

_____.

_____.

_____.

_____.

_____.

_____.

_____.

_____.

_____.

_____.

_____.

_____.

Honor one another above yourselves.

ROMANS 12:10 NIV

God Will See

Knowing that God sees my work inspires me to . . .

_____

_____

_____

_____

_____

_____

_____

_____

_____

_____

_____

_____

_____

_____

The famed artist Michelangelo was summoned to Rome by Pope Julius II to work on a painting project. Michelangelo wanted to refuse the task, which involved painting a dozen figures on the ceiling of a small chapel in the Vatican. Michelangelo was a trained painter, but his true passion was sculpture. However, when pressed, Michelangelo reluctantly accepted the task.

The artist's rivals hoped he would fail in his assignment, knowing that painting was not his first love. But once Michelangelo agreed to do the job, he poured himself into it. He expanded the scope of the project from a simple depiction of the twelve apostles to include more than four hundred figures and nine scenes from the book of Genesis.

For four agonizing years, Michelangelo lay on his back painting the Sistine Chapel's ceiling. His neck, shoulders, and back ached. Paint dripped into his eyes. His vision was damaged. Later, Michelangelo would call this time "tortured years" that made him feel "as old and as weary as Jeremiah."

However, the fruits of this agony are beautiful. Art historians note that artists like Raphael adapted their styles to reflect Michelangelo's influence. What drove Michelangelo's commitment to excellence and beauty? "No one will ever see this corner of the chapel," someone called up to him as he worked one day. His reply was simple: "God will see."

o o o o o

All hard work brings a profit, but mere talk leads only to poverty.

PROVERBS 14:23 NIV

Nothing great in the world has been accomplished without passion.

Give It Your All

now where or how you will
hear... ...will change your life. A fifteen-
year... ...ball player was attending a
sum... ...all camp run by a man named
Easy... ...y. At one point, Macauley told
his ... ...ters, "Just remember that if
you ... ...ing at your game to the
utm... ...ability, there will be someone
out ... ...where with equal ability who is
doi... ...And one day you'll play each
oth... ...have the advantage."

... ...rds profoundly affected at least
on... ...ung Bill Bradley. Bradley lived
th... ...e worked hard on his game
an... ...excellent high-school
ho... ...star college player at
Pr... ...driven, he elevated his talents
to... ...level and became a key
m... ...great New York Knicks' teams.

... ...wasn't enough for Bradley.
A... ...rom basketball, he entered
p... ...n for the office of president of
th... ...tes.

... ...e you doing to "work on your
g... ...spects of your life? What are
y... ...distinguish yourself from others
w... ...the same craft that you do? If
y... ...compete against them, who
w... ...he advantage?

o o o o o

...e *anything less than your*
...*t is to sacrifice the gift.*

To gain the advantage, I commit to . . .

_____.

_____.

_____.

_____.

_____.

_____.

_____.

_____.

_____.

_____.

_____.

_____.

_____.

_____.

Hard work brings prosperity;
playing around brings poverty.

PROVERBS 28:19 TLB

First Things First

What are the biggest "rocks" in my life today?

_____

_____

_____

_____

_____

_____

_____

_____

_____

_____

_____

_____

_____

A time-management expert addressed a group of business students. He pulled out a one-gallon Mason jar and set it on the table. Then he produced a dozen fist-sized rocks and carefully placed them into the jar. Then he asked, "Is this jar full?"

Everyone said yes. Then he reached under the table and pulled out a bucket of gravel. He dumped it in and shook the jar. He asked the group again, "Is the jar full?"

By this time the class was on to him. "Probably not," one student answered. Then the instructor reached under the table and grabbed a bucket of sand. He dumped the sand, which went into all of the spaces between the rocks and the gravel. He asked, "Is this jar full?"

"No!" the class shouted.

Next, he grabbed a pitcher of water and began to pour it in until the jar was filled to the brim. "What is the point of this illustration?" he asked.

One student offered, "No matter how full your schedule is, you can always fit some more things into it!"

"No," the speaker replied, "The truth this illustration teaches us is: If you don't put the big rocks in first, you'll never get them in." Ask yourself, "What are the 'big rocks' in my life?" Put those in your jar first.

o   o   o   o   o

"Where your treasure is, there your heart will be also."

MATTHEW 6:21 NIV

Our greatest danger in life is in permitting the urgent things to crowd out the important.

Short and Sweet

...le believe that important
me... ...ecisions must be conveyed
wit... ...iage and fanfare. The humble
and ...ent Abraham Lincoln wasn't
on... ...eople. On April 7, 1865, with
the ...aging, Lincoln needed to
co... ...ith one of his generals on the
fr... ...credibility as president—and
th... ...future—hung in the balance. He
w... ...essage to inspire but also to be
c... ...hat he wrote:

... Grant,

... Sheridan says, "If the thing is
... think Lee will surrender." Let
... be pressed.

Lincoln

... was a brilliant, effective commu-
... knew that few things are as effec-
... ...licity and directness. His famous
... Address is another example of
... ...mmunication. Too many words can
... ...re of one's time than is necessary
... ...erve the deliverer of the message
... ...n the receiver. What's more, lengthy
... ...can become confused and diluted,
... original intent altogether.

... ...ou communicate at home, school,
... follow Lincoln's example. There's
... to complicate your message with
... ...jargon or equivocation. Say what
... ...h. Then send that e-mail, write that
... end that phone call. Keep it short
... ...le.

o o o o o

Brevity is the soul of wit.

HOW do I rate as a communicator?

_____.

_____.

_____.

_____.

_____.

_____.

_____.

_____.

_____.

_____.

_____.

_____.

_____.

_____.

A fool's voice is known by his many words.

ECCLESIASTES 5:3 NKJV

Take Courage

Knowing God is with me gives me the courage to . . .

_____

_____

_____

_____

_____

_____

_____

_____

_____

_____

_____

_____

_____

_____

An auto racer who set the world speed record. A fighter pilot who recorded the most aerial-combat victories against the Germans in World War I. A man who survived a plane crash and spent twenty-two days on a raft in the Pacific Ocean. What do these three have in common?

They are all the same person: Eddie Rickenbacker. When Eddie was twelve, his father died. So Eddie quit school to become the family breadwinner, doing whatever he had to do to help the family survive.

As a teen, he started working as a race-car mechanic. By the time he was twenty-two, he was racing himself. Two years later, he set the world speed record at Daytona.

When World War I began, Eddie tried to enlist as an aviator but was told he was overaged and undereducated. He eventually talked his superiors into sending him to flight training. By the war's end, he had logged 300 combat hours and survived 134 aerial encounters, shooting down twenty-six enemy planes.

When asked the secret to his success, Rickenbacker cited courage. "Courage," he told them, "is doing what you're afraid to do. There can be no courage unless you're scared."

Fear is natural. It can overcome you, or you can say, as Eddie Rickenbacker did a thousand times, "I'll fight like a wildcat!"

o o o o o

Be strong and courageous.
DEUTERONOMY 31:6 NIV

Courage is fear that has said its prayers.

God Can Show You New Things

the Swiss were the kings of
watc_____ They built the best timepieces
mon_____ By the 1940s, they
prod_____ ____rcent of the world's watches.

_____ate 1960s, an inventor
app_____ading Swiss watch company
with_____ _____ a new kind of watch. This
firm_____ ____ inventor's idea, as did every
oth_____ _____ npany he courted.

_____ng his design had merit, the
ma_____ Japan. And a company there
wa_____ y the invention—a digital
wa_____ e of the company was Seiko.
Se_____ oducing digital watches, which
to_____ e 80 percent of all watches
pr_____ same percentage once
cla_____ Swiss.

_____ arket leaders may not be
to_____ Only those who have the
fo_____ nticipate the future and improve
th_____ s and/or services can compete
in_____ dly changing, innovation-driven
s_____ companies that have a sizable
le_____ competitors will eventually get
p_____ quit moving forward.

_____ panies—or individuals—to thrive,
i_____ e to embrace new ideas, different
_____ g things. When it comes to new
_____ tive and keep an open mind.

o o o o o

____te where the puck is going
____be, not where it has been.

HOW can I tap into God's creativity?

_____.
_____.
_____.
_____.
_____.
_____.
_____.
_____.
_____.
_____.
_____.
_____.
_____.
_____.
_____.
_____.

From now on I will tell you of new things,
of hidden things unknown to you.

ISAIAH 48:6 NIV

Focus and Dedication

I can improve in my
area of interest by . . .

· _____

· _____

· _____

· _____

· _____

· _____

· _____

· _____

· _____

· _____

· _____

· _____

· _____

· _____

· _____

If you met Tony Gwynn on the street, you might not guess he is a professional athlete. At 5'11" and 220 pounds, he's a bit on the chubby side. But if you watched him play baseball, you'd have no doubt about his athletic prowess. For many years, he has been baseball's most consistent hitter. He has eight batting titles to his credit—if it weren't for injuries, he'd have more.

What makes Gwynn such as exceptional hitter? Focus and dedication. Several times each season, Gwynn devours Ted Williams's book, *The Science of Hitting,* a book he's been reading since college. And he watches count-less hours of videotapes on hitting. He also loves to talk about hitting with his peers, and he's been known to arrive at social events with a batting glove hanging from his pocket.

And when he's not playing, talking, or watching baseball, you might find Gwynn playing Ping-Pong or some other activity that will increase his hand-eye coordination.

You may feel that you lack some of the natural physical or intellectual tools to excel in your area of interest. But if you are willing to focus on the details that lead to excellence, you could be a big hit in your chosen area!

○ ○ ○ ○

Luck is what happens when preparation meets opportunity.

Whatsoever a man soweth,
that shall he also reap.
GALATIANS 6:7

Am I passionate enough about the important things?

[...]ster Wunderman was fired
fron[...] a New York advertising
firm [...] was discouraged and hurt,
part[...]use he knew that he could
lear[...] the agency's leader, Max
Sac[...] next morning, Wunderman
ret[...] office and worked just as he
had [...]—but without pay.

[...] ignored the young former
em[...] month or so. Then, he finally
rel[...] proached Wunderman one
day [...] OK, you win. I never saw a
ma[...]ed a job more than he
wa[...]"

[...]an made the most of his
se[...]. He continued to learn from
Sa[...] eventually went on to become
o[...]untry's most successful ad
ex[...]me credit him with being the
fa[...]t marketing.

[...]d of initiative and boldness are
y[...] take to gain the attention and
c[...] your teachers, boss, and
c[...] bad do you want to learn? And
c[...] a vocation—or a passion?
S[...] proaching what seems like
o[...]k with extraordinary intent can
[...]elievable results.

o o o o

*[...] name for people who aren't
[...] about their work: unemployed.*

Isn't it wonderful all the ways in which this distress has goaded you closer to God? You're more alive, more concerned, more sensitive, more reverent, more human, more passionate, more responsible.

2 CORINTHIANS 7:11 THE MESSAGE

Choose the Right Team

What effect does the "team" I'm on have on me?

. _____

. _____

. _____

. _____

. _____

. _____

. _____

. _____

. _____

. _____

. _____

. _____

. _____

. _____

In his book *The Mind of Watergate*, psychiatrist Leo Rangell, M.D., relates what he calls a "compromise of integrity" as he analyzes the relationship between former President Richard M. Nixon and several of his closest confidants. He records a conversation between investigative committee member Senator Howard Baker and young Herbert L. Porter:

Baker: "Did you ever have any qualms about what you were doing? Did you ever think of saying, 'I do not think this is quite right.' Did you ever think of that?"

Porter: "Yes, I did."

Baker: "What did you do about it?"

Porter: "I did not do anything."

Baker: "Why didn't you?"

Porter: "In all honesty, probably because of the fear of the group pressure that would ensue, of not being a team player."

There's nothing wrong with being a team player, as long as you choose the right team! You will become like your friends, even as they change and become a little more like you. Therefore, choose your friends cautiously and thoughtfully.

o o o o o

The rotten apple spoils his companion.

Children who obey what they have been taught are smart, but friends of troublemakers disgrace their parents.

PROVERBS 28:7 NCV

How can I accentuate my strengths?

_____ .
_____ .
_____ .
_____ .
_____ .
_____ .
_____ .
_____ .
_____ .
_____ .
_____ .
_____ .
_____ .

knew he wanted to be an
ente   orked hard on a magic act,
whic   egan to try out on audiences.
How   of the tricks invariably went
wro   ould have become discour-
age   ened to and watched his
aud   lly. He noticed that the
cro   rupt with laughter when a
tric   n.

sai   e to the audiences, Martin
sai   rough my act and started
tak   e things that went right."

               other words, performed the
ult   trick. He turned his illusionist
ac   edy routine and became the
cc   tand-up act. And he's gone on
to   uccessful comedic actor, direc-
tc

               are so focused on accom-
p   es of tasks that we don't take
ti   the effectiveness—or neces-
s   we are doing. If we fail, we
c   t as a signal to give up entirely.
               r teachers, your coaches, your
b   nt? What do they respond to
r   astically and appreciatively? Is
               u are striving to give them, or
               ely trying to pull a non-existent
               a hat?

o o o o

_rience is not what happens
_man; it is what a man does
th what happens to him.

> Wise people can also listen and learn;
> even smart people can find good
> advice in these words.
>
> PROVERBS 1:5 NCV

Where can my light shine most brightly?

. _____

. _____

. _____

. _____

. _____

. _____

. _____

. _____

. _____

. _____

. _____

. _____

One night in 1837, a young woman named Florence believed she heard God's voice informing her that she had a mission. Nine years later, that mission began to take shape when a friend sent her information about the Institution of Protestant Deaconesses in Germany. She entered the institution to learn how to care for the sick.

In 1853, Florence became superintendent of a woman's hospital in London. When the Crimean War broke out the following year, she volunteered at once to care for British soldiers, leaving for Constantinople in haste. Once there, she was given charge of nursing at a military hospital. Even though the doctors were hostile toward her and the hospital was deplorably filthy, she dug in her heels and began to care for her patients as best she could.

First she used provisions she had brought with her from London. Then she spearheaded a correspondence campaign to resupply the hospital. She spent many hours each day in the wards, caring for the soldiers who entered the hospital. The comfort she gave on night rounds earned her the nickname "The Lady with the Lamp."

This woman's selfless giving eventually made her name synonymous with compassionate nursing care. She was Florence Nightingale.

o o o o o

"You are the world's light—a city on a hill, glowing in the night for all to see. Don't hide your light! Let it shine for all; let your good deeds glow for all to see, so that they will praise your heavenly Father."

MATTHEW 5:14-16 TLB

God can do tremendous things through people who don't care who gets the credit.

Get Better Not Bitter

Who are the "unlovable" people God wants to love through me?

_____.

_____.

_____.

_____.

_____.

_____.

_____.

_____.

_____.

_____.

_____.

_____.

_____.

_____.

the ... ... tougher commandment than
the ... ...ructs us to love our enemies?
Not ... ...m, or simply do kind things
for ... ...em. Those obnoxious, cruel,
hate... ...he teacher who treats you
unfa... ...ow student who pretends to
be ... ...hen stabs you in the back. The
unh... ...er who unfairly criticizes you
and ... ... to your boss. That bully who
is c... ...ude. Or that certain someone
wh... ...nnoying.

... ...tep in loving our enemies is
pra... ...m (not for their humiliation,
do... ...struction, by the way). And
wh... ...for our enemies, we need to
pr... ...or our own attitudes and
be... ...r theirs. That way, even if our
pr... ...change our enemies' ugly quali-
ti... ...change us.

... ...e first thing to pray for is simply
th... ...ace to want to love our enemies.
... ...g for these people, we may
c... ...ze that they are no less attrac-
t... ...r loved by God than we are.
A... ...xperience what hard work it is
t... ...able people, we will value God's
l... ...ore than ever.

o o o o o

_...wrestles with us strengthens
...rves, and sharpens our skill.
...r antagonist is our helper._

> "Love your enemies! Do good to them!
> Lend to them! And don't be concerned about
> the fact that they won't repay. Then your
> reward from heaven will be very great, and
> you will truly be acting as sons of God: for
> he is kind to the unthankful and to those
> who are very wicked."
> LUKE 6:35 TLB

Am I courageous enough to speak what I believe?

_____

_____

_____

_____

_____

_____

_____

_____

_____

_____

_____

_____

_____

_____

A nineteenth-century preacher named Peter Cartwright was preparing his sermon one Sunday when he was warned that U.S. President Andrew Jackson would be in the congregation. He was told to keep his remarks benign so as not to offend the president.

During his message, Cartwright acknowledged his famous guest. "I have been told that Andrew Jackson is in the congregation," he said. "And I have been asked to guard my remarks. What I must say is that Andrew Jackson will go to hell if he doesn't repent of his sin."

Some people in the audience cringed. Others gasped. What would become of this outspoken pastor? What penalty might he face?

After the service, Jackson strode up to Cartwright. The noble preacher stood his ground. "Sir," the president said, "if I had a regiment of men like you, I could whip the world."

It's not always easy to speak the truth, especially if you're intimidated by the size or import of your audience. It's much easier to say what we believe people—especially our friends—will want to hear. When you don't say what you truly believe, not only are you speaking untruthfully to others, but you are betraying your own ideas and convictions. Speak what you believe—the results of such honesty might just surprise you.

○ ○ ○ ○ ○

The LORD detests lying lips, but he delights in men who are truthful.

PROVERBS 12:22 NIV

One man with courage makes a majority.

... of a Mexican restaurant in
Calif... ...t they had devised a clever
prom... ...began offering free lunch for
life ... ...ho would get a tattoo of the
rest... ...—a red-sombrero-clad fellow
ridi... j... ...ered ear of corn. The manager
rea... ...t people in their right minds
wo... ...my the Corn Man perma-
ner... ...o their skin?"

...ks that followed, forty-plus
pe... ...orting Jimmy on various parts
of ... ... In a panic, the manager did
so... ...th, calculating that just to feed
th... ...emblazoned with Jimmy would
co... ...urant $5.8 million over the
c... ...next fifty years. With a face as
r... ...sombrero, the manager halted
t... ...n at fifty people.

...fornia eatery could have learned
a... ...The Big Texan Steak Ranch in
... ...s. This establishment offers a
... ...e steak dinner to any patron
... ...f down the steak—plus a salad,
... ...tail, potato, and roll—in an hour

... a few people have accomplished
...st fail and have to pay $54.13
... ...eals. On the average, only one
... ...ight succeeds. That means for
... ...meal it gives away, The Big Texan
... ...378.91.

○ ○ ○ ○ ○

...u fail to plan, you plan to fail.

Whom do I trust to help me make wise plans?

_____ .
_____ .
_____ .
_____ .
_____ .
_____ .
_____ .
_____ .
_____ .
_____ .
_____ .
_____ .
_____ .
_____ .
_____ .
_____ .
_____ .

"Suppose one of you wants to build a
tower. Will he not first sit down and
estimate the cost to see if he has
enough money to complete it?"

LUKE 14:28 NIV

Excuses

HOW truthful am I regarding absences?

People have to miss work occasionally for a variety of reasons. However, some of the reasons are more intriguing than others. Consider, if you will, these actual "excuses" gleaned from voice-mail messages, memos, and e-mails:

- Please excuse me for missing work today. I forgot to get the Sunday paper off the porch, and when I found it on Monday, I thought it was Sunday.

- Please excuse me for missing work today. I was ill and had to go get shot.

- I am calling to inform you that I will be absent from work. I have to go get three teeth taken out of my face.

- Hi, this is Robert. Please excuse me from work on January 28, 29, 30, 31, and 32. Also 33.

- I will not be coming into the office tomorrow. I am being bothered by very close veins.

- This is Mary, calling to notify you that I won't be at work on Monday because I am very tired. I spent the weekend with the Marines.

o o o o

A good laugh is sunshine in a heart.

A happy heart is good medicine and a cheerful mind works healing.

PROVERBS 17:22 AMP

...ng are actual signs from
busi... ...d the world:

- ... ...n department store: "Bargain
  ... ...Upstairs."

- ... ...arm supplies store: "Horse
  ... ...cents pre-packed bag, 20
  ... ...it yourself."

- ... ...secondhand shop: "We
  ... ...nything—bicycles, washing
  ... ...etc. Why not bring your wife
  ... ...get a wonderful bargain?"

- ... ...town hall in the U.K.: "The
  ... ...s closed until opening. It will
  ... ...sed after being opened. Open
  ... ..."

- ... ...marquee: "Smarts is the most
  ... ...disco in town. Everyone is
  ... ..."

- ... ...a dry cleaner's window:
  ... ...eaving their garments here for
  ... ...n thirty days will be disposed

- ... ...a health-food shop window:
  ... ...due to illness."

- ... ...air shop door: "We can repair
  ... ...(Please knock hard on the
  ... ...he bell doesn't work.)"

- ... ...a washroom in a London office
  ... ..."Toilet out of order. Please use
  ... ...ow."

○ ○ ○ ○ ○

...aughter is the joyous
...versal evergreen of life.

What comical situations have I witnessed lately?

_____ .

_____ .

_____ .

_____ .

_____ .

_____ .

_____ .

_____ .

_____ .

_____ .

_____ .

_____ .

_____ .

_____ .

> A glad heart makes a cheerful countenance.
>
> PROVERBS 15:13 AMP

Use It or Lose It

HOW does God want me to use my gifts?

_____
_____
_____
_____
_____
_____
_____
_____
_____
_____
_____
_____
_____
_____
_____

Imagine receiving a gift from a wealthy person who is renowned for his taste in selecting perfect and valuable presents for everyone on his list. Wouldn't this be a gift you would be eager to open?

Sadly, many people have been given gifts from the perfect Giver, but they never bother to open them or use them for their intended purpose.

God has given each of us abilities. And He never makes a mistake. His gifts are never the wrong size or style or inappropriate in any way. No one has ever needed to return a gift from God. If we open these Heaven-sent gifts, we can then use them in a way that will benefit others and bring glory to our Creator. Do you know what your true gifts are? Are you using them? Or are they lying dormant, gathering dust? If so, it's time to tear into that aging wrapping paper.

Putting your God-given talents to work is one of the most satisfying things you can do. As you do what God created you to do, you gain a deep sense of purpose and become closer and more grateful to the One who gave you your talents. Few things are as beautiful as Creator and creation working together. Do what you can with what you've been given.

o o o o

_Talent is like an arm or a leg—
use it or lose it._

Do not neglect your gift.
I TIMOTHY 4:14 NIV

HOW would God have me overcome envy?

___ referred to as the "big
gree_____ for nothing. God hates
jealo___ ___ that it made His top-ten
list—___ ___mmandments. He etched in
stor_ ___ing words: "You shall not
cov_ ___bor's wife, or his manservant
or _ _____ his ox, or donkey, or anything
tha_ ___ your neighbor."

___ terms, this commandment
fro_ ___of Exodus could read, "You
sha_ ___ your friend's boyfriend; your
gir_ ___ularity status; or a friend's
tr_ ___s, grades, etc."

___l God's children, and we
sh_ ___pare our "blessings" with those
o_ ___en we envy what others have,
w_ ___ves of the joy and contentment
w_ ___d in what God gives us. The
e_ ___alousy is so powerful that it
c_ ___ squelches the positive energy
___ ___using to better ourselves—in
___ ___thletic abilities, or musical
___ ___vaste energy that we could use
___ ___ers.

___ your heart. If you find yourself
___ ___joice in the success of others,
___ ___ instead of focusing on what
___ ___, ask God to remind you of the
___ ___ngs, gifts, and talents He has given
___ ___eep in mind, they are all grace
___ ___is they are all free and unearned.

o o o o

___ takes the joy, happiness, and
contentment out of living.

> Where envying and strife is, there is
> confusion and every evil work.
>
> JAMES 3:16

HOW can I walk in God's peace?

_____

_____

_____

_____

_____

_____

_____

_____

_____

_____

_____

_____

_____

The apostle Paul instructed believers to "Be anxious for nothing" (Philippians 4:6 NASB). Think about that. Paul says the child of God shouldn't worry about anything! And Paul didn't give this advice lightly. He was in prison at the time he wrote it. In fact, he spent a lot of time in chains at various "gray-bar hotels"—separated from those he loved.

He had his well-publicized "thorn in the flesh" to contend with as well.

Paul was a man who endured beatings and stonings. He even had disagreements with one of Jesus' original disciples, Peter. Ultimately, his staunch faith in God and his outspokenness about it got him beheaded.

Despite all his trials, Paul knew God could bring peace. God doesn't always untie all the knots in our lives. But He does give us the grace to live with the knots. So remember, there is nothing you face that is too difficult, too troubling, or too frightening for God. Follow Paul's example. He put it this way: "The Lord is near. Do not be anxious about anything, but in everything, by prayer and petition, with thanksgiving, present your requests to God. And the peace of God, which transcends all understanding, will guard your hearts and your minds in Christ Jesus" (Philippians 4:5-7 NIV).

o o o o

Anxiety is the misuse of the imagination.

May the Lord of peace himself give you peace at all times and in every way.

2 THESSALONIANS 3:16 NIV

...ng the grueling Tour de
Fra... cyclist Lance Armstrong went
on ... e feat in the year 2000.
Ar... both of these races and a
sc... after battling cancer, a cancer
so ... that it had spread throughout
his ... to his brain.

... remarkable victory in the 1999
T... e, Armstrong said that he
v... been able to win if not for the
c... rive, the perseverance, and the
c... he developed while battling his
... ny made him strong enough to
... nd harder—and with more deter-
... han all of his opponents.

... athletes like Armstrong train, they
... lift weights to the point of
... re. Although this approach actually
... vn muscle fibers, it is beneficial
... e body adapts to the stress and
... e damaged fibers to be stronger

... ainly, the pain and trials that
... us come from many different
... But it could be that God allows
... ply to give us a chance to grow
... and better able to overcome our
... and become all He intended us to be.
... rmstrong knew the truth of the
... an proverb, "In the presence of trials,
... uy crutches. But others grow wings."

o o o o o

...at feeling—the finish line, the last
...le of meters—is what motivates me.
...could bottle that up and sell it, I'd be
the richest man is the world.

I will exchange my weakness for
God's strength by . . .

_____ .
_____ .
_____ .
_____ .
_____ .
_____ .
_____ .
_____ .
_____ .
_____ .
_____ .
_____ .
_____ .
_____ .
_____ .
_____ .
_____ .
_____ .

He gives power to the tired and worn out,
and strength to the weak.

ISAIAH 40:29 TLB

Whom You Hang With

With what kind of companions do I spend my time?

_____

_____

_____

_____

_____

_____

_____

_____

_____

_____

_____

_____

_____

_____

Companionship choices are difficult to make. Jesus spent time with many people of low reputation, even to the point of being accused of being a low-life himself. Yet we are cautioned by a familiar proverb that "bad company corrupts good character." The key to following Jesus' example and protecting ourselves lies in discernment.

First, we should spend as much time as possible with Godly people who will encourage us to grow closer to our Creator. Second, as we befriend troubled people, we must be careful to do so on our terms as much as possible. Certainly, in the classroom we don't have total control over whom we hang around. But we do have to exercise control over the setting. It's unwise to join in or stand silently by while a group of friends gossips maliciously about someone else at school.

And it's foolish to be around when classmates are abusing school equipment or resources (e.g., viewing pornography on the Internet, cheating, using drugs, and the like).

At school we are known largely by the company we keep. There's nothing wrong with trying to be a positive influence among people who need a good role model. But, when swimming with the sharks, we must constantly ask ourselves, "Am I drawing these individuals to God, or are they drawing me away from Him?"

o o o o o

He who walks with the wise grows wise,
but a companion of fools suffers harm.

PROVERBS 13:20 NIV

Your companions are like buttons on an elevator. They will either take you up or take you down.

One for the Father

... ollege football coach Knute
Rock ... Dame once gleaned a
mar... rmance from his team by
urgi... Get out there, and win one
for ... a deceased former player. They
gave ... someone they cherished.
Ho... e motivation can we muster by
ded... fforts to God, the One who
cre... oves us unconditionally?

... e days when the yearning for
co... popularity, or the praise of
yo... s not motivate you at school,
yo... our Heavenly Father should. In
re... your ultimate Coach, your
ul... nce.

... you're doing something
a... c, or career-oriented, do it for
... as the One you serve, beyond
y... your teachers, your friends—or
y... bition. Dedicate the work to
... to honor Him for the talents
... you.

... g God, you can't help but serve
... d you—and you will know that
... g the best you can do. However
... turn out, He will be proud of
... u will know the joy of pleasing
... Give it all you've got—for the
... atters most.

o o o o

... our work is, there let our joy be.

HOW can I keep God as my primary motivation?

_____.
_____.
_____.
_____.
_____.
_____.
_____.
_____.
_____.
_____.
_____.
_____.
_____.
_____.
_____.
_____.
_____.
_____.

Serve the Lord with gladness!

PSALM 100:2 AMP

Take Time to Refuel

HOW can I ensure that I get enough rest on a regular basis?

_____

_____

_____

_____

_____

_____

_____

_____

_____

_____

_____

_____

_____

_____

_____

God doesn't sweat. He doesn't get tired or suffer with aching muscles. He never needs to take an aspirin or use Bengay. Yet what did He do after creating the world? He rested. He took the time to step back, cease working, and enjoy His creation. If an all-powerful Being took the time to rest, that should speak volumes to us mere mortals.

We need to rest occasionally. We need to take time to recover physically, emotionally, and spiritually from life's demands. We need time to take stock of where we've been, where we are, and where we're headed. We need to take the time to be a friend, a son or daughter, a child of God.

Various studies—including a very recent one at the University of Chicago—reveal that those who fail to recharge their mental and physical batteries once in a while are more susceptible to illness and stress-related problems such as ulcers—and to mistakes. Many forget that activity, however productive it might seem, doesn't equal a quality life.

Additionally, in resting we find the time and the right frame of mind to contemplate God's wonders and to thank Him for His grace and kindness to us. We gather the energy to run the next miles on our journey with Him and toward Him.

o o o o o

He lets me rest in the meadow grass and leads me beside the quiet streams. He restores my failing health.

PSALM 23:2 TLB

Even the best racehorse has to stop for oats once in a while.

Better Double-check

...the next time you type up
you... ...fill out a job application.
The... ...weren't careful enough!

- ...raduate degree in unclear

- ...vious position, I saved the
  ...$29,000 a year by removing
  ...al pants from the reception
  ...the cafeteria."

- ...ous job was serving as a
  ...ist in a lawyer's office."

- ...tectural experience includes
  ...golf curses."

- ...d for twelve years as an
  ...ed security guard."

- ...nteer experience includes deliv-
  ...males to senior citizens."

- ...y last job because my souse is in
  ...y and had to relocate."

- ...e to work for a company that
  ...Judo-Christian values."

- ...t job was assistant manager at
  ...Plumbing and Hating Specialists."

- ...ademic scholarship I earned
  ...ith a $5,000 award and a plague."

- ...of my experience to this point
  ...en as a blue-color worker."

- ...rt of the city maintenance crew, I
  ...d bad roads and defective brides."

- ...graduating from college, I worked
  ...othing store for seven moths."

- ...areer goal is to shave my talents
  ...growing company."

- ...obbies include raising long-eared
  ...as pets."

○ ○ ○ ○ ○

*...s achieved much who has lived
...aughed often, and loved much.*

Don't Put It Off

I am reminded that I need to . . .

. _____

. _____

. _____

. _____

. _____

. _____

. _____

. _____

. _____

. _____

. _____

. _____

. _____

. _____

Cindy, a young writer, grinned as she read her prose on the computer screen. The words were flowing smoothly from her brain to her fingers. *I'm even impressing myself,* she thought, a bit sheepishly. *This is the best short story I have ever written. Only a few more pages and I'll be done.*

She thought about pausing briefly to save her work, but she was on a roll. She feared the sudden inability to regain the rhythm she had found. *I'll save it as soon as it's finished,* she reasoned.

As Cindy plunged into the next paragraph, her cursor suddenly stopped blinking. Her pulse quickened. "Come on," she said, "don't do this to me, please. Not now!" Cindy waited a few moments, then hit her space bar. Nothing. Panicking, she hit "return." No response. Her screen was frozen like the arctic tundra.

She pounded furiously on her space bar and moved her mouse frantically across its pad, but she knew it was futile. *Why didn't I take a minute to save this?* she thought.

Cindy sighed deeply. All that appeared on the screen was the story title: "Ready or Not."

Cindy shook her head, then phoned her husband to tell him she'd be home late. Then she faced the almost-blank screen and began typing. Again.

○ ○ ○ ○

Make the most of every opportunity.
COLOSSIANS 4:5 NIV

Procrastination is the thief of time.

...oted a small airplane and
ofte[n] ...rvices to hunters in the
Car[...] ...ness. One season, he was
app[...] ...eb and Jake, two moose
hun[...] ...s took the duo to the wilds.

[...] [Th]omas returned to fetch his
clie[nts] ...ed their gear and two gigantic
m[...] ...rry, fellas," he told them. "I
ca[...] ... here with the two of you, all
yo[...] ...those two Bullwinkles!"

[...]t?" Jeb asked.

[...] the load will be too heavy for
m[...] ...ill never get off the ground."

[...] understand this," Jake said,
e[...] ..."Last year each of us got a
[...] ...he pilot was willing to load
[...] ...n his plane."

[...] Thomas said tentatively, "I guess if
[...] it last year, uh, I can too."

[...] [lo]aded up the plane, and Thomas
[...] ...gines. The pontoon plane rose
[...] ...unsteadily. As it approached a
[...] ...became apparent to Thomas that
[...] ...ever clear this obstacle. Sure enough,
[...] ...ashed partway up the mountain.

[...] ...[fortu]nately, no one was hurt. As the trio
[...] ...om the wreckage, Jeb asked,
[...] ...e we, Jake?"

[...] ...urveyed the area. "Oh, about a mile
[...] ...n we got last year. Hey, Thomas,
[...] ...etter pilot than that last guy we had!"

o o o o o

[Wi]sdom is oft times nearer when
we stop than when we soar.

Do I trust my internal instincts as much as I should?

_____ .

_____ .

_____ .

_____ .

_____ .

_____ .

_____ .

_____ .

_____ .

_____ .

_____ .

_____ .

_____ .

_____ .

_____ .

As dead flies give perfume a bad smell, so
a little folly outweighs wisdom and honor.
ECCLESIASTES 10:1 NIV

When things look bleakest, I . . .

. _____

. _____

. _____

. _____

. _____

. _____

. _____

. _____

. _____

. _____

. _____

. _____

. _____

Some years ago, a large American shoe manufacturer sent two of its sales reps to different parts of the Australian outback. The company hoped that it could drum up some business among the Aborigines. It was a risky venture, but the firm realized how many new customers could be gained if the venture were successful.

After each rep had spent a few weeks in the outback, the shoe company received two faxes: "There is no hope for new business here," reported one rep. "The Aborigines don't even wear shoes! It's not part of their culture. Couldn't we have researched this earlier and saved me the trip? This has been a colossal waste of time. I can't wait to get back home."

The second rep filed a different report: "Wow! What an incredible opportunity we have here in the outback! Did you know that Aborigines don't wear shoes at all? That means we have no competition from another manufacturer! We'll have thousands of new customers! Thanks for this great opportunity! It was an ingenious idea to send me here!"

As you can see, one person's obstacle is another person's opportunity. All it takes is some optimism and a little bit of soul (or sole).

o o o o

Give me the ability to see good things in unexpected places and talents in unexpected people.

"Everything is possible for him who believes."

MARK 9:23 NIV

Invest in Yourself

__ __ high-school student ponder-
ing __ __ __ here is some information
wo__ __ __ ng. According to Speaker's
Ide__ __ __ Americans today (78 percent)
are __ __ __ graduates than at any time in
hist__ __ __ e a high-school diploma is a
sol__ __ __ esn't distinguish one from the
pa__ __ __ ercent of Americans have a
de__ __ __ high school. A college degree
is __ __ __ to make you more competi-
tiv__ __ kforce.

__ __ __ level also weighs heavily on
th__ __ __ a person gets and how much
m__ __ __ she will make. Average earnings
fo__ __ __ ool graduate are about twelve
th__ __ __ ars a year. Over the same time
p__ __ __ erage worker with a bachelor's
d__ __ __ rn twice that amount. And you
c__ __ __ e number again for the average
e__ __ __ h a doctorate.

__ __ __ ing the next educational level
s__ __ __ reach financially, consider check-
i__ __ __ many scholarships and financial
a__ __ __ available. And if the time
__ __ __ or scheduling seems
__ __ __ g, there are many programs
__ __ __ ifically to the needs of people
__ __ __ nsider full-time work schedules.

__ __ g on your educational founda-
__ __ __ h considering. It won't just make
__ __ __ r; it will probably make you
__ __ __ oo.

o o o o o

__ __ st in knowledge. The interest
__ __ t earns will astound you.

HOW much education do my dreams require?

_____ .
_____ .
_____ .
_____ .
_____ .
_____ .
_____ .
_____ .
_____ .
_____ .
_____ .
_____ .
_____ .
_____ .
_____ .
_____ .

Wise men store up knowledge.

PROVERBS 10:14 NIV

What methods do I use to motivate others?

_____
_____
_____
_____
_____
_____
_____
_____
_____
_____
_____
_____
_____
_____

It's intriguing to watch how two different cultures approach a common business exercise. The exercise involves pairing people off, placing or drawing a line between them, then instructing both members of the pair to convince the other to cross the line. The participants are allowed to use any persuasive means necessary—except physical force—to achieve their goal.

Americans attack the persuasion with vigor and ingenuity. They plead, cajole, intimidate, bargain, tempt, shame, berate, and negotiate. However, for all their efforts, very few U.S. players ever persuade their partners to cross the line.

Japanese business people take a different tack. One of them will simply and quietly say to his counterpart, "If you will cross this line, so will I. That way, we both achieve our goals." Then, each person crosses the line, and both win.

The culture in the U.S. is often marked by the familiar "looking out for number one" approach. Often, even if we wish to distance ourselves from this way of achieving our goals, we can find ourselves pulled into this way of thinking. Yet this mindset leaves everyone wanting. As our world gets smaller but also more complex, it's important to remember the effectiveness of cooperation.

○ ○ ○ ○ ○

"You're blessed when you can show people how to cooperate instead of compete or fight. That's when you discover who you really are, and your place in God's family."
MATTHEW 5:9 THE MESSAGE

Politeness goes far, yet costs nothing.

Smile!

... pastor began a custom during
his S... ...ce—a custom he continued
for ... . Before dismissing the
chil... ... or church, he invited them all
to t... ... he sanctuary to march past
his ... ...eir way to the special kid-
ori... ... e. As the kids walked past him,
the ... ... e a point to smile at each one.
In ... ... them smiled at him. "It was
on... ... points of the service," he
on...

... ...ay, however, the pastor became
dis... ... ...ng the youth exodus. He forgot
to ... ... e curly-haired, four-year-old girl.
Th... ... e line of children and ran back
to ... ... Sobbing uncontrollably, she
th... ... into her mother's arms.

... ... service, the pastor sought out
th... ... find out what had happened.
S... ... to him that after her child quit
c... ... ...d, "Mommy, I'm so sad. I smiled
a... ... le didn't smile back at me!"

... ...tor reflected, "To that child, I
s... ... ...d. I had failed with my smile, and
t... ... ...nt dark for her."

... ... each person you encounter
... ...ubtful that anyone will confuse
... ...d, but smiling is one way to
... ...d's love.

o o o o o

*... ...rfulness or joyfulness is the
... ...re under which all things thrive.*

Today I will remember to smile at others because . . .

_____ .

_____ .

_____ .

_____ .

_____ .

_____ .

_____ .

_____ .

_____ .

_____ .

_____ .

_____ .

_____ .

_____ .

_____ .

_____ .

The LORD make his face shine upon you and
be gracious to you; the LORD turn his face
toward you and give you peace.

NUMBERS 6:25 NIV

Kindness Can Transform a Life

What kind gesture can I extend to someone whose situation seems "hopeless"?

._____

._____

._____

._____

._____

._____

._____

._____

._____

._____

._____

._____

._____

._____

._____

._____

._____

Many years ago, a child known as "Little Annie" was locked in the dungeon of a mental institution near Boston—her doctors' last resort for the "hopelessly insane." At times, Annie seemed to fit the label. She was known to behave like an animal and viciously attack those who came near her "cage." At other times, she sat in a daze.

An elderly nurse, however, didn't see Annie as an animal. She began to take her lunch breaks outside Annie's cell. She hoped to find some way to communicate God's love to this troubled girl. One day, she left her dessert, a brownie, next to Annie's cell. Annie didn't acknowledge the gesture at the time, but when the nurse returned the next day, all that remained of the brownie were crumbs. From then on, the nurse brought Annie a brownie every Thursday.

As the months passed, the institution's staff noted changes in Annie's behavior. She was removed to a more humane room. Ultimately, this once hopeless case was told she was able to return home.

Annie declined. A young adult by this time, she chose to stay at the institution to help others. One of the people she taught and nurtured was Helen Keller. As you've probably guessed, Annie's last name was Sullivan.

o o o o o

Be kind and compassionate to one another.

EPHESIANS 4:32 NIV

A part of kindness consists of loving people more than they deserve.

The Worry Chart

...e made a "worry chart" on whic... ...ed all of his troubles and woe... ...ar of this worrisome task, he dec... ...late the results.

...hat 40 percent of his anx... ...d out to be things that were unl... ...pen. Thirty percent were about dec... ...d made—and could not un... percent of his worries were ba... ...le's criticisms of him, and 10 pe... ...bout his future health (including... ...ulcer from too much worrying). O... ...e latter 10 percent were items he... ...ntrol over. Finally, the businessm... ...d that only 8 percent of his past ye... ...had been legitimate.

...e you worrying about today? H... ...onverting your worry time to p... ...It's amazing how much worry c... ...ted when we talk to God about ... ...s and, in effect, give them over to ... ...don't add worrying about how ... ...ur list of concerns. If you can't ... ...o express your troubles, God ... ...heart and mind and hears you ... ...ou don't speak. Just sit quietly ... ...His goodness.

o o o o o

...ry is like a rocking chair—
...gives you something to do
but gets you nowhere.

What do I need to put on my worry chart?

_____ .
_____ .
_____ .
_____ .
_____ .
_____ .
_____ .
_____ .
_____ .
_____ .
_____ .
_____ .
_____ .
_____ .
_____ .
_____ .

"Who of you by worrying can
add a single hour to his life?"
MATTHEW 6:27 NIV

No Excuses

In the game of life, what do I need to do to ensure I will succeed?

_____
_____
_____
_____
_____
_____
_____
_____
_____
_____
_____
_____
_____
_____
_____

Charles Oakley, forward for the New York Knicks and an NBA All-Star, has a reputation for being one of basketball's best rebounders. It's his toughness, however, that has probably contributed the most to his outstanding sports career.

While other professional players seem to have frequent injuries or are sidelined for other reasons, Oakley has had very few injuries over the course of his career, even though he has absorbed a great deal of physical punishment on the court. He is often pushed and fouled. He puts in miles each game running up and down the court. He frequently dives into the stands for loose balls, to the extent the courtside media teases him about being a working hazard. According to Oakley, his tenacity and energy have their origin in his grandfather, Julius Moss.

Moss was a farmer in Alabama who did most of his field work by hand. "Other people had more equipment than he did," Oakley says. "He didn't have a tractor, but he got the work done. No excuses." Moss, who died in 1990, developed all sorts of aches and pains in his life, but he laughed at them and went about his business. Oakley saw a lesson in that: Nothing should prevent him from earning a day's pay.

Being focused, dedicated, and disciplined will make the difference between a mediocre life and a great life.

○ ○ ○ ○ ○

In a race, everyone runs but only one person gets first prize. . . . To win the contest you must deny yourselves many things that would keep you from doing your best.
I CORINTHIANS 9:24-25 TLB

No horse gets anywhere until he is harnessed. No life ever grows great until it is focused, dedicated, disciplined.

D... t Be Too Quick to Speak

... encountered two rather
dens... ...ring a day of job interviews.
He g... ...ch a task. Later, the men met
at a ... ...o compare notes.

... ...at manager stupid!"
excla... ...mus No. 1. "He gave me a
five-... ...en told me to go buy him a
Pors... ...mmy didn't even tell me what
colo... ...!"

... ...that's bad," replied ignoramus
No. ... ...e doing the interview in this
con... ...n, see, and he says, 'Go up to
my ... ...ee if I'm there. If I'm not
ther... ...k and tell me.' What a moron!
The ... ...one right there in the confer-
enc... ...could have called up to his
offi... ...he was there. He didn't have
to ...

... ...ok his head sadly. "Sure glad I
did ... ...ob. Who wants to work for
an ...

... ...u," his companion said. Turning
to ... ..., the first man asked for a
pe... ...a.

... ...u like that cut into six or
eig... ...he waitress asked.

... ...ake it six," the second man
re... ...t think we're hungry enough
fo...

○ ○ ○ ○ ○

...ide noisy, inside empty.

Am I guilty of sounding like a fool? When?

_____ .
_____ .
_____ .
_____ .
_____ .
_____ .
_____ .
_____ .
_____ .
_____ .
_____ .
_____ .
_____ .
_____ .
_____ .
_____ .

> A wise man doesn't display his knowledge,
> but a fool displays his foolishness.
>
> PROVERBS 12:23 TLB

Don't Be Too Quick to Judge

What standard do I use in evaluating others?

_____

_____

_____

_____

_____

_____

_____

_____

_____

_____

_____

_____

_____

_____

A medical-school professor once posed this medical/ethical question to his students: "Here's a family history—the father has syphilis. The mother has TB. They already have had four children. The first is blind. The second has died. The third is deaf. The fourth has TB. Now the mother is pregnant again. The parents come to you for advice. They are willing to abort their child if you decide they should. What do you say?"

After students shared various individual opinions, the professor placed them into groups to make final decisions. After deliberating, every group reported that it would recommend an abortion to the parents.

"Congratulations," the professor told his class. "You just took the life of Beethoven!"

What is the lesson for us? A person's inherent value and potential don't depend on family background or social station. God has created each person with worth and skill and promise. The way we treat people at home, at school, and on the job shouldn't be tainted by prejudice that's based on race, economic status, appearance, or handicap. This may seem like stating the obvious, but we might be surprised if we honestly examined the way we evaluate others.

Every person has potential to add music to the great symphony called life.

o   o   o   o

Thou didst form my inward parts; Thou didst weave me in my mother's womb.

PSALM 139:13 NASB

_You must look into people,
as well as at them._

] Can!

What are some of the short-term goals I can set?

[...]dini, who won fame as an
esc[...]rly in the twentieth century,
issu[...]ge wherever he went. He
clai[...]ld be locked in any jail cell in
the[...]d set himself free within
mi[...]d done it over and over in
ev[...]isited.

[...], however, something seemed to
go[...]dini entered a jail cell in his
st[...] The heavy metal doors clanged
sh[...]m, and he took from his belt a
c[...]ce of strong but flexible metal.
H[...]rk on the lock to his cell, but
s[...]emed different about this particu-
l[...]orked for thirty minutes, but
[...]ened. An hour passed. This was
[...]time that Houdini normally freed
[...]he began to sweat and pant in
[...]. Still, he could not pick the lock.

[...]after laboring for two hours,
[...]nd feeling a sense of failure
[...]round him, Houdini leaned against
[...]e could not unlock. To his amaze-
[...]ung open! *It had never been locked!*

[...]many times are challenges impossi-
[...]ors locked—only because we
[...]are? When we focus our minds
[...]y toward them and strike the word
[...]m our vocabulary, those impossible
[...]into attainable goals.

○ ○ ○ ○ ○

*[...] in people is caused more by lack
[...]etermination than lack of talent.*

I can do all things through Christ
which strengtheneth me.

PHILIPPIANS 4:13

_____ .
_____ .
_____ .
_____ .
_____ .
_____ .
_____ .
_____ .
_____ .
_____ .
_____ .
_____ .
_____ .
_____ .
_____ .
_____ .

What life-giving words can I speak to others?

_____

_____

_____

_____

_____

_____

_____

_____

_____

_____

_____

_____

_____

_____

Shortly after arriving in Major League Baseball, pitcher Orel Hershiser was called to the office of Los Angeles Dodgers General Manager Tommy Lasorda. Hershiser feared the meeting wouldn't be pleasant. He had begun his career as a relief pitcher, and his performance had been disappointing.

Lasorda, however, didn't dwell on his pitcher's past. He said instead, "You don't believe in yourself! You're scared to pitch in the big leagues! Who do you think these hitters are, Babe Ruth? Ruth's dead! You've got good stuff. If you didn't, I wouldn't have brought you up. You gotta go out there and do it on the mound. Be a bulldog—that's gonna be your new name. Bulldog Hershiser. I want you, starting today, to believe you are the best pitcher in baseball."

Bulldog Hershiser wrote in his autobiography, *Out of the Blue*, "I couldn't get over that Tommy Lasorda felt I was worth this much time and effort. He believed I had big league stuff." In Hershiser's next game, he pitched three innings and gave up only one hit. He went on to one of the longest pitching careers in recent Major League history.

As you talk with your friends and teammates, focus more on their future than their past. All of us have way more potential than we have history.

o o o o o

> Words kill, words give life; they're either poison or fruit—you choose.
> PROVERBS 18:21 THE MESSAGE

> *Good words are worth much and cost little.*

It [...]n't Take Much to Sound like a Fool

Not[...] tive to guard your tongue?
Not[...] nous quotes from some
fam[...]

- [...] ntly on a tour of Latin
  [...] d the only regret I have was
  [...] t study Latin harder in school
  [...] converse with those
  [...] former VP Dan Quayle
- [...] big country, inhabited by
  [...] ese."—former French
  [...] Charles deGaulle
- [...] contract isn't worth the
  [...] written on."—film executive
  [...] oldwyn
- [...] his game is ninety percent
  [...]—baseball manager Danny Ozark
- [...] ping to turn this team around
  [...] ndred and sixty degrees."—
  [...] ll star Jason Kidd
- [...] nore and more people are thrown
  [...] ork, unemployment results."—
  [...] U.S. President Calvin Coolidge
- [...] are more like they are now than
  [...] r were before."—former
  [...] nt Dwight Eisenhower
- [...] the pollution that's harming the
  [...] ment. It's the impurities in our air
  [...] er that are doing it."—Dan Quayle
- [...] resident has kept all of the
  [...] es he intended to keep."—aide
  [...] ner President Bill Clinton,
  [...] e Stephanopolous

o o o o

[...] people speak when they have
[...] ng to say; foolish people speak
[...] e they have to say something.

When was the last time I remember sticking my foot in my mouth?

_____.
_____.
_____.
_____.
_____.
_____.
_____.
_____.
_____.
_____.
_____.
_____.
_____.
_____.
_____.
_____.

The wise of heart will heed
commandments, but a babbling
fool will come to ruin.

PROVERBS 10:8 NRSV

Even the Most Awesome Have Experienced Failure

HOW do I typically respond to rejection or failure?

_____

_____

_____

_____

_____

_____

_____

_____

_____

_____

_____

_____

_____

_____

_____

If you've been passed over for a place on the basketball team or in the drama club, don't be too discouraged. Consider the following:

- Michael Jordan was cut from his high-school basketball team.
- After his first screen test, Fred Astaire received the following assessment from an MGM executive: "Can't act. Slightly bald. Can dance a little."
- A football "expert" said of two-time Super Bowl-winning coach Vince Lombardi, "He possesses minimal football knowledge. Lacks motivation."
- In screenings before test audiences, the pilot for _Seinfeld_ received low marks for its story line and main characters.
- Walt Disney was fired from a newspaper because he lacked ideas. Later, he went bankrupt several times before he built Disneyland.
- A young Burt Reynolds was told he couldn't act. His pal Clint Eastwood was told he would never make it in the movies because his Adam's apple was too big.

Certainly you can learn from rejection and disappointment. You may discover weaknesses you need to bolster to reach your maximum potential. On the other hand, the person making the assessment might be flat-out wrong. Let rejection fuel your determination. And hang on to those negative letters and reports. Someday, you might want to frame them.

○ ○ ○ ○ ○

"LET not your heart be troubled."

JOHN 14:1

There is no failure except in no longer trying.

...rising public figure said, "I am ... I ever been in favor of mak... jurors of Negroes, nor of qual... to hold office, nor to inter-mar... people.... There is a physi-cal ... between the white and black race... elieve will forever forbid the two ... together on terms of social and ... uality."

... wever, this man's views cha... s it was the courage and int... saw two hundred thousand me... isplay in battle. Perhaps the Go... he so often spoke changed his mi... eart. Whatever the case, four ye... racist statement, Abraham Lin... the Emancipation Pr... clearing the path for the Th... endment, which ended slavery in ... States.

... ately, racism is still an evil that m... with every day. Imagine how th... God, who created us all and lo... live in harmony.

... chool, there are probably p... many ethnic backgrounds—p... eflect the rich diversity of an i... eator. Remember, when God lo... on us, He only sees one race—t... ce.

o o o o o

...must learn to live together ...brothers, or we will perish together like fools.

Live in harmony with one another.

I PETER 3:8 NIV

Who needs me today?

. _____

. _____

. _____

. _____

. _____

. _____

. _____

. _____

. _____

. _____

. _____

. _____

. _____

. _____

> When God's children are in need,
> you be the one to help them out.
>
> ROMANS 12:13 TLB

Once, a young orphan girl, despondent and lonely, walked through a meadow and saw a small butterfly caught in a thorn bush. The more the butterfly struggled to free itself, the deeper the thorns cut into its fragile body.

Filled with compassion, the girl released the butterfly. But, instead of flying away, the butterfly transformed into an angel and said gently, "To reward you for your kindness, I will do whatever you would like."

The girl thought for a moment, then replied, "I want to be happy!"

"Very well," the angel said. Then the heavenly creature leaned close to the girl and whispered something in her ear.

Many years later, as the orphan lay on her deathbed after a full and happy life, her friends gathered around her. "Won't you tell us your secret now," they pleaded.

With a labored smile, the woman answered, "An angel told me that no matter where I went in life, I would find people who needed me—people rich or poor, young or old, meek or self-assured—and meeting those needs would bring me happiness and satisfaction."

Somewhere in your school or sphere of influence, there is someone who needs you. Are you willing to be an angel and meet that need?

o o o o o

Do a good deed; meet a need.

Real Beauty

How can I ensure that my inner self is as beautiful as I want my outer appearance to be?

_____.

_____.

_____.

_____.

_____.

_____.

_____.

_____.

_____.

_____.

_____.

_____.

_____.

_____.

_____.

_____.

...oy, plagued by feelings of
uglin... ...to a mirror and studied his
refle... ...e nose, thick lips, tiny gray
eyes... ...hands and feet. The boy was
so ... ...out his appearance that he
beg... ...work a miracle and turn him
into... ...e man. He vowed that if God
wo... ...n him, he would give his
Cr... ...t he now possessed and all
tha... ...earn in the future.

...ian boy was Count Tolstoy,
wh... ...o become one of the world's
m... ...authors. He is best known for
his... ...nd Peace. In one of his books,
To... ...s that through the years he
di... ...t the physical beauty he once
cr... ...the only beauty in life. Nor is it
th... ...of beauty. Ultimately, Tolstoy
g... ...d the beauty of a strong charac-
t... ...nost pleasing in God's eyes.

...ople today spend large sums on
t... ...appearance. Designer clothes,
h... ...dy piercing, even cosmetic
s... ...racter, in contrast, can't be
l... ...plied or worn. It is a matter of
...right, standing up for what's
...eloping the qualities that you
...th the physical eye.

o o o o o

...e beauty of character is
...beauty that never fades.

Don't be concerned about the outward beauty that depends on jewelry, or beautiful clothes, or hair arrangement. Be beautiful inside, in your hearts, with the lasting charm of a gentle and quiet spirit which is so precious to God.
I PETER 3:3-4 TLB

See a Need and Meet It

What are some of the needs that I see around me?

_____

_____

_____

_____

_____

_____

_____

_____

_____

_____

_____

_____

_____

_____

Some thought Les Goldberg was crazy when he cashed in his personal investments to buy a home to lease to the homeless. But Goldberg, a retired engineer, felt that investing in the homeless would bring rich dividends—not necessarily monetary ones.

Goldberg retired from his job to enter a life of service. He works on six service boards and leads a crew of homeless people on various odd jobs and in charity work. He has never regarded the homeless as irresponsible or unreliable. He sees them simply as people. And the home that he purchased is used as a temporary homeless shelter and a drop-in center—a place where homeless people can pick up their mail, make phone calls, pursue job leads, and receive donated goods.

At any given time, four homeless people live at the house, paying a small rent to help offset expenses. And house rules are strict: no alcohol, no drugs, and no loitering.

Les Goldberg, by the way, is not some wealthy philanthropist who gives from his abundant resources. Prior to retiring, he worked for twenty years designing and installing fire sprinklers. His annual income was about twenty-five thousand dollars per year, very modest by today's standards. Goldberg is simply a man who saw a need and found a way to meet it.

○ ○ ○ ○ ○

How does God's love abide in anyone who has the world's goods and sees a brother or sister in need and yet refuses help?

1 JOHN 3:17 NRSV

You need not have a lot to give a lot.

Can I be trusted to be honest in even the littlest things?

consultants competed vigor-
ousl   y vacated management
posi   ge investment firm. After
care   ering each candidate's merits,
a te   tives made its decision. They
dec   y the lucky consultant of his
pro   lunch.

noon hour, one of the direc-
tor   e manager-to-be ahead of him
in l   mpany cafeteria, separated by
sev   ustomers. The director watched
the   select his food, including a small
sq   er. As soon as the candidate
pla   -cent pat of butter onto his
pla   y placed a dinner roll on top of
it   m the cashier.

rnoon, the executive team met
in   oom, then summoned the
d   g man. He walked to the board-
r   hope. He imagined his large new
o   ostantial raise, his own adminis-
t   nt, and the management bonus.
H   her than promote the candidate,
t   ent team fired him.

isn't a selective quality. People
t small matters tend to lie about
as well. So invest in honesty. You
ith whom you live and hang out
dividends that truth brings.

○ ○ ○ ○ ○

h up on your honesty; it will
elp you fight truth decay.

He that speaketh truth sheweth forth
righteousness: but a false witness deceit.

PROVERBS 12:17

Follow Instructions

HOW quickly do I submit to authority?

Baseball manager Earl Weaver had a firm rule: "No one steals a base unless I give the steal sign." Superstar Reggie Jackson wasn't happy with that rule, believing he knew enough to judge when he could swipe a base. One day, while standing restlessly near first base, Reggie decided to steal second, even though Weaver hadn't given him the sign.

As the pitcher hurled the ball, Reggie rocketed toward second base. The pitcher had a slow delivery, and the catcher didn't have a great arm. He easily beat the catcher's throw to second base. He smiled, feeling vindicated in his judgment.

Weaver, however, wasn't smiling. He took Jackson aside later and explained why he hadn't given the steal signal. Lee May, the batter who followed Jackson, was a major power hitter, and once Jackson had stolen second and left first base open, the opposing team intentionally walked May, thus killing his chance for a base hit or home run that would have put points on the scoreboard. What's more, the batter who followed May hadn't been successful against the opposing pitcher, so Weaver had to pinch-hit for him—a move that depleted the bench strength.

Jackson had been successful in his individual endeavor, but Weaver was calling the game with the entire team's mission in mind.

○ ○ ○ ○ ○

> Obey your leaders and submit to their authority.
>
> HEBREWS 13:17 NIV

You can't see the big picture if your nose is pressed against it.

Today I will walk in the God-kind of love by . . .

_____.

_____.

_____.

_____.

_____.

_____.

_____.

_____.

_____.

_____.

_____.

_____.

_____.

_____.

F ... s for a Happy Day:

1. ... not strike back. If a class-
... g, or other person is rude,
... or unkind, I will not respond
... nner.

2. ... ask God to bless my
... I encounter a longtime rival
... person—or anyone who
... harshly or unfairly—I will
... God to bless him or her.

3. ... I be careful about what I say. I
... lly choose and guard my
... king certain that I don't spread
... malign anyone in any way.

4. ... ll go the extra mile. I will find
... hare another's burdens. I will
... to make life more pleasant for
... I encounter.

5 ... ill forgive. I will forgive the
... injuries that come my way
... d I will try to put past hurts
... s behind me, once and for all.

... u've had time to digest these
r u ... py day, tomorrow you will
le ... e. These ideals may seem a little
l o ... are guaranteed to help you
k ... itude straight and your relation-
s ... igned.

o o o o o

*... ve is ... profound concern for
... being of another, without any
... ontrol that other, to be thanked
... other, or to enjoy the process.*

Love is very patient and kind, never jealous or envious, never boastful or proud, never haughty or selfish or rude. Love does not demand its own way. It is not irritable or touchy. It does not hold grudges and will hardly even notice when others do it wrong.
I CORINTHIANS 13:4-5 TLB

Another Happy Day

Today, I will practice the golden rule by . . .

. _____

. _____

. _____

. _____

. _____

. _____

. _____

. _____

. _____

. _____

. _____

. _____

. _____

. _____

. _____

. _____

Five More Rules for a Happy Day:

1. Today I will do something nice for someone, but I will do it secretly. I will reach out anonymously to bless the life of another person.
2. Today I will treat others as I wish to be treated. I will practice the golden rule—do unto others as you would have them do unto you—with everyone I meet.
3. Today I will raise the spirits of someone who is discouraged. My smile, my words, my expressions of hope and support—all can make a difference to someone who is struggling with discouragement or depression.
4. Today I will nurture my body. I will eat less. I will eat healthy foods. My staples will not be Cokes and pizza. I will be grateful for, and respectful of, my body.
5. Today I will grow spiritually. I will use breaks, lunch, and down times to pray and meditate. I will seek a quiet place, a quiet moment, so that I can rejuvenate myself spiritually.

There are difficult people in most aspects of life, those who tear others down to build themselves up. Resist the urge to stoop to their standard. Instead, rise above it by aligning yourself with God's standard.

o o o o o

"Love your neighbor as yourself."

MATTHEW 19:19 NLT

It's not hard to make decisions when you know what your values are.

A Wise Response

British leader Winston
Chu... ...t finished a rousing speech.
Upo... ...ords, the crowd that gathered
to h... ...pted with thunderous
appl... ...the clapping and cheering
fade... ...unimpressed by Churchill's
rhe... ...im "the raspberry." The rest
of t... ...sat in suspense, awaiting the
po... ...man's response to the rude
ma... ...looked at his tormentor and
sp... ...I agree with you. But what are
we... ...many?"

...s reply was a hit with the throng,
an... ...ly tense situation was diffused.

...Vinston, you may occasionally
fa... ...someone who openly opposes
y... ...on an issue—perhaps in a
c... ...g manner. It's tempting to
b... ...y and lose your composure.
... ...ave been led to believe that in
... ...w our strength, we must fight
... ...But don't forget the power of
... ...humility when dealing with criti-
... ...eness.

...ble promises that a soft answer
...wrath. Certainly there will be
...you must forcefully defend
...your position on an important
...atchful, however, for the times
...ng fire with fire will only make
...ot and miserable and do nothing
...the situation.

o o o o o

*...er than other people if you can,
but do not tell them so.*

How can I develop this keen sense of diplomacy?

_____.

_____.

_____.

_____.

_____.

_____.

_____.

_____.

_____.

_____.

_____.

_____.

_____.

_____.

_____.

The person with understanding is always
looking for wisdom, but the mind of
a fool wanders everywhere.

PROVERBS 17:24 NCV

Determine to Learn Something from Everyone

What can I learn from the people in my life?

._____

._____

._____

._____

._____

._____

._____

._____

._____

._____

._____

._____

._____

A business manager who was confronted with frequent ethical dilemmas or problems was fond of saying, "What would Phil do?" Whether in large meetings or one-on-ones, when a problem would arise, she would thoughtfully utter those four words. This behavior piqued the curiosity of the manager's colleagues.

After a blistering debate about downsizing the company, one of them spoke up: "Okay, I have to ask you. You repeatedly say, 'What would Phil do?' whenever you're confronted with a difficult issue. Who is Phil? He must be a very wise man if you consider his example whenever you have to make an important decision. Was he one of your mentors?"

The manager laughed and shook her head. "Mentor is probably not the best term," she noted. "Phil was a former manager of mine—a completely unprincipled, profane, and egotistical man. He rarely made a good decision, and even his few good decisions weren't made for the right reasons. So, when I ask myself 'What would Phil do?' I consider the answer. Then I do exactly the opposite. That formula has yet to fail me."

Wherever you find yourself in life, you will have opportunities to make hard decisions. Perhaps you've witnessed someone you are determined not to be like. Just remember, whether a person is a positive or negative role model, you can learn some lesson from everyone you meet.

○ ○ ○ ○

Enter not into the path of the wicked, and go not in the way of evil men.

PROVERBS 4:14

Every man is my teacher; I learn something from everyone that I meet.

olfer named Ken Venturi
playe   noles under the watchful eye
of hi   legend Byron Nelson. Venturi
hit s   ot with the appropriate
pow   sion. At the end of the
eigh   Venturi had carded a blistering   strokes under par. Such a
scor   ce Venturi atop the leader
boa   najor professional golf tourna-
mer   nowever, wasn't overwhelmed
by t   enomenon's performance. "I
see   ght things you need to
cor   d Venturi.

Thr   amateur and professional
car   villing to make the small
adj   t separate the good players
fro   ones. And he was able to win
or   : major amateur and profes-
sio   naments as a result.

               n: The elite people in any disci-
pli   t there's more to success than
an   :otal—whether it's a golf score,
a t   r an award for music competi-
tic   lly analyzing each phase of your
gif   ou can probably identify areas
in   :an improve—even if you're
kn   outstanding at what you do.

               uble-bogey your life away. Listen
to   respect.

o o o o o

a way to do it better, find it.

What pointers have wise people given me?

_____ .

_____ .

_____ .

_____ .

_____ .

_____ .

_____ .

_____ .

_____ .

_____ .

_____ .

_____ .

_____ .

_____ .

_____ .

_____ .

He who ignores discipline despises
himself, but whoever heeds correction
gains understanding.

PROVERBS 15:32 NIV

HOW well do I get along with others?

_____

_____

_____

_____

_____

_____

_____

_____

_____

_____

_____

_____

_____

_____

Andrew Carnegie was able to assemble the greatest private-enterprise leadership team of his day. To accomplish this goal, he searched the world for the top men and women in their various fields of expertise.

At one point, he found a chemist in Germany who was the best of the best. Carnegie more than doubled his salary, and he gave him a new house and a five-year contract. However, three months later, Carnegie called the chemist into his office and fired him. He bought out the rest of his contract and paid his moving expenses back to Germany.

Why forfeit such a substantial investment and fire an elite scientist? Because, as Carnegie discovered, this chemist was impossible to get along with. He constantly argued with others on the leadership team and hindered their progress.

Explaining his decision, Carnegie strongly declared, "I will not have anyone work for me, especially in a leadership position, who does not have the quality of being able to get along with others."

Expertise in an area will get you only so far in life. It is important to develop and practice your technical skills but not at the expense of people skills. Or, as another Carnegie, Dale, might put it, don't discount the value and necessity of "making friends and influencing people."

o o o o

It is good and pleasant when God's people live together in peace!

PSALM 133:1 NCV

The greatest quality that an individual can possess is the ability to get along with others. It is a quality that I am willing to pay more for than any other.

What is the quality of my work?

...ociation excitedly put tog...s mailing touting its new pr...ervices. One executive looked ov...rials and declared them ready to...printer, then on to thousands o..."Shouldn't we have someone in t...department look this over for e...dministrative assistant asked.

..y," the executive snorted. "I can't ...picky people. They're always ...out the grammatical errors in our ...iving me crazy! I mean, who cares ...splaced comma here or there? We ...t this mailing out next week. We ...d any delays!"

..he mailing went to the printer, then ...association's vast mailing list of ...nd prospective customers. The ...on beefed up its inbound telephone ...er service staff in anticipation of ...d business. But the company was ...when no calls came in about the ...Within a couple of weeks, an editorial ...ember found a copy of the brochure ...as the centerpiece of the mailing.

"Hey," she said to the editor-loathing ...tive, "did you know that you have our toll-...order number wrong in this brochure?"

As this association learned the hard way, ...hardly ever a good idea to short-cut ...lity control. Good work is more impor-...t than a job done hastily. Whatever your ...k, take that extra couple of minutes to ...eck over your work to insure it is ...mpleted with excellence.

o o o o

Take time for all things: great haste makes great waste.

Be not wise in thine own eyes.

PROVERBS 3:7

Don't Be Afraid of a Little Hard Work

HOW can I turn around a difficult situation in my life?

_____
_____
_____
_____
_____
_____
_____
_____
_____
_____
_____
_____
_____
_____

After five years as a sales manager, Amanda could proudly state that she had reached her quarterly sales goals every time. Her territory had grown to include the entire state in which she lived. And she had built an excellent reputation among her peers and competitors. Then, suddenly, she was assigned to a neighboring state. Amanda was dismayed to learn that her predecessor hadn't worked very hard, so the territory was undeveloped. Assessing her new position, Amanda decided she had been demoted. Her first impulse was to quit.

Instead, she reasoned that hard work had produced results in the past, so why not try it now? She put in long hours and lots of miles during the next few months. And, by the end of the third quarter, her results surpassed those she had enjoyed in her previous territory! She had turned a trial into a triumph.

The company rewarded Amanda by naming her as a regional vice president, with a territory that included both her former and current states. Had she stayed with the old position, Amanda wouldn't have been able to prove her ability to turn around a poor territory, and she wouldn't have earned her promotion.

So, learn from Amanda, and keep your hand to the plow. You never know how fertile even the toughest soil may be!

o o o o o

Hard work means prosperity; only a fool idles away his time.

PROVERBS 12:11 TLB

Opportunity is missed by most people because it is dressed in overalls and looks like work.

Don't Get in a Hurry

...enior basketball player finished
his ... flourish. He racked up
impr... tics, won several post-season
hon... his team into the NCAA
tou... he had to do was make a
dec... at a spring camp, and he was
cer... No. I draft choice in the NBA.

...tely, he broke his nose before
the ... ad to reduce his training
re... ear a protective face guard.
Th... thought about skipping the
ca... g himself time to heal. But, as
th... w near, he decided to attend. He
e... his face guard because he
d... e scouts to think he was "soft."
... y, as he scrimmaged with other
... s, the ex-college star couldn't
... d off his aching—and vulnera-
... le played tentatively and passively.
... n attendance wrote him off as a
... t. And when the first-round draft
... called out weeks later, this player's
... ot among them.

...sson: First impressions are lasting.
...ociety, there is constant pressure
... However, in our haste we should
...et that there's nothing to be gained
... out front with a less-than-
...performance. In an effort to be
...n't be too early. It just might help
...face."

○ ○ ○ ○ ○

...ever is in a hurry shows that the
...g he is about is too big for him.

Why am I in a hurry?

_____ .
_____ .
_____ .
_____ .
_____ .
_____ .
_____ .
_____ .
_____ .
_____ .
_____ .
_____ .
_____ .
_____ .
_____ .

He has made everything
suitable for its time.
ECCLESIASTES 3:11 NRSV

A Bit of Humor

Which of these nuggets do I need to work on?

_____

_____

_____

_____

_____

_____

_____

_____

_____

_____

_____

_____

_____

_____

_____

Rejoice evermore.

I THESSALONIANS 5:16

Things They Probably Aren't Teaching You at School:

- Always remember, you are special and unique. Just like everyone else.
- Never test the depth of the water with both feet.
- It is far more impressive when others discover your good qualities without your help.
- If you tell the truth, you don't have to remember so much.
- If you lend a person ten dollars and never see that person again, it was probably worth it.
- The "good" things that come to those who wait are what's left behind by those who got there first.
- Good judgment comes from bad experience, and a lot of that experience comes from bad judgment.
- The quickest way to double your money is to fold it in half and put it back into your pocket.
- There are two theories about arguing with others. Neither one works.
- Never miss a good chance to shut up.
- Generally speaking, you aren't learning much when your mouth is moving.
- Anything worth taking seriously is worth making fun of.
- Diplomacy is the art of saying "good doggie" while looking for a big stick.
- The older you get, the better you get, (unless you're a banana).

o o o o o

Always laugh when you can;
it is cheap medicine.

What is my primary motivation for doing what I do?

...wood carver sat on his front porc... ...nonade and enjoying the view... ...afternoon. Around him on the p... ...various creations. A friend of th... ...opped by for a quick visit and... ...ed to see the artisan relaxing. "It's... ...the afternoon," he observed. "A l... ...r a break, isn't it?"

...swallowed a mouthful of lem... ...awned. "This isn't a break," he said... ...or the day."

...a young marketing executive, was... "What do you mean? It's too ear... ...to stop. You need to produce mo... ...rve more figures, you can ma... ...ney. You could even hire an ass... ...p you with the business end of thi... ...d buy new tools. You could bu... ...you wouldn't have to carve he... ...ouse."

...uld I want to do all of that?" th... ...ed.

...can make more money!" his fri... ...ed.

...at would I do with all that e... ..."

...enjoy life, of course!"

...d carver took another sip of le... ...ned back in his chair, and closed h... ...re he drifted off for a nap, he n... ...ntentedly, "What do you think I..."

...e and hard work are admirable ... ...if the only motivation is to make ..., you may be missing the point. ...not "out there" somewhere; it ...d right where you are today.

o o o o o

...piness is not a destination, but a journey.

Keep your lives free from the love of money and be content with what you have.

HEBREWS 13:5 NIV

Attention to Detail

HOW well do I pay attention to details?

_____

_____

_____

_____

_____

_____

_____

_____

_____

_____

_____

_____

_____

_____

A man was brought to trial for illegal possession of a narcotic drug. His chances didn't look good. He was caught red-handed while being stopped for a traffic violation.

The police had spotted the narcotic lying in plain sight in the man's vehicle. And he had a previous drug conviction. However, as the defense attorney examined the papers related to the arrest and subsequent criminal charges, he smiled, whispered to his client, then approached the presiding judge. The defense lawyer pointed out that whoever had typed up the papers had misspelled the name of the drug the defendant allegedly had in his car. The erroneous spelling constituted the name of a narcotic but not the one with which the defendant had been caught. Thus, the defense lawyer argued, the case had to be thrown out. His client was never in possession of the drug listed in the official documents. So, due to a lack of attention to detail, a guilty man went free, and a police officer's work went for naught.

While the situation may not be as extreme, failing to take the details into account in your life or on your job can have severe consequences. If you think details don't matter, just ask a lucky law-breaker or an angry cop.

o o o o o

Good is not good where better is expected.

"Keep alert and pray."
MATTHEW 26:41 TLB

Keep It Simple

How can I simplify my life?

...o you solve problems? This
brief ... o you gauge (and improve)
your ... ving ability. The questions seem
simp... carefully before answering.

1. ...u put a giraffe into the refrig-
...

2. ...u put an elephant into the
...r?

3. ...ing is hosting an animal
... One animal is missing—
...?

4. ...to a river that is known to be
...y crocodiles. How do you
...?

KE...

1. ...Open the refrigerator, jam the
...and close the door.
...you tend to do simple things
...rly complicated way?

2. ...Open the refrigerator, take the
...t, put the elephant in, and close
... Did you remember to remove
...e?
...o you think through the reper-
...of your actions?

3. ...The elephant is missing because
...n the refrigerator!
...ow good is your memory and
... continuity?

... :You can swim across safely. All
...codiles are at the Lion King's
...conference.
...How good is your ability to learn
...from previous mistakes?
...idn't fare well on this quiz, don't
...ut 90 percent of business profes-
...rrectly answered all four
...Children, on the other hand,
...vered them all correctly.

o o o o

...ge is a process of piling up facts;
...m lies in their simplification.

> He that walketh with wise men
> shall be wise: but a companion
> of fools shall be destroyed.
>
> PROVERBS 13:20

Don't Insist on Your Own Way

Am I guilty of doing my own thing? How can I change that?

. _____

. _____

. _____

. _____

. _____

. _____

. _____

. _____

. _____

. _____

. _____

. _____

. _____

. _____

Major General Charles Lee was the most seasoned officer on George Washington's staff. Early in the American Revolution, Washington instructed Lee to take his forces north. Washington sent a second letter, then a third, but Lee continued to delay. Irritated, Washington wrote: "My former letters were so full and explicit that I expected you would have been sooner in motion." Still, Lee found reasons to procrastinate.

Finally, Lee began to move, but he suggested he would lend greater aid by remaining on the British rear to harass them from behind. Washington wrote back, "I cannot but request and entreat you to march and join me with all your whole force, with all possible expedition."

Still, Lee chose to do his own thing. Then, while eating breakfast in a tavern one morning, he was found unprotected and unprepared. British troops found him and captured him. In the end, Lee brought trouble on himself and the entire army. Even after he was released and in command of the Continental Army, he continued to insist on doing things his way. His willfulness resulted in a military disaster at Monmouth in 1778, after which he was court-martialed.

If you constantly do things on your own terms, you may not be court-martialed, but you could be courting danger of another kind—losing the confidence and respect of others.

o o o o o

A rebel is destroyed by lack of common sense.

PROVERBS 10:21 TLB

Delayed obedience is disobedience.

One Step at a Time

What is the step I should be taking today?

_____ .
_____ .
_____ .
_____ .
_____ .
_____ .
_____ .
_____ .
_____ .
_____ .
_____ .
_____ .
_____ .
_____ .

you think," Thomas Edison was   "is the first requisite for succ   field or any other?"

nventor replied, "The ability to appl   cal and mental energies to one prol   ntly, without growing weary." Wh   rd to schoolwork or in other area   y people run into problems in one   they spurn Edison's wisdom and   ect aside and turn to another. The   xpedience. Determination, cor   e quality that enables a person to   confident this is the right dir   ing to make it work!"

ation is the choice to press ah   er what obstacles appear. Th   s a way. The appearance of ob   ld not be a surprise to any of us   the very laws of nature warn us   ery action there is an equal and op   ion." Any movement will meet w   asure of friction.

hould expect obstacles and re   t don't let them stop you from ac   what you know needs to be d   ination is the power to climb o   s. An accomplished mountain c   nce asked, "How did you ever c   huge peak?"

ing one foot ahead of the other,"

○ ○ ○ ○ ○

evable steps can overcome impossible obstacles.

I want to suggest that you finish what you started.

2 CORINTHIANS 8:10 TLB

Make Sure You Have All the Facts

HOW can I keep from judging others too quickly?

_____

_____

_____

_____

_____

_____

_____

_____

_____

_____

_____

_____

_____

An ancient Arabian tale:

An old dervish (monk) encountered two anxious merchants. "You have lost a camel!" the dervish called.

"Indeed we have," they replied, puzzled.

"Was it not blind in its right eye and lame in its left leg?" asked the dervish.

"It was," the men responded.

"Had not your camel lost a tooth, and was it not loaded with honey on one side and corn on the other?"

"It was," the merchants remarked. "Please take us to it immediately."

The dervish frowned, "I have never seen your camel."

"Certainly you have!" shouted the angry merchants. "You shall answer before the cadi (magistrate)."

Before the cadi, the dervish explained, "I knew I had crossed the tracks of a stray camel because I found no human footprints. I knew the animal was blind in one eye because it had cropped the vegetation on one side of the path but not the other. I perceived it was lame in one leg from the faint impression made by one foot in the sand. I concluded the animal had lost a tooth because a small tuft of herbage remained uninjured wherever it grazed. As to the beast's burden, the ants informed me it was corn on one side and the clustering of flies that it was honey on the other."

The cadi readily set the dervish free.

○ ○ ○ ○

The fool has his answer on the edge of his tongue.

What a shame—yes, how stupid!—to decide before knowing the facts!

PROVERBS 18:13 TLB

...omas Edison had an intrigu-
ing ... ...rating his creative successes.

"aft... ... summertime," Edison said,
"aft... ...ade something which was
suc... ...d to engage a brick-sloop at
Per... ...nd take the whole crowd
dov... ...hing banks on the Atlantic for
tw...

...ch excursion, Edison sat
pa... ...his fishing pole and line. But he
ho... ...n. He continued fishing into the
nig... ...inued the second day and also
th... ...ght. He was determined to
ca... ...ut he failed. As they reached the
e... ...llotted time, Edison's compan-
io... ...m to put away his gear, so they
c... ...e. But he would not. Finally,
E... ...perated coworkers pulled up the
a... ...ailed away, thus compelling him
t...

...ison been the sole person making
...s, he would have continued until
...oal.

...s determination was woven into
...er of his being. He was deter-
...e lab, and he was determined on
...was his character. Character is not
...anner of behavior you adopt in
...n set aside at home. It should
...every part of your life.

o o o o o

...hing great was ever achieved
without character.

What characteristics permeate my life?

_____ .
_____ .
_____ .
_____ .
_____ .
_____ .
_____ .
_____ .
_____ .
_____ .
_____ .
_____ .
_____ .
_____ .
_____ .
_____ .

A man is known by his actions.

PROVERBS 21:8 TLB

What kind of employee am I?

_____

_____

_____

_____

_____

_____

_____

_____

_____

_____

_____

_____

_____

_____

Dear Business Associate:

For now, I have chosen to be your customer. No matter what part of the organization you're in—no matter what job you perform—you are part of my customer service experience. You determine whether or not I'll be back.

When I call or visit your place of business, I expect to be treated well by the people who wait on me. But I judge your business by a lot more than just how I'm dealt with by the "customer-service people." I look at everything. I ask questions: Is the facility clean and well maintained? Is the product or service of good quality? Did the shipment arrive on time and in good condition? Was the payment processing handled efficiently and correctly? Were the shelves well stocked and organized? Are written communications and phone messages clear and easy to understand? How long was I put on hold or passed from department to department?

Chances are you'll never know me personally. You may never even see me. But you ought to appreciate me immensely. I am, after all, the reason the business for which you work exists—the reason you have a job. Do your part to make my experience a good one, and I'll be back to give you my hard-earned money.

Sincerely,
Your Customer

Even though it is doubtful you are a business owner, it is quite likely that you do have a job. Even now, begin to develop a good work ethic, and treat your place of employment as though it were your very own company. Excellent workers are hard to come by; make sure your place is secure.

o o o o o

Serve wholeheartedly, as if you were serving the Lord, not men.

EPHESIANS 6:7 NIV

Give the world the best you have, and the best will come back to you.

... s not a very popular word. It is, ho... of the most critical character qual... e that leaders must exemplify by e... military has a saying: "A seni... er regard his rank. The junior mus... et it."

...ords, before leaders can exp... e from those under them, the... tain exemplary obedience to tho... m. If one of your friends sees you... g about a coach's directives, tha... l immediately recognize your spi... on. Even if you comply with the... our attitude will provide justifi-cat... e under your leadership to ba... structions.

... to effectively lead is to be even m... ul and obedient to your author-iti... expect others to be to you. Al... e your position or power to bu... nstead, earn respect through y... ge, integrity, and work ethic. Sh... ple that compliance is a matter o... vital part of a person's depend-a... oductivity, as well as a measure o... haracter.

...ates and employees can't be ... to do their jobs as instructed, t... on of the team or company is at ... anization has achieved excellence ... chy and disorganization.

o o o o o

who has learned to obey
know how to command.

What kind of example do I set for those I lead?

_____ .
_____ .
_____ .
_____ .
_____ .
_____ .
_____ .
_____ .
_____ .
_____ .
_____ .
_____ .
_____ .
_____ .
_____ .
_____ .

This is love: that we walk in
obedience to his commands.
2 JOHN 6 NIV

Be Adaptable

Am I flexible enough to change with the times?

_____
_____
_____
_____
_____
_____
_____
_____
_____
_____
_____
_____
_____
_____

With technology so rapidly changing, it is more important than ever that people be open minded and stay flexible and adaptable. Consider this story of one who refused to go with the flow.

A hard-working paste-up artist named Mark had worked for many years at a magazine. He was an expert with an X-acto knife, ruler, and waxer machine as he carefully trimmed columns of copy and pasted them onto art boards to send to the printer. In his spare time, Mark began to read about the advent of desktop publishing and its effect on the magazine and book industries. The company offered to send Mark to school to learn the new technology. But he declined, convinced that he could still work faster and better than a computer-based artist.

The test came when Mark and his computer-based competitors were given sixteen-page sections of the magazine to produce. Those using the new technology produced quick, error-free work. In his haste, Mark forgot to paste a key paragraph into one story and duplicated a sentence in another. When the waxer clogged, Mark knew he was in trouble.

While relieving him of his job, Mark's manager said sadly, "Mark, you are like a great builder of covered wagons. Unfortunately, people today are driving comfortable cars powered by internal-combustion engines, not a team of mules."

Mark is still looking for a publisher who appreciates old-style methods. He tells friends, "I think this desktop publishing thing might just be a fad. Someday, publishers will need people like me again."

o o o o o

Pride leads only to shame;
it is wise to be humble.

PROVERBS 11:2 NCV

'Tis not knowing much, but what is useful, that makes a wise man.

...ewton wasn't the first person
to b... ...the head by a falling apple or
to d... ...causes objects to tumble
tow... ...ut there's a reason he's
cre... ...scovering the theory of gravity.
He ... ...er the phenomenon later
kno... ...y. He calculated and hypothe-
size... ...Newton's famous *Principia* went
to ... ...dically changed humanity's
un... ...of the universe. The ability to
thi... ...entrate is what turns inspiration
int... ...and practical application.

...a few tips to build your brain
to ... ...levels:

- ...n is like a muscle. Exercise it by
...a topic and contemplating it
...ly. Don't discard the topic when
...stuck for answers. That's like
...down a barbell every time it
...o feel a little heavy.

- ...tion builds creativity. Feed your
...ion by reading great books,
...fine artwork, or watching
...ive films or TV programs.

...your thoughts. This will keep you
...d—and prevent you from forget-
...y ideas and insights.

...word puzzles, memory games, and
...searches are great ways to
...nge and develop your mind.

...need a break from all the thinking,
...mind and enjoy an apple. Isaac
...ould approve.

o o o o o

...Isaac Newton. He was a guy who
...rstood the gravity of a situation.

_____ .
_____ .
_____ .
_____ .
_____ .
_____ .
_____ .
_____ .
_____ .
_____ .
_____ .
_____ .
_____ .
_____ .
_____ .

Finally, brothers, whatever is true, whatever
is noble, whatever is right, whatever is
pure, whatever is lovely, whatever is
admirable—if anything is excellent or
praiseworthy—think about such things.
PHILIPPIANS 4:8 NIV

The Trouble Tree

What troubles do I need to hang on my tree?

_____

_____

_____

_____

_____

_____

_____

_____

_____

_____

_____

_____

_____

_____

_____

A young couple hired a carpenter to help them restore an old farmhouse. During a rough first day on the job, a flat tire made him lose an hour of work, his electric saw quit, and finally, his ancient truck refused to start when it was time for him to go home.

While the couple drove him home, the carpenter sat in stony silence. On arriving, he invited them in to meet his family. As the threesome walked toward the front door, the carpenter paused briefly at a small tree, touching the tips of the branches. As he opened the door to his home, the carpenter underwent an amazing transformation. His tanned face relaxed. He smiled as he hugged his two small children and kissed his wife.

Afterward, he walked the couple to their car. They passed the tree, and the husband asked, "Why did you touch the tree like that earlier?"

"Oh, that's my trouble tree," the carpenter replied. "I can't help having troubles on the job, but troubles don't belong in our home. So I hang them up on the tree every night. In the morning, I pick them up again." He smiled, "Funny thing though, when I come out in the morning, there aren't nearly as many as I remember hanging up the night before."

o o o o o

Life is what we make it, always has been, always will be.

Cast all your anxiety on him because he cares for you.

I PETER 5:7 NIV

Virtue without Vices

HOW do I want to be remembered?

_____.
_____.
_____.
_____.
_____.
_____.
_____.
_____.
_____.
_____.
_____.
_____.
_____.
_____.
_____.
_____.
_____.

Sou   gressmen for the seceding
Sta   s formed the Confederate
Jef   ica, they chose U.S. Senator
Da   to be their leader. Little did
fai   hat the clerical assistant who
be   d by his side would be remem-
      ro for generations to come.

      stant, an experienced soldier
n   t E. Lee, had been confined to a
d   nond, Virginia. There he obedi-
e   out the president's instructions
      plaint. It was not until June of
      than a year after the fighting
      Lee entered the battlefield.

      gh history has demonstrated Lee
      uperior strategist, he deferred to
      egularly cleared his own plans
      before implementing them. With
      rship in the field, the Confederate
      lled its enemy for the first time and
      ding northward.

      s written of Lee: "He possessed
      tue of the great commanders,
      heir vices. He was a foe without
      iend without treachery . . . a neigh-
      out reproach; a Christian without
      y. . . . He was a Caesar without his
      ; a Frederick without his tyranny; a
      on without his selfishness; and a
      gton without his reward. He was
      t to authority as a servant and loyal
      ority as a true king, [yet] submissive to
      Socrates."

o o o o o

_Stature comes, not with height,
but with depth._

The fear of the LORD is the instruction of
wisdom; and before honour is humility.

PROVERBS 15:33

What am I joyful about today?

_____

_____

_____

_____

_____

_____

_____

_____

_____

_____

_____

_____

_____

_____

_____

Irrefutable Principles of Life:

- A clear conscience should never be confused with a bad memory.
- Sweeping the room with a glance doesn't qualify as tidying one's bedroom.
- Letting it all hang out is unwise; you might not be able to get it tucked back in.
- Age is a very high price to pay for maturity.
- A closed mouth gathers no foot.
- Whine doesn't improve with age.
- Experience is a wonderful thing. It enables you to recognize a mistake when you make it again.
- One who thinks logically provides a nice contrast to the real world.
- Just when you start to win the rat race, scientists will develop bigger, faster rats.
- Jumping to conclusions, running your mouth, and ducking responsibility don't count as fitness exercises.
- It is better to light one small candle than to be seen with no makeup under fluorescent lighting.

o o o o o

Take laughter home, and make a place in your heart for her.

My soul shall be joyful in the LORD.

PSALM 35:9

Whom do I need to seek for support?

Ranger was misnamed. He wasn't ... all. He didn't defeat the bad guys ... from danger by himself. He had ... his faithful friend, Tonto—not to ... fast and trusty horse, Silver. Hur... ust aren't designed to conquer life ... n. Whether it's figuring out a diffi... ith concept, getting over a bre... boyfriend or girlfriend, or cop... pression or an eating disorder, sor... s require a call for help.

... be one of those people who has... king for help. If so, just remember ... ssistance you need is available, re... whether it's physical, emotional, fin... chnical. It may take a little re... ulnerability to connect with th... selor, friend, coworker, or family m... ending up an SOS when you ne... re sign of maturity—not w... ding the support or guidance y... make a great difference in the w... orm at school and on the job, t... think about your life, and, p... t importantly, the way you live.

... e afraid to reach out when you r... e. And remember, the person you s... m today might be the one who r... expertise, guidance, or moral ... ewhere down the road.

o o o o o

in a bundle are unbreakable.

> Two are better than one, because they
> have a good return for their work:
> If one falls down, his friend can help
> him up. But pity the man who falls
> and has no one to help him up!
> ECCLESIASTES 4:9-10 NIV

Keep Confidences

HOW good am I at keeping confidences?

_____

_____

_____

_____

_____

_____

_____

_____

_____

_____

_____

_____

_____

One of the primary characteristics of a valued friend and employee is the ability and determination to keep confidences. "Why" is simple. Trust is a key factor in every relationship. People want a friend, someone with whom they can feel safe. In fact, the word *confidential* is derived from the same root word as *confidence*. If you can keep a confidence, people will have confidence in you.

So learn to put a lock on your lips and keep secrets—secret! When you encounter the compulsion to whisper what you've been told to someone else (and you will), remember that trust builds relationships, but betrayal tears them apart. Your family, friends, teachers, and your boss will respect you, value you, and know they can depend on you when you prove you are trustworthy in the safekeeping of confidential matters. This respect and value can only serve to enhance your life.

Certainly, if someone is planning to do something illegal or harmful, you must exercise discretion as to what is the greater good— breaking a confidence or letting harm come to someone. But, for the most part, confidential matters belong in a vault to which only you have the key. It's a key of trustworthiness, hanging from a key chain of sound judgment.

o o o o o

The human heart has hidden treasures, in secret kept, and silence sealed.

Set a watch, O LORD, before my mouth; keep the door of my lips.

PSALM 141:3

Turn a Deaf Ear

What would I do if I didn't let others discourage me?

_____.

_____.

_____.

_____.

_____.

_____.

_____.

_____.

_____.

_____.

_____.

_____.

_____.

_____.

_____.

the   frogs was hopping through
                  denly, two of them plunged
into   As the other frogs circled the
dee   uickly concluded that their
amp   nds were doomed. Frantically,
the   tunate frogs began leaping with
all   h. "Give it up," some of their
col   d them. "You are as good as
dea   two frogs kept jumping.

fro   lf hour, one of the trapped
co   discouraged, curled up in a dark
ot   pit, and waited to die. But the
cc   t jumping, even though his
o   ontinued to jeer. Finally, with
pi   nge, he leaped to the rim of the
                 himself to safety.

i   vhat a hop!" one of the naysay-
t   mented. "I guess it was a good
                 ored us."

                 w-safe frog simply looked at his
                 with a puzzled expression on his
                 hen, through a series of frog sign-
                 tures, he explained to the others
                 deaf. He didn't hear their
                 g words. And, in fact, when he had
                 rantic gestures, he assumed they
                 ing him on!

                 sson: You can accomplish amazing
                 you turn a deaf ear (or two) to
                 raging words of negative-thinking

o o o o o

ubt indulged soon becomes
doubt realized.

It is God's will that by doing good you should silence the ignorant talk of foolish men.

I PETER 2:15 NIV

Which area do I need to work on the most?

_____

_____

_____

_____

_____

_____

_____

_____

_____

_____

_____

_____

_____

Suggestions for Success:

- Find a job you love. This alone will determine 90 percent of your career happiness.
- Be wise always as to how you spend your time and your talent.
- Give people more than they expect—and do so cheerfully.
- Be the most positive, encouraging, and kind-hearted person you know.
- Be forgiving toward others and toward yourself. No one is perfect.
- Be generous—and not just with money.
- Cultivate a grateful heart.
- Be persistent about developing and exercising persistence.
- Discipline yourself to save money, regardless of your financial situation. Don't wait till the "next raise" to start saving.
- Treat everyone just as you want to be treated.
- Determine that you will constantly improve your skills and learn new ones.
- Commit yourself to quality.
- Understand that happiness isn't based on position, money, or possessions.
- Be loyal.
- Be honest.
- Be a self-motivated, self-starting person of action.
- Be decisive. Some decisions won't turn out the way you hope, but indecision rarely leads to anything good.
- Stop blaming others. You are responsible for your life, your happiness, your well-being.
- Be courageous. You don't want to look back on your life someday and live with the regret of what might have been.
- Take good care of those you love.
- Don't do anything that wouldn't make your mom and dad—or your brothers and sisters—proud of you.

o o o o o

Whatever you are, be a good one.

Commit to the LORD whatever you do, and your plans will succeed.

PROVERBS 16:3 NIV

One Brave Soul

Whom do I know that could use a good laugh?

_____ .

_____ .

_____ .

_____ .

_____ .

_____ .

_____ .

_____ .

_____ .

_____ .

_____ .

_____ .

_____ .

_____ .

_____ .

... president held a retreat for his st... ...ey arrived, the president asked them ... ... down by the lake. "Resort offici... ...ked this lake with a couple-hund... ..." he told them. "They were reluc... ...ade it worth their while. I want to d... ... most courageous people on my t... ...ring one thousand dollars to anyc... ...ough to swim across."

... ...bassed. Staff members whi... ...ach other and shook their hea... ...ldenly, a young woman plunged into ... With screams of terror, she beg... ...g madly across the lake. At last ... ...d the far shore and pulled her ... ...y. Her clothes were torn. She wa... ...ith bite marks.

... ...e staff raced around the lake an... ...t her side. "You see? I knew th... ... brave soul among all you co... ...president pontificated. "Jennifer he... ...ne thousand dollars richer. Je... ...re anything you would like to sa... ...up?"

... ...nnifer struggled to her feet. "... ...d slowly, "I have four words I w... ... say."

"... ...ell," the president responded. "... ...listen to brave Jennifer's four in... ...ords."

... ...at Jennifer faced the staff, cleared ... ...nd screamed, "WHO PUSHED ...

○ ○ ○ ○ ○

... ...most wasted day is that in ... ...ch we have not laughed.

THERE IS A right time for everything . . .
A time to laugh.
ECCLESIASTES 3:1,4 TLB

Leaders Learn to Share the Effort

HOW can I become a more effective leader?

_____

_____

_____

_____

_____

_____

_____

_____

_____

_____

_____

_____

_____

_____

Often in our society, the independent, self-reliant leader is revered. Such people live by adages like "If you want something done right, you have to do it yourself." Being responsible for your actions is certainly admirable, as is the ability to get things done without forming a committee. If you are the leader of a club, youth group, or athletic team, however, it's important not to overlook the wisdom and efficiency of delegating.

Thomas Edison, for example, is viewed by many as a lone genius, toiling away in his laboratory. In reality, he was not a hermit-inventor. He kept a large team working on as many as forty-five inventions at a time.

This system required expert management and precise scheduling. "We had all the way from forty to fifty men," Edison said of his system. "They worked all the time. Each man was allowed from four to six hours sleep." While Edison's work schedule was a bit harsh, his principle is sound. One man simply couldn't have managed forty-five or fifty inventions and experiments simultaneously.

If you are a natural-born leader and find yourself leading various groups or projects, you can build a delegation of key people who can help reach your goals in a shorter time span. You will probably find that your peers appreciate your trust in them—and the opportunity to learn new skills and to be a part of the team effort.

○ ○ ○ ○

I know your eagerness to help, and I have been boasting about it.
2 CORINTHIANS 9:2 NIV

Leadership: The art of getting someone else to do something you want done because he wants to do it.

D___ Your Life Need a Lift?

K___ ___ Enjoying Your Life:

- ___ the value of time. Grab it, use ___ savor every moment of it.
- ___ that it's easier to prevent bad ___ forming than it is to break ___ they are formed.
- ___ive the road to success, ___ letting others travel with you. ___ will be more fun.
- ___ld have a good reason for ___ out; you don't necessarily need ___ eason for remaining silent.
- ___ items you can wear to school ___ k, your facial expression is the ___ portant.
- ___ eing paranoid or overly sensitive.
- ___ both praise and constructive ___ n with grace.
- ___ d in what you stand for. Be careful ___ ou fall for.
- ___ give up on miracles. They do happen.
- ___ rain on other people's parades. ___ a drip would do that.
- ___ postpone joy.
- ___ vays to truthfully compliment ___ s on a job well done.
- ___ eal!
- ___ ose to give others the benefit of ___ doubt.
- ___ aud the achievement of others.
- ___ 't forget to say "Thank you!"

o o o o o

___ays do right. This will gratify some people and astonish the rest.

What three things do I want to work on today?

_____.
_____.
_____.
_____.
_____.
_____.
_____.
_____.
_____.
_____.
_____.
_____.
_____.
_____.
_____.
_____.
_____.
_____.

Let the wise listen and add to their learning.

PROVERBS 1:5 NIV

What idea do I need to retool?

_____

_____

_____

_____

_____

_____

_____

_____

_____

_____

_____

_____

_____

_____

_____

Television producer Sherwood Schwartz was frustrated. He had created a television show that he felt was a winner. However, network executives from CBS had shown Schwartz's pilot program to test audiences, and they were underwhelmed at the show's content and its attempts at humor.

Some producers give up and move on to the next idea when faced with such rejection, but Schwartz believed that his idea, while admittedly campy and silly, had merit. So he tinkered with his show, rewriting scenes and replacing characters. He replaced a cutesy character named Bunny, for example, with a wholesome farm girl named Mary Ann.

Schwartz's retooled show was a hit with test audiences. And, since its network debut in 1964, _Gilligan's Island_ has been on the air ever since, thanks to its popularity in the syndication market.

It doesn't take a Professor to realize that you shouldn't cast away your ideas merely because they aren't quickly accepted. Have courage. Even something that seems like a shipwreck at first could make you a Skipper (CEO), a Millionaire, or a Movie Star.

o   o   o   o

The largest room in the world is the room for improvement.

Lazy hands make a man poor, but diligent hands bring wealth.

PROVERBS 10:4 NIV

HOW can I convert my frustration into determination?

"...hout exaggeration," Thomas
Ediso... ..., "when I say that I have
cons... ...e thousand different theories
in co... ...th the electric light, each one
of th... ...ble and apparently likely to
be tr... ...wo cases only did my experi-
men... ... truth of my theory."

...s Edison developed 2,998
faile... ...long with his two successful
exp... ...e entire story of the lightbulb
is a ... ...s tale of repeated trial and
failu... ...ugh it all, Edison was watching
atte... ...d learning.

...Edison's lead. When failures
mo... ...ck. Re-examine your goal. Then
tur... ...nergy of frustration into a
ren... ...mination to keep striving
tow... ...al. Determination is a decision
no... ...is a foundational principle of
go... ...r.

Ed... ...esson can be learned from
th... ...re determined you become,
th... ...ful you must be in handling
yo... ...As Edison's various attempts
to... ...cotton thread for a lightbulb
fil... ...he became increasingly deter-
m... ...ute force was not the key for
m... ...delicate filament work. He had
to... ...s determination with great
pa... ...e handling a fragile component.
In... ...ore intent a person becomes,
th... ...ient he or she must be to keep
fr... ...the goal of earnest efforts.

...develop and test your own
b... ...remember how many failures
E... ...o endure to achieve success. If
... ...ng to emulate his patience and
... ...on, you may be shocked at your

o o o o o

...ce and diligence, like faith,
remove mountains.

Patience is better than pride.

ECCLESIASTES 7:8 NIV

Over and beyond the Call of Duty

How can I ensure that I finish a task, no matter what?

_____

_____

_____

_____

_____

_____

_____

_____

_____

_____

_____

_____

_____

_____

Mr. Boswell, the owner of a hardware store, was looking for a young man to hire. Several dozen young men responded to his ad, but he eventually narrowed his choice down to three: Ted, John, and Bob. Then he devised a final test. He gave each of them a new screwdriver set with an innovative design and told them to deliver it to Mr. C.M. Henderson at 314 Maple Street.

After a while, Ted phoned the store to ask whether the number was actually 413, rather than 314. Later, he returned saying there was no house at that address.

When John came back, he reported that 314 Maple was a funeral parlor and that Mr. Henderson had lived at 314-1/2 but had moved away.

Bob took longer than the other two young men. Like John, he also discovered that Mr. Henderson had moved away, but he had managed to secure his new address and had gone there. Mr. Henderson didn't recall ordering the screwdriver, but when Bob pointed out its unique features and told him the price, Mr. Henderson decided he wanted the screwdriver and paid for it on the spot.

Which young man was hired? Bob, of course. He was given a task to do, and he did it. Leaders don't let any obstacles stop them from reaching their goals. Persistence and patience produce payoff.

○ ○ ○ ○

Be diligent so that you will receive your full reward.

2 JOHN 8 NLT

The secret of success is to do the common things uncommonly well.

What am I willing to sacrifice to attain my dreams?

_____.
_____.
_____.
_____.
_____.
_____.
_____.
_____.
_____.
_____.
_____.
_____.
_____.
_____.
_____.

...rents were brutally
mur... ...rth Vietnam, Ri moved to
Sout... ...While there, Ri went to
scho... ...tually became a building
con... ...prospered greatly until he was
arre... ...on a trip north. After being
imp... ...North Vietnam for three years,
he f... ...ed and made his way south,
only... ...ged as a spy for the north!
Wh... ...ed that the United States was
pul... ...outh Vietnam, he gave all his
wo... ...sions in exchange for passage
on... ...rcrowded fishing boat. He was
lat... ...o on the high seas by an
An... ...and was taken to the
Ph... ...ce there, he lived in a refugee
ca... ...years until he was allowed to
co... ...United States.

...arrived in the U.S., Ri's cousin
of... ...him and his wife jobs in his tailor
sh... ...ough their net pay was only $300
a... ...were determined to succeed. For
tw... ...ey lived in the back room of the
ta... ...d took sponge baths, so they
c... ...ery penny possible.

...two years, they had saved $30,000
a... ...out the cousin's business. It was
c... ...t they rented an apartment.

...Ri is a millionaire. Hard work and
f... ...can bring a dream into reality!

o o o o o

_...way to get to the top is to
get off your bottom._

The lazy will not get what they want, but
those who work hard will.

PROVERBS 13:4 NCV

Never Give Up

What obstacles do I need God's help to overcome?

. _____

. _____

. _____

. _____

. _____

. _____

. _____

. _____

. _____

. _____

. _____

. _____

. _____

. _____

. _____

In the 1880s, some of the finest engineers in the world were called in to give their opinions about the possibility of building a railroad through the Andes Mountains. One by one, groups of engineers were presented with various possible routes, and one by one they reported the job couldn't be done. Finally, as a last resort, a Polish engineer named Ernest Malinowski was consulted. Malinowski had a tremendous reputation, but by this time, he was sixty years old.

Malinowski not only assured the representatives of the participating nations that the job could be done, but that he was the man for the job. Thus, at the start of his seventh decade, he began overseeing the building of the highest railroad in the world.

The railroad wound its way through the Andes, through sixty-two tunnels, and across thirty bridges. One tunnel was 4,000 feet long and 15,000 feet above sea level. Revolutions held up construction twice, and once, Malinowski had to flee for his life to Peru. In spite of all the obstacles, the feat was accomplished and is considered one of the great engineering marvels of the world.

Obstacles are meant to be hurdled.

Never, never, never give up.

o o o o

This is accomplished from start to finish by faith.

ROMANS 1:17 TLB

The most rewarding things you do in life are often the ones that look like they cannot be done.

A[im t]o Do What You Love to Do

Oct[ober]

[...] asil L. Gildersleeve of Johns
Hop[...] [univers]ity was once interviewed for
the [...] [Even]ing Post. At the time, the
elde[...] [schola]r was considered to be the
grea[...] scholar in the nation, and his
wor[...] honored by numerous organi-
zatio[...] [soci]eties around the world.

[...] [interv]iewer asked Professor
Gil[...] [wh]at he considered to be the
high[...] [o]r compliment he had ever
rec[...] [th]ought for a moment and then
rep[...] [lie]ve it was when one of my
stu[...] 'Professor, you have so much
fur[...] [own] mind!'"

[...] [a]l researchers have discovered
th[...] [pe]ople enjoy their work and feel it
is [...] they are more productive, more
o[...] [impr]ovement, and more concerned
ab[...] [qua]lity of their work. As their levels
o[...] [productivit]y and quality rise, they become
m[...] and actually begin to earn
m[...] —either through promotions,
p[...] a broader customer base. As
t[...] increases, they tend to enjoy
t[...] [e]ven more!

[...] [pe]ople to be truly effective, they
[...] [pl]easure in their work. Find
[...] [y]ou sincerely enjoy doing, then do
[...] [succe]ss will surely follow!

[...] [lov]e what you do and feel that it
[...] [ma]tters—how could anything
be more fun?

How can I turn what I really love doing into a career?

_____.
_____.
_____.
_____.
_____.
_____.
_____.
_____.
_____.
_____.
_____.
_____.
_____.
_____.
_____.
_____.

> When you eat the labor of your hands,
> You shall be happy, and it shall
> be well with you.
> PSALM 128:2 NKJV

Finish What You Start

HOW good am I at finishing what I start?

_____
_____
_____
_____
_____
_____
_____
_____
_____
_____
_____
_____
_____
_____

The Brooklyn Bridge, which links Brooklyn to Manhattan Island, is one of the most famous bridges in the world. At the time it was first conceived in 1883, however, bridge-building experts throughout the world told the designer, a creative engineer by the name of John Roebling, that his idea wouldn't work.

Roebling convinced his son Washington, who was also an engineer, that his idea had merit. The two of them developed the concept, resolved the problems others had forecast, and enthusiastically hired a crew to build their bridge.

After only a few months of building, a tragic on-site accident took John's life and severely injured Washington, who became unable to talk or walk. Everyone thought the project would have to be abandoned since the Roeblings were the only ones who knew the dynamics of building the bridge.

Washington, however, could still think, and he had a burning desire to see the bridge finished. As he lay in his hospital bed, he had an idea. He would communicate with the engineers by using one finger to tap out in code on his wife's arm what he wanted her to tell them.

Washington tapped out his instructions for thirteen years until the bridge was built!

Leaders are not only self-starters, they are finishers.

○ ○ ○ ○ ○

I have fought a good fight, I have finished my course.

2 TIMOTHY 4:7

The test of a first-rate work is that you finish it.

James J. Corbett made many
mem...   ...ements during his colorful
care...   ...aps his most famous was
whe...   ...ked, "What is the most
imp...   ...g for a man to become
a ch...

...eplied, "Fight one more round."

...successful people have that
per...   ...omas Gray wrote seventy-five
dra...   ...y Written in a Country
Ch...   ...efore he was satisfied with his
po...   ...piece. S. N. Behrman, an
A...   ...wright, wrote plays for eleven
ye...   ...he sold one. Somerset Maugham
ea...   ...ve hundred dollars in his first
te...   ...a writer. While working full-time
in...   ...nrico Caruso studied voice for a
t...   ...before he became a successful
p...   ...eorge Gershwin composed
a...   ...undred melodies before he sold
...   ...—for five dollars. During his first
...   ...a writer, Zane Grey couldn't sell
...   ...y.

...be discouraged if your dream
...he true immediately. Continue to
...r craft or talent. Study and learn.
...xperience. Keep working. The
...s to those who are willing to fight
...e round!"

o o o o o

...ams don't work unless you do.

Am I willing to pay the price to make my dreams come true?

_____ .
_____ .
_____ .
_____ .
_____ .
_____ .
_____ .
_____ .
_____ .
_____ .
_____ .
_____ .
_____ .
_____ .
_____ .
_____ .
_____ .

The desire of the sluggard puts him to
death, For his hands refuse to work.

PROVERBS 21:25 NASB

Don't Always Take No for an Answer

"Where there's a will ... there's a way" means I ...

_____

_____

_____

_____

_____

_____

_____

_____

_____

_____

_____

_____

_____

_____

Irwin, a junior naval officer, was discharged from military service after he was diagnosed with cancer—standard military procedure at the time. The loss of his job was quite a blow, but he was determined to get back both his health and his job. With faith and dogged determination, he battled the disease that tried to take over his body. At one point, he was given only two weeks to live, but eventually his cancer was brought under control.

Irwin then focused his attention on his desire to become a naval officer. He discovered, however, that regulations forbade reinstatement of a person discharged with cancer. Everyone told Irwin, "Give up. It would take an act of Congress to get reinstated." Their advice gave him an idea—he would pursue an act of Congress!

President Harry S Truman eventually signed into law a special bill that allowed Irwin W. Rosenberg to re-enlist and become a rear admiral in the United States Seventh Fleet!

The thought, "Where there's a will ... there's a way" is applicable to nearly every circumstance in life. When our will lines up with God's will, we will be able to accomplish anything with His help!

o o o o

Clear your mind of can't.

This is the confidence that we have in him, that, if we ask any thing according to his will, he heareth us: And if we know that he hear us, whatsoever we ask, we know that we have the petitions that we desired of him.
I JOHN 5:14-15

C__nue Setting New Goals

What is my next goal?

_____ face the temptation to
slack _____ ey have achieved a goal. At
that _____ sy to let go of yesterday's
inse___ _____ insufficiencies and accept the
illusi__ _____ has arrived.

_____ al athletes are especially aware
of t___ ___ f such complacency. Even
whil__ _____ g at their peak performance,
they _____ hallenge of preparing
the _____ the time when their skills fade
and _____ on ends. Those who don't
pre___ _____ settle into marginal careers,
and _____ bottom.

_____ 60s, Dave Bing was the NBA's
lea___ _____ in his second year as a Detroit
Pis___ _____ he is still considered one of
ba___ _____ eatest players.

_____ ught ahead. Before he went pro,
he _____ Syracuse University. His advisors
su___ _____ skip the serious courses and
e___ _____ " degree. Bing refused and took
t___ _____ ss classes instead.

_____ his pro years, he continued his
e___ _____ eading voraciously on road trips
a___ _____ ff-season jobs at a bank, a steel
___ _____ Chrysler Corporation. Today, he
___ _____ of three multimillion-dollar
___ _____ that employ more than three
___ _____ ople, and he is one of the most
___ _____ black businessmen in the nation.

_____ let one success keep you from
___ _____ to bigger and better things.
___ _____ set new goals, and you will attain
___ _____ never dreamed were possible.

○ ○ ○ ○ ○

_____ ss travels so slowly, that poverty
soon overtakes him._

Yet a little sleep, a little slumber, a little
folding of the hands to sleep: So shall
thy poverty come as one that traveleth;
and thy want as an armed man.

PROVERBS 24:33-34

What do I need to sacrifice for the good of those I lead?

._____

._____

._____

._____

._____

._____

._____

._____

._____

._____

._____

._____

._____

In *Miracle on the River Kwai,* Ernest Gordon tells how Scottish soldiers were forced by their Japanese captors to work on a jungle railroad. They worked in deplorable conditions, under barbarous guards.

One day, a shovel was declared missing. The officer in charge became enraged, demanding that the missing shovel be produced, or he would kill all of the men. The officer pulled his gun. It was obvious he meant what he said.

After several tense moments, a man finally stepped forward. The officer put his gun away, picked up the shovel, and beat the man to death right in front of the other prisoners. They were allowed only to pick up his bloody corpse and carry it with them to a second tool check. There, the tools were recounted, and all shovels were accounted for—there had never been a missing shovel. There had simply been a miscount at the first checkpoint.

Word of the incident quickly spread through the entire prison camp. An innocent man had been willing to die to save the others. The incident had a profound effect, binding the prisoners together in deep loyalty. It was that loyalty, in part, that gave the men strength to survive until they were liberated.

Personal sacrifice is inspiring to others. It brings hope and encouragement to weary souls. It produces growth and maturity. There is no true leadership without some kind of sacrifice.

o o o o o

What is your life? It is even a vapor that appears for a little time and then vanishes away.

JAMES 4:14 NKJV

Life is a coin. You can spend it any way you wish, but you can only spend it once.

once so ugly and clothed so
shab   was continually tormented by
his s   He turned to reading in
orde   their taunts. At eighteen, he
took   bricklayer. He decided,
how   e did not want to be a bricklayer   vright. He forged a new path
in h   as eventually honored by
Que   n I and decorated by King
Jam   Ben Johnson, one of the most
brill   ghts in England's history.

             dsmith was the son of a poor
pre   as considered to be a sensitive
but   d. His schoolmaster labeled
him   lockhead." He earned a college
deg   duated at the very bottom of
his   as rejected from becoming a
pre   ied law and again was rejected.
He   a suit of clothes to take an
exa   become an assistant in a
ho   ailed at that as well.

             n poverty, was often ill, and
on   ned his clothes for food. The
on   vanted to do more than
an   o write. And so he forged a new
tra   d, he rose above his past to rank
an   eatest writers of all time.

             es a way will open up for you.
A   s, you may have to open it up!

○ ○ ○ ○ ○

follow where the path may
-go instead where there is
path and leave a trail.

What path does God seem to be opening up for me?

_____.

_____.

_____.

_____.

_____.

_____.

_____.

_____.

_____.

_____.

_____.

_____.

_____.

_____.

_____.

He restoreth my soul: he leadeth me in the
paths of righteousness for his name's sake.

PSALM 23:3

Dare to Dream Big

What do I desire that seems beyond my reach?

. _____

. _____

. _____

. _____

. _____

. _____

. _____

. _____

. _____

. _____

. _____

. _____

. _____

. _____

Cathy Guisewite is the creator of the very popular syndicated cartoon strip "Cathy." In the comic strip, Cathy routinely has encounters with her mother, who is always full of advice for her unmarried, career-oriented daughter. In real life, Cathy's mother has been known to offer her advice from time to time.

Guisewite once said: "I believe very strongly in visualizing goals way beyond what seems humanly possible. I got this from my parents. When my mother first suggested I submit some scribbles to a syndicate, I told her I knew nothing about comic strips. Mom said, 'So what? You'll learn.' When I pointed out that I didn't know how to draw, she said, 'So what? You'll learn.' All parents believe their children can do the impossible. They thought it the minute we were born, and no matter how hard we've tried to prove them wrong, they all think it about us now. And the really annoying thing is that they're probably right."

When we face challenges that lie just beyond our ability, we enter into the realm of faith and hope. It is as we face new frontiers in our lives that we truly encounter what our Creator has endowed us to do. Don't be afraid to desire to accomplish more in life.

○ ○ ○ ○ ○

These things I plan won't happen right away. Slowly, steadily, surely, the time approaches when the vision will be fulfilled. If it seems slow, wait patiently, for it will surely take place. It will not be delayed.
HABAKKUK 2:3 NLT

Lord, grant that I may always desire more than I can accomplish.

Octo...

his b... ...n expelled from college, and ...mpts had failed. Now, as he stoo... ...ndswept shores of Lake Mich... ...ntry night, the thirty-two-year... ...e last look at the sky above him ...red to cast himself into the free...

...verpowering moment. He felt a ru... ...s he saw the starry heavens, and ...t seared his mind, *You have no righ... ...e yourself. You do not belong to you...* ...ster Fuller walked away from the ...arted over.

... point on, he embarked on a jou... ...d him into careers as an inventor... ...mathematician, architect, poet, an... ...st. He eventually won dozens of ...egrees and a Nobel Prize no... ...uller invented the geodesic do... ...two dozen books, circled the gl... ...en times, and told millions ab... ...ams for the future. He seldom re... ...self in lectures that sometimes la... ...o four hours on topics that r... ...education to the origin of life.

... Buckminster Fuller encountered h... ...e day he began to find meaning f...

...s always a reason to hope. Hope ... ...strength to walk away from ... ...nove on to success.

o o o o o

...is a vigorous principle; it sets ...head and heart to work and ...ates a man to do his utmost.

> He will not break the bruised reed,
> nor quench the dimly burning flame.
> He will encourage the fainthearted,
> those tempted to despair.
>
> ISAIAH 42:3 TLB

Doing the Right Thing

For me, doing the right thing means . . .

. _____

. _____

. _____

. _____

. _____

. _____

. _____

. _____

. _____

. _____

. _____

. _____

. _____

. _____

Illinois is considered one of the most prosperous states in the nation today. Many regard an action taken by Stephen Douglas as the origin of that prosperity.

The nation was undergoing a financial depression in the mid 1800s, and state governments began to panic about their potential financial losses. Pennsylvania refused to pay its debts, although it was considered a rich state at the time. Illinois, a poor state at that time, felt justified that it might also take this route in confronting its debt.

When Stephen Douglas heard of this possibility, he opposed the idea with all his might. Although he was seriously ill, he insisted that he be carried on a stretcher to his place in the state legislature. Lying on his back, he made a historic resolution: "That Illinois be honest." His motion touched the deepest sense of morality in every member of the legislature. It was overwhelmingly adopted. The practice of repudiation was dealt a deathblow. The result was that Illinois had to find a new way out of its financial slump—a way that turned out to be one of investment, growth, and, eventually, prosperity.

Doing the right thing always pays off, usually not right away, but the momentary relief of an easy solution is nothing compared with the eternal joy of choosing right.

o o o o o

Do what is right and good in the sight of the LORD, so that it may go well with you.
DEUTERONOMY 6:18 NRSV

Efficiency is doing things right.
Effectiveness is doing the right thing.

Develop Efficiency

... s told of the manager of a
min... ...seball team who became
com... ...usted with his center fielder's
perf... ...om where he sat in the
dug... ...w was a lot of running
aro... ...sed catches—activity but not
mu... ...vity. The center fielder always
see... ...e "faded" to the wrong side of
the... ...e but not having any effect. The
ma... ...ually ordered the player to the
du... ...umed the position himself!

...ball that came his way took a
ba... ...it the manager right in the
m... ...xt hit was a high-fly ball to
ce... ...the manager lost in the glare of
th... ...unced off his forehead. The third
ba... ...e his way was a hard line drive
th... ...ed valiantly, only to have the ball
s... ...ve his outstretched glove.

...the manager ran back to the
d... ...ed the center fielder by his
u... ...shouted, "You've got center field
s... ...p that even I can't do a thing
...

...cy isn't a matter of excessive
... ...a matter of doing only the motion
... ...o get the job accomplished.

... ...f the attributes that makes a leader
... ...nowing which motions to perform.

○ ○ ○ ○

...equate activity with efficiency.

I can be more efficient by . . .

_____ .
_____ .
_____ .
_____ .
_____ .
_____ .
_____ .
_____ .
_____ .
_____ .
_____ .
_____ .
_____ .
_____ .

Let all things be done decently and in order.

I CORINTHIANS 14:40

Laughter Makes Life Better

What makes me laugh?

. _____

. _____

. _____

. _____

. _____

. _____

. _____

. _____

. _____

. _____

. _____

. _____

. _____

. _____

The world always looks brighter when viewed with a smile.

> Laugh a little now and then
> It brightens life a lot;
> You can see the brighter side
> Just as well as not.
> Don't go mournfully around,
> Gloomy and forlorn;
> Try to make your fellow men
> Glad that you were born.
>
> —Unknown

It actually takes more muscles to frown than it does to smile. Beyond that, laughter has other very practical therapeutic results. It sends endorphins to the brain, which bring about a sense of well-being and calm. It energizes the body. It releases one's mind from depression and turns it toward goals, dreams, and triumphs. It makes time go by faster and menial chores more enjoyable.

Furthermore, when shared with friends and family, laughter builds relationships. At the end of a busy, tiring day, a happy home is a refuge for each family member, young and old.

Find a reason to enjoy a hearty laugh today!

o o o o o

A sense of humor is the pole that adds balance to our steps as we walk the tightrope of life.

Let all those that put their trust in thee rejoice: let them ever shout for joy, because thou defendest them: let them also that love thy name be joyful in thee.

PSALM 5:11

...lake Wesley, a former NHL
hock... ...eemed to have it all—money,
luxu... ...nd pretty wife, and three
sons... ...when the injuries of his sport
caus... ...xperience constant pain,
Blak... ...painkillers, then alcohol, and
ever... ...s. He became increasingly
irre... ...s a father and husband, so his
wif... ...sons back home to Oregon
unt... ...his life head-on.

...s coach that his eight-year
car... ...er until he straightened out his
life... ...d himself alone in a dark, seedy
ho... ...red and angry, he hit bottom. At
th... ...remembered the Lord. Falling
to... ...he yielded his life—including the
a... ...of his failures and sins—to the
G... ...an, with no strings attached.

...minutes, his healing had begun.
B... ...ed months of counseling and
r... ...n, but an inner work had started
t... ...ted in complete restoration of his
f... ...is life.

...pent with God today will be the
...rows into a new tomorrow.

o o o o o

...urpose of Christ's redeeming
...k was to make it possible for
...men to become good—deeply,
radically, and finally.

What good work do I need God to complete in me?

_____.
_____.
_____.
_____.
_____.
_____.
_____.
_____.
_____.
_____.
_____.
_____.
_____.
_____.
_____.
_____.
_____.

Being confident of this very thing, that he
which hath begun a good work in you will
perform it until the day of Jesus Christ:

PHILIPPIANS 1:6

You Can Make a Difference

Today I can make a difference by . . .

_____

_____

_____

_____

_____

_____

_____

_____

_____

_____

_____

_____

Can one person really make a difference in the world today?

One New Yorker thought so. He was determined to be complimentary to every person he saw every day. A friend asked him, "Do you even compliment cab drivers?"

The man said, "Certainly! If I am nice to one cab driver, he's likely to be nice to his next twenty fares, at a minimum. If they are in turn nicer to the shopkeepers, waitresses, and their own families, that one gesture of goodwill might influence at least a thousand people!

"Now, if only three people whom I talk to today have a happier day because of what I say to them, I might indirectly influence the attitude of three thousand people. If a few of those I talk to are teachers or people who have contact with more than the usual number of people . . . why my good mood might touch more than ten thousand lives. Not one other thing I do today is likely to have that kind of impact!"

Pass on a portion of what you have today. If you have nothing but your own smile, goodwill, and joy—pass it on! You can make a difference.

o o o o o

An unused life is an early death.

"Tell them what great things the Lord has done for you."

MARK 5:19 NKJV

Aim High

Three things I am aiming for are . . .

_____ .

_____ .

_____ .

_____ .

_____ .

_____ .

_____ .

_____ .

_____ .

_____ .

_____ .

_____ .

_____ .

_____ .

_____ .

rly age, Larry lived and
brea   ort of golf. As a teenager, he
was   one of the top sixteen young
golf   ation. Then, at the beginning
of h   ar of high school, Larry was
in a   le accident. He suffered
sev   , but the most devastating was
tha   m had to be amputated just
bel   ow.

            never heard of a one-armed
go   again, he didn't know that it
cc   ne! As Larry began to swing a
fe   at the rehab center, his mother
ar   ogist sought out someone who
c   a prosthetic hand for him. After
s   hs of practice with his new hand,
L   all one day. When it landed more
t   ndred yards away, he knew he
             He rejoined his high-school team,
             better than before, and is now
             a golf scholarship!

             think of your missing limb as
             that makes you a lesser person,"
             told an audience of children who
             nbs. "Think of it as something that
             you stronger. I would love to be the
             olfer with a prosthetic hand. But I
             that if I don't succeed, I won't be a
             only fail if we don't try."

○ ○ ○ ○ ○

_the long run people hit only
what they aim at._

I do not run uncertainly
(without definite aim).

I CORINTHIANS 9:26 AMP

What can I do to become more enthusiastic?

._____

._____

._____

._____

._____

._____

._____

._____

._____

._____

._____

._____

._____

._____

._____

A young man once placed this ad in a New York City newspaper:

Inexperience is the most valuable thing a man can bring to a new job. A man of inexperience, you see, is forced to rely upon imagination and verve, instead of timeworn routine and formula. If you're in the kind of business which is penalized by routine and formula thinking, then I'd like to work for you. Inexperience is my forte. I'm twenty-five years old and have the ability to become enthusiastic and emotionally involved in my work.

He was immediately hired by a chain of photo studios.

Be enthusiastic today about every area of your life—your family, your friends, your school, your work, your hobbies, your church, but especially your dreams and your potential to achieve them. Enthusiasm fuels hope and joy. People gravitate toward a person who radiates hope and joy, bringing with them unique opportunities, sound advice, and valuable resources.

o o o o o

Enthusiasm is contagious. It's difficult to remain neutral or indifferent in the presence of a positive thinker.

Ye shall go out with joy, and be led forth with peace: the mountains and the hills shall break forth before you into singing, and all the trees of the field shall clap their hands.

ISAIAH 55:12

...up in Puerto Rico, the son of a sug... ...ntation foreman. He lived with his f... ...t in a three-room shack with a di... ...no toilet. His first job, at the age... ...to drive oxen to plow the can... ...t hours a day for one dollar, wit... ...s. Juan looks back on those days as... ...important in his life.

...the cane fields that he learned to... ...work hard, and be loyal and re... ...his employers. His job and small in... ...a great source of self-esteem. At a... ...got a job at a golf course s... ...s for golfers.

...gan to dream of playing golf and ...ugh money to buy a bicycle. The ...eamed, the more he thought, *Why* ...de a club out of a guava limb and a ...e, and then he hammered an empty ...a ball. Next, he dug two small ...e ground and hit the ball back and ...een them. He practiced "golf" with ...ntensity he had put into his job in ...ield, only this time he was driving ...with a club, rather than oxen with a ...ntually, he became a very good golfer.

...is thirty-one years as a pro golfer, ...i Chi" Rodriguez won twenty-four ...ents and earned four million dollars.

...matter how or where you started ...fe, you can use your circumstances ...r benefit. Difficult circumstances can ...ou more determined to succeed if you ...he right attitude.

○ ○ ○ ○ ○

...xperience is not what happens to people, it's what people do with what happens to them.

I am determined to succeed at . . .

————————————————— .
————————————————— .
————————————————— .
————————————————— .
————————————————— .
————————————————— .
————————————————— .
————————————————— .
————————————————— .
————————————————— .
————————————————— .
————————————————— .
————————————————— .
————————————————— .
————————————————— .
————————————————— .
————————————————— .
————————————————— .

Whatever is born of God overcomes the world; and this is the victory that has overcome the world—our faith.

I JOHN 5:4 NASB

What can I do to develop more common sense?

._____

._____

._____

._____

._____

._____

._____

._____

._____

._____

._____

._____

._____

._____

After Thomas Edison's fame had become international, he was advised to have scientists come to his lab and help him understand just why some of his inventions had worked. Edison didn't see much use for it, but being open-minded, he consented to the idea. As a result, a brilliant research scientist from Germany came to his lab to explain to him the principles behind some of his innovations.

Edison handed the man a globe that had been twisted into a gourd-like shape and said, "Give me the cubic content of this."

Weeks passed, and eventually Edison sought out the man to ask him why he hadn't replied. The scientist began to give him a lengthy explanation about the difficulties of solving such a problem with higher mathematics. Edison then picked up the globe, took it over to a nearby sink, and filled it with water. He poured the water into a measuring tube, and holding up the tube, he said, "This is the cubic content."

The solutions to most problems are probably far more simple than we think they might be. They usually stem from an understanding of basic principles—the whys of life.

o o o o

The person who knows "how" will always have a job. The person who knows "why" will always be his or her boss.

How much better it is to get wisdom than gold! And to get understanding is to be chosen rather than silver.

PROVERBS 16:16 NKJV

How do I want my world to look?

... to designer Judyth van
Am... ...r of *Home Art: Creating
Rom... ...agic With Everyday Objects,*
"Yo... ...d a lot of money—just a little
ima... ...o do what I do." Judyth often
find... ...rials she works with at flea
ma... ...e instance, she took an old
fra... ...d it with macaroni shells, hiding
th... ...acks and chips, and painted it in
"s... ...ors. In another case, she covered
th... ...warped pine table—a junk-shop
fi... ...astic ivy and fruit to give it an
e...

...does she get her ideas? "I have
r... ...e says, "but I've always wanted to
...onal touch on things. . . . Don't be
...periment. The point is to
...things to your own style, your own
...g, and in the process, make life
...sing."

...began her business by designing
...welry, and gloves and then went on
...te homes. Today she is able to
...rself full-time to her design work in
...k City.[21]

...around today. How do you wish the
...look? It is out of your own vision
...can begin to brighten your world.

o o o o o

...evelop the hunter's attitude . . .
...herever you go, there are ideas
waiting to be discovered.

_____

_____

_____

_____

_____

_____

_____

_____

_____

_____

_____

_____

_____

_____

_____

_____

Give her of the fruit of her hands; and let
her own works praise her in the gates.

PROVERBS 31:31

Live in the Present

What are my immediate goals?

._____
._____
._____
._____
._____
._____
._____
._____
._____
._____
._____
._____
._____
._____
._____

Charlie Brown comes up to bat. He is determined, as always, to do well. Someday, just maybe, his team will win a game. And someday, just maybe, he might be a baseball hero.

Strike three! Charlie Brown has struck out once again. He returns to the sidelines and slumps down on the bench. "Rats! I'll never be a big-league player. I just don't have it! All my life I've dreamed of playing in the big leagues, but I know I'll never make it."

Lucy turns to console him in her inimitable way. "Charlie Brown, you're thinking too far ahead. What you need to do is set more immediate goals for yourself."

Charlie looks up, appearing to brighten at the prospect of something positive that might come from all the negatives he has been experiencing. "Immediate goals?"

"Yes," Lucy advises, "start with the next inning. When you go out to pitch, see if you can walk out to the mound without falling down!"

Too often, we allow ourselves to stumble over our daily chores because our minds are in the clouds, dreaming about the person we will become someday. It's okay to dream about tomorrow, but be sure to live in the present.

o o o o

Take first things first. That process often reduces the most complex human problems into manageable proportions.

This is the day the Lord has made.
We will rejoice and be glad in it.
PSALM 118:24 TLB

Determination

What am I determined to accomplish with God's help?

...ll of France in World War II, a fable... ...rculate about the fate of Engla... ...ry was told that in July 1940, Hitle... ...olini invited Churchill to Paris for a... ...ference. They met at a tea table... ...mous carp pool. The führer ope... ...og: "England is finished, Chu... ...this document admitting defeat, and... ...will have peace tomorrow!"

...said quietly, "I don't agree that we... ...e war."

...unded the table and cried,

"Ri...

...t settle this with a wager?" Ch... ...d.

...sponded, "What's the bet?"

...I said, "See these big carp in the po... ...ager that the first to catch one w... ...customary fishing equipment w... ...inner."

...nd Mussolini agreed, and the fü... ...y pulled out a revolver and e... ...the nearest fish. The water c... ...e bullets. Next, Mussolini jumped i... ...l and tried to catch a carp with ...ds. He failed. "Your turn, ...said Hitler.

...ill began to repeatedly dip his ...the pool and toss the water over his ...What are you doing?" cried Hitler.

...hill replied, "It will take a long ...e are going to win the war!"

○ ○ ○ ○

...eople succeed because they are ...ed to, but most people succeed ...ause they are determined to.

_____ .
_____ .
_____ .
_____ .
_____ .
_____ .
_____ .
_____ .
_____ .
_____ .
_____ .
_____ .
_____ .
_____ .
_____ .
_____ .

We're so proud of you; you're so steady and determined in your faith despite all the hard times that have come down on you.

2 THESSALONIANS 1:3 THE MESSAGE

Jesus Is Our Why

What is my "why" for pressing on?

. _____

. _____

. _____

. _____

. _____

. _____

. _____

. _____

. _____

. _____

. _____

. _____

. _____

. _____

When Everett Alvarez Jr. was given only thirty seconds to prepare a five-minute speech, he quickly thought back through his life. He recalled a time when he searched through his neighbor's trash for empty soda pop bottles to turn in at the corner grocery for a penny each.

All day, he carried bottles to the store in his red wagon, until he had a small mountain of coins—just enough to buy a card and a candy bar. They were surprise birthday presents for his mother. When he returned home, his mother demanded, "Where have you been? I've been searching everywhere for you!"

As his mother continued her questioning, Ev blubbered through his tears, "I was collecting bottles to get you these." He handed her the unsigned card and the candy bar that had nearly snapped in two in his pocket. His mother then began to cry as she proudly placed the gifts on a window ledge, so all the neighbors might see.

Ev's speech spoke to the hearts of his audience—a group of fellow prisoners of war at the infamous Hanoi Hilton prison camp in North Vietnam. For many of the men, it was the heritage of sacrificial family love that was their "suit of armor," the "why" that enabled them to survive years of nightmarish torture.

o o o o o

Never forget your promises to me your servant, for they are my only hope. They give me strength in all my troubles; how they refresh and revive me!

PSALM 119:49-50 TLB

The person who has a why to live can bear almost any how.

Divide and Conquer

...e, a well-known author and
prof...   wrote that he learned the
most ...   sson of his life when he was
only ...   ears old. It came from his
pian...

...y times a week do you
prac...   w long do you practice each
time...   her asked.

...d that he usually tried to
prac...   a day, generally for an hour or
mo...   her warned, "Don't do that.
Wh...   w up, time won't come in long
str...   tice in minutes, whenever you
car...   —five or ten before school,
aft...   tween chores. Spread your
pr...   ghout the day, and music will
be...   t of your life."

...back, John saw that advice as a
go...   against burnout. He also saw it
as ...   ve a complete life as a creative
w...   from his regular teaching duties.
H...   e bulk of his most famous work,
H...   while commuting between his
h...   e university.

...e a day count, make each minute
c...

o o o o o

...hing is particularly hard if
...u divide it into small jobs.

What things would I enjoy more if I did them in small increments of time?

_____ .
_____ .
_____ .
_____ .
_____ .
_____ .
_____ .
_____ .
_____ .
_____ .
_____ .
_____ .
_____ .
_____ .

> [Abram] divided his forces against them
> by night, he and his servants, and
> defeated them, and pursued them.
>
> GENESIS 14:15 NASB

Determine to Be a Real Friend

I can turn my jealousy
into love by . . .

. _____
. _____
. _____
. _____
. _____
. _____
. _____
. _____
. _____
. _____
. _____
. _____
. _____
. _____
. _____

A friend loves at all times.
PROVERBS 17:17 NRSV

F. B. Meyer, a minister in England, once told of the following experience to a few of his friends:

It was easy to pray for the success of G. Campbell Morgan when he was in America. But when he came back to England and took a church near to mine, it was something different. The old Adam in me was inclined to jealousy, but I got my heel upon his head, and whether I felt right toward my friend, I determined to act right. My church gave a reception for him, and I acknowledged that if it was not necessary for me to preach Sunday evenings, I would dearly love to go and hear him myself. Well, that made me feel right toward him. But just see how the dear Lord helped me out of my difficulty. There was Charles Spurgeon preaching wonderfully on the other side of me. He and Mr. Morgan were so popular, and drew such crowds, that our church caught the overflow, and we had all we could accommodate.

When we give up being jealous of a friend, we often find in its place a deeper friendship and a greater blessing.

o o o o

It is the character of very few people to honor without envy a friend who has prospered.

Working Together

...n who once lived in a conva-
lesc... ...ad each suffered an incapaci-
tatir... ...aggie's stroke had caused
para... ...r left side. Rachel's stroke had
cau... ...ent damage to her right side.
Bot... ...vere devastated by what had
hap... ...hem, since they assumed they
wo... ...e able to pursue a pastime they
ha... ...enjoyed throughout life—
pl... ...ano.

...e day, Maggie and Rachel met
a... ...lking about their lives. When they
r... ...both had an interest in music, an
i... ...d. When approached with the
i... ...valescent center's director
...m a piano and helped each
...on an elongated bench in front of
...layed the right-hand notes, while
...ed the left-hand ones! Not only
...nake beautiful music together, but
...ed a long and endearing friendship.

...s design for us is that we work
...live together, and have fun together.
...e choose to share our time and
...th others, we will reap the rewards
...d peace.

o o o o o

*Brotherhood: helping yourself
by helping others.*

With whom would I make a good team?

_____ .
_____ .
_____ .
_____ .
_____ .
_____ .
_____ .
_____ .
_____ .
_____ .
_____ .
_____ .
_____ .
_____ .
_____ .
_____ .

Together you are the body of Christ, and
each one of you is a part of that body.
I CORINTHIANS 12:27 NCV

True Success

HOW can I find time to develop strong relationships?

_____

_____

_____

_____

_____

_____

_____

_____

_____

_____

_____

_____

_____

_____

_____

_____

_____

Writing in *Brown Book Magazine* in 1904, Bessie Anderson Stanley gave this eloquent definition of success:

> He has achieved success who has lived well, laughed often and loved much; who has enjoyed the trust of pure women, the respect of intelligent men and the love of little children; who has filled his niche and accomplished his task; who has left the world better than he found it, whether by an improved poppy, a perfect poem, or a rescued soul; who has never lacked appreciation of earth's beauty or failed to express it; who has always looked for the best in others and given them the best he had; whose life was an inspiration; whose memory a benediction.

Our true sense of identity—which gives our life meaning and a genuine sense of success—is not bound up in tasks, deadlines, or sports victories. It lies in relationships—the day-to-day associations we have at home, at school, and in church—as well as our relationship with our Heavenly Father. It is as we relate to people—family, friends, adults, peers—that we develop a true sense of who we are.

o   o   o   o

What advantage does man have in all his work Which he does under the sun? A generation goes and a generation comes, But the earth remains forever.

ECCLESIASTES 1:3-4 NASB

Never allow your sense of self to become associated with your sense of job. If your job vanishes, your self doesn't.

The Bare Essentials

... *...rious Island,* a novel by Jules
Ver... ...ory of five men who escape a
Civ... ...n camp by hijacking a hot-air
bal... ...uickly, they realize the wind is
ca... ...out over the ocean. As the
ho... ...ey see the horizon receding and
re... ...hey are also losing altitude. Since
th... ...way of heating the air in the
b... ...begin to throw some of the
e... ...nt overboard. Shoes, coats, and
... ...e reluctantly discarded, yet they
... ...the balloon begins to rise.

... ...they draw dangerously close to the
... ...and begin to toss their food
... Better to be aloft and hungry! Yet a
... ...the balloon begins to descend, and
... one of the men suggests they tie
... the ropes that connect the balloon
... ...sket in which they are riding and then
... ...e ropes and cut away the heavy
... he very floor they had been standing
... away, and the balloon rises once again.

... ddenly, they spot land. With not a
... to spare, they jump into the water
... im to an island. Their lives are
... —not because of any great heroics, but
... se they had learned what they could
... ithout.

... We often say "I have to have" this or
... however, there are few things in life we
... y cannot do without. God has promised
... eet all our needs. There are things we
... want, but they are not to be confused
... h things we must have. Happiness is
... owing the difference and being content
... ere you are.

○ ○ ○ ○ ○

*To have what we want is riches; but
to be able to do without is power.*

Do I need to re-evaluate what I really need?

_____.

_____.

_____.

_____.

_____.

_____.

_____.

_____.

_____.

_____.

_____.

_____.

_____.

_____.

_____.

_____.

Not that I was ever in need, for I
have learned how to get along
happily whether I have much or little.

PHILIPPIANS 4:11 TLB

Undefeatable Determination

What projects do I need to see through to completion?

_____
_____
_____
_____
_____
_____
_____
_____
_____
_____
_____
_____
_____
_____
_____

Every athlete who goes into training conducts himself temperately and restricts himself in all things. They do it to win a wreath that will soon wither, but we [do it to receive a crown of eternal blessedness] that cannot wither.

I CORINTHIANS 9:25 AMP

As a young boy, Fritz wanted nothing more than to play the violin. He listened with rapt attention to violin music. His parents encouraged his interest by paying for him to have lessons. Fritz didn't make as much progress as they had hoped he would, however, and after a few years, he eventually quit the lessons.

Over the next several years, through college and young adulthood, Fritz studied medicine, but he failed to complete medical school. He joined the army and failed to be promoted. He tried and quit many other pursuits. Realizing that the little bit of success he had enjoyed in life had been related to the violin, he went back to his violin instructor and said, "I want to play."

She said, "Fine, I'll take you back as a student but only if you acquire the irreplaceable quality that is necessary for you to become a great violinist. You must exhibit undefeatable determination."

This time, Fritz Kreisler persevered in his pursuit of music—the first time he had truly persevered in anything he had attempted—and eventually Carnegie Hall was filled with his music.

o o o o o

We improve ourselves by victories over our self. There must be contests, and we must win.

...ungry for success. At the age
of th... ...ed his own business, drove a
spor... ...a house at the beach and a
con... ...the office, and was part
own... ...t. He was tall and good-
look... ...oit the eligible bachelor, and he
see... ...ined to date as many women
as ...

...e of thirty-one, Don was
str... ...cancer. Everything in his life
abo... ...ged. To his credit, he was able to
ma... ...leap in his life from living for
hir... ...cording to his own will to
ex... ...need for God and a desire to
liv... ...g to God's will.

...evaluated his priorities and four
y... ...aid: "I've been in several hospitals
a... ...mber of different treatments. I've
b... ...ission twice, and twice the
c... ...returned. I've seen people die, and
I... ...ople live. And above all, I've
... ...t's important and what's not."

...g the course of his illness, Don
... ...e of the women he had been
... ...a year later, his wife gave birth to
... ...Don says of his life today, "I
... ...rade what I've been through. Having
... ...ot living. Loving and knowing
... ...t's living. The fact is, whether I'm
... ...arth or in Heaven, loving and
... ...God is all that matters."

o o o o

...nd man exist for each other, and
...er is satisfied without the other.

How can I develop this kind of relationship with God?

_____ .

_____ .

_____ .

_____ .

_____ .

_____ .

_____ .

_____ .

_____ .

_____ .

_____ .

_____ .

_____ .

_____ .

_____ .

I count everything as loss compared to
the possession of the priceless privilege
(the overwhelming preciousness, the
surpassing worth, and supreme advantage)
of knowing Christ Jesus my Lord.

PHILIPPIANS 3:8 AMP

Care Before You Preach

Do people sense I really care about them?

_____

_____

_____

_____

_____

_____

_____

_____

_____

_____

_____

_____

_____

_____

_____

When Jim was diagnosed with cancer, his company heartlessly dumped him. In battling the disease, he used up all of his insurance fund and his life savings. A church deacon went to visit Jim and asked boldly, "Have you prepared for your life after death?"

Jim became irate, and swearing at the man he said, "All you Christians think about is what's going to happen after I die. If your God is so great, why doesn't He do something about the real problems of life?" He bitterly complained that he was leaving his wife penniless and his daughter without money for college. Then he ordered the man to leave his house.

The man thought about what Jim had said and soon returned. "I offended you, and I'm sorry," he said. "I've been working on your problems. A realtor I know has agreed to sell your house and give your wife his commission. Some of us will make your house payments until the house is sold. The earnings from your house should pay for your daughter's college. Also, the owner of an apartment building up the street has offered to give your wife a unit, with free utilities, plus a monthly salary in exchange for managing the complex."

Jim cried like a baby. He could finally hear the Gospel message with an open heart.

o o o o

If I have the gift of prophecy and can fathom all mysteries and all knowledge, and if I have a faith that can move mountains, but have not love, I am nothing

I CORINTHIANS 13:2 NIV

People don't care how much you know, until they know how much you care . . . about them.

...d and Dorothy Hustead
deci... ...e to a town that had four
thin... ...chool, a Catholic Church, a
doc... ...opportunity. They wanted to
ope... ...n pharmacy. They eventually
ch... ...uth Dakota, as the perfect
loc... ...hers, however, Wall seemed to
be... ...dle of nowhere—somewhere
be... ...Black Hills and the Badlands.

...year was a tough one—thick
d... ...heat, and strong winds. In their
d... ...ve on to a more welcoming
p... ...throat-parched travelers rarely
s... ...en, Ted and Dorothy came up with
a... ...y made a sign that read: FREE ICE
'... ...WALL DRUGSTORE. The sign
...nething of a novelty. They made
...and put them farther and farther
...—eventually, as far as Europe, India,
...pt, and the North Pole!

...ruggists, of course, made "free" ice
...lable for their customers. But
...lse had thought to advertise the
...entually, some four to six thousand
...rs a day stopped at Wall Drugstore.

...en you take a step toward your
...ou open yourself to creative ideas
...tions. Taking that big step gives you
...d optimism, which are essential
...ts for creativity. Dream big, step big,
...big things.

o o o o o

*Nothing is ordinary if you
know how to use it.*

I need to apply more
creativity to . . .

_____ .
_____ .
_____ .
_____ .
_____ .
_____ .
_____ .
_____ .
_____ .
_____ .
_____ .
_____ .
_____ .
_____ .
_____ .

I am wisdom, and I am smart. I also
have knowledge and good sense.
PROVERBS 8:12 NCV

Always Do Your Best

What steps can I take to ensure that I do a thorough job no matter what?

_____

_____

_____

_____

_____

_____

_____

_____

_____

_____

_____

_____

_____

_____

_____

_____

When Daniel Webster was just beginning his career as a lawyer, he took a case for a fee of twenty dollars. The case turned out to be a very difficult one, and in preparing for it, Webster had to make a trip to Boston, which in itself cost more than Webster was going to earn as a fee. He was determined, however, to do a thorough job on the case and win it, which he did. In retrospect, it seemed like a small case, but at the time, it was a big victory.

Years later, a large company approached Webster on short notice, asking him to undertake a case for which they were willing to pay a very handsome fee—in fact, a fee quite stunning at the time. As Webster reviewed the case, he found that it was almost identical to the one he had researched and won nearly twenty years before for the fee of only twenty dollars. He took the case, and just as before, the verdict was in favor of his client.

A familiar phrase holds great truth: "Nothing is lost in God's economy." He uses all our efforts that are motivated by goodwill and a generous and faithful heart. Sometimes the reward is immediate. Sometimes it can take a lifetime, but the reward will most definitely come.

o o o o o

Be great in the little things.

These things I have told you are all true. Insist on them so that Christians will be careful to do good deeds all the time, for this is not only right, but it brings results.

TITUS 3:8 TLB

[...]uring a crisis at the Telegu
Miss[...], a civil engineer named John
E. C[...]ed to go to the mission to
hel[...]onary board of the American
Ba[...]nary Union had some misgivings
ab[...]ivil engineer who had never
g[...]nary would want to go to India,
b[...]ired his zeal, so they authorized
h[...]

[...]me, it became apparent why God
[...]im to India. During the great
[...]876-77, Clough supervised the
[...]he Buckingham Canal. His position
[...]m to hire thousands of starving
[...]thus, secure them wages and a
[...]buying food. Because of this practi-
[...]saving act, the Telegus were open to
[...]what Clough truly desired to give
[...]pies of the Scriptures and the life-
[...]message of Jesus Christ.

[...]ly God can truly see the beginning
[...]ending of any situation or circum-
[...]He alone knows the very best person
[...]h job in His kingdom. God is always in
[...]cess of preparing you for your next
[...]rom where you are, it may not look
[...]e most logical way to go, but once you
[...]the step, it will become apparent why
[...]e there.

○ ○ ○ ○ ○

*Christian action should be defined
as an action of God mediated
through a person.*

How can I be quicker to obey God when I don't understand why?

_____.
_____.
_____.
_____.
_____.
_____.
_____.
_____.
_____.
_____.
_____.
_____.
_____.
_____.
_____.
_____.
_____.
_____.

Many are the plans in a man's heart,
but it is the LORD's purpose that prevails.
PROVERBS 19:21 NIV

When Is Enough, Enough?

What steps can I take to learn to be happy now?

. _____

. _____

. _____

. _____

. _____

. _____

. _____

. _____

. _____

. _____

. _____

. _____

. _____

. _____

. _____

He who loves money will not be satisfied with money, nor he who loves abundance with its income. This too is vanity.

ECCLESIASTES 5:10 NASB

A film editor once said, "I had this date the other night with a woman who wanted to walk along the beach. I'm wearing a $1200 suit, a $75 tie, a $150 shirt, and a pair of $200 shoes. It costs me $15 to clean my suit and $6 to have my shirt hand-washed.

"I don't even want to think about what it would cost if I should get a drop of spaghetti sauce on my tie. And this woman wants me to roll up my pants and walk along the beach! All I can think about is how much it's going to cost me if she wants to sit down on the sand. Here's the bottom line that I have to ask myself: 'Can I afford to wear my own clothes?'"

Another man, a lawyer, once said, "I don't think I'm trapped on this treadmill forever, but I'm certainly involved with it right now. . . . It's the old merry-go-round of how much money is enough money? And it's never enough. Three years ago I thought, *Just a little more.* . . . Now I make twice as much, and it's still not enough."[22]

Money should be a means toward living a generous, giving life—not an end in itself. When having money becomes their only goal, people not only hoard it, but they close themselves off to genuine living.

As a teen, you might think this doesn't apply to you. But as you prepare for college and a future career, remember money is merely a tool, and, in and of itself, it brings no lasting fulfillment.

o o o o

Many people have found the acquisition of wealth only a change, not an end, of miseries.

ber of years, Jamie
Buc ... riodically worked with healing
eva ... ryn Kuhlman. He wrote the
foll ... ping with Criticism:

... gh Miss Kuhlman was very
... criticism, she never let it
... from her goal. Instead, she
... help her get there. . . . Shortly
... went on nationwide television
... weekly program, she received a
... m a public-school official. . . . "I
... and love your program," he
... it would have been much better,
... r, if you didn't have to spend so
... me tugging at your skirt trying to
... down over your knees. It was
... distracting. Why don't you wear a
... ress instead?" Kathryn read the
... "You know, he's right," she said to
... ecretary. She never wore another
... t-length dress on her TV program.

... lesser person would have responded
... nger or passed it off as just another
... ess remark. But she was not that sort
... er person. She heard. She coped. She
... help her toward her goal of communi-
... g. All of which was possible because
... e was no root of bitterness to give a bad
... e to everything that came into her life
... ch presented another viewpoint.[23]

o o o o o

*I am defeated, and know it, if I meet
any human being from whom I find
myself unable to learn anything.*

What do I do with the criticism given to me?

_____ .

_____ .

_____ .

_____ .

_____ .

_____ .

_____ .

_____ .

_____ .

_____ .

_____ .

_____ .

_____ .

_____ .

_____ .

A wise man will hear, and will increase
learning; and a man of understanding
shall attain unto wise counsels.

PROVERBS 1:5

Don't Be Distracted

HOW can I develop this kind of focus?

._____

._____

._____

._____

._____

._____

._____

._____

._____

._____

._____

._____

._____

._____

._____

._____

> Stay grounded and steady . . .
> tuned in to the Message, careful
> not to be distracted or diverted.
> COLOSSIANS 1:21 THE MESSAGE

On a cold Saturday morning in January, in a small Wisconsin town on the southern shore of Lake Superior, an annual dogsled derby was about to begin. The course had been staked out by little fir trees secured to the ice.

The racers were all children—from large boys with several dogs and big sleds to one little boy who had only a small sled and one small dog. On the signal, the sleds took off, and the little fellow was soon so far behind he hardly seemed to be in the race. Then, about halfway through the course, the second-place team tried to move into first place. The sleds came too close, and the dogs began to fight. As each subsequent sled came upon the fight, more dogs became involved. The scene was soon one big, seething knot of kids, sleds, and dogs. All thought of racing had vanished from the minds of the sledders. However, the one little fellow and his small dog managed to skirt the others and went on to win the race!

Part of any success is refusing to become distracted. Pursue your goals today without wavering or hesitating. Keep your eyes on the finish line.

o o o o o

Success seems to be largely a matter of hanging on after others have let go.

You Attitude Can Change the State of Things

didr ...tinually complained that she
the ...ough money, couldn't afford
eve ...wanted, and therefore, wasn't
cou ...mount to anything. A
en ...to her, "You're throwing your
ge ...omplaining instead of using it to

th ...n don't understand. The job is
...not me," Cheryl countered.

n ...nselor said, "Your low-paying job
c ...oblem, and your boss may
...much, but if you are continually
...ou are causing yourself more
...either the job or the boss."

...t can I do?" she asked.

...ounselor said, "You can't control
...or the job, but you can control how
...bout them. Change your attitude."

...yl took her advice. When she
...whining about her life, people around
...ed. She got a promotion, and with
...job status, she was more marketable.
...several months, she was transferred
...ne department into a position with
...gher pay and a more supportive boss.

...ful is a state of *attitude*. A change in
...e will change the state of things!

○ ○ ○ ○ ○

*If you keep saying that things
are going to be bad, you have
a chance of being a prophet.*

I will improve my
attitude by . . .

_____ .
_____ .
_____ .
_____ .
_____ .
_____ .
_____ .
_____ .
_____ .
_____ .
_____ .
_____ .
_____ .
_____ .
_____ .
_____ .
_____ .

Thou art snared with the words of
thy mouth, thou art taken with
the words of thy mouth.
PROVERBS 6:2

Knowing God will one day welcome me home makes me feel . . .

. _____

. _____

. _____

. _____

. _____

. _____

. _____

. _____

. _____

. _____

. _____

. _____

. _____

. _____

On their way home from a lifetime of service as missionaries in Africa, an elderly couple found themselves on the same ocean liner as President Teddy Roosevelt, who was returning from a big-game hunting expedition.

The couple watched in awe at the fanfare given the president and his entourage. When the ship docked in New York, a band was waiting to greet him, the mayor was there to welcome him, and the newspapers heralded his return.

Meanwhile, the missionary couple slipped quietly off the ship and found a cheap apartment. They had no pension, they were in poor health, and they were discouraged and fearful. The husband, especially, could not seem to get over how the president had received such acclaim, while their decades of service had gone without notice or reward. "God isn't treating us fairly," he complained bitterly to his wife.

"Why don't you pray about it?" his wife advised.

A short time later, the wife noticed a change in her husband's demeanor. "What happened?" she asked.

The man replied, "The Lord put His hand on my shoulder and simply said, 'But you're not home yet!'"

○ ○ ○ ○ ○

In heaven a crown is waiting for me which the Lord, the righteous Judge, will give me on that great day of his return. And not just to me, but to all those whose lives show that they are eagerly looking forward to his coming back again.

2 TIMOTHY 4:8 TLB

In heaven, to be even the least is a great thing, for all will be great.

... years ago, a young man was
wo... ...ard as a section hand for a
rail... ...any. His superiors offered him
the ... ...ty to work in the shipping office
for ... , and he jumped at the chance.

... ...at time, the superintendent
as... ...ng substitute clerk for some vital
fa... ...res. "Have them on my desk when
I ... three days," he said. The young
... now anything about bookkeeping,
... ...ed three days and three nights
... ...ep. He had the facts and figures
... the superintendent returned.

... ...oung man, of course, won the
... of his superintendent, and as soon
... ...anent position opened, he recom-
... ...ne young man for the job. Over
... young man was promoted many
... each time, he was applauded for his
... ...ness and trustworthiness. He eventu-
... ...me vice-president of the Ralston
... ...ompany in Saint Louis, Missouri.

... ...ve each difficult task and each
... ...e chore or request your best effort.
... ...l be rewarded not only according to
... ...ks you complete, but also for the way
... ...h you complete them!

o o o o o

*...w me a person who cannot bother to
...little things, and I'll show you a person
...ho cannot be trusted to do big things.*

HOW thorough am I at doing the little things?

_____ .
_____ .
_____ .
_____ .
_____ .
_____ .
_____ .
_____ .
_____ .
_____ .
_____ .
_____ .
_____ .
_____ .
_____ .
_____ .

Work hard so God can approve you.
Be a good worker, one who does
not need to be ashamed.

2 TIMOTHY 2:15 NLT

When I look at the bigger picture, I see . . .

_____

_____

_____

_____

_____

_____

_____

_____

_____

_____

_____

_____

_____

_____

_____

A small-town chamber of commerce once invited a man to address their annual banquet. The speaker was asked to be motivational, since the town's economy had been bad that year, and people were discouraged.

During his presentation, the speaker took a large piece of white paper and made a black dot in the center of it with a marking pen. He then held the paper up before the audience and asked, "What do you see?"

One person replied, "I see a black dot."

The speaker said, "Fine. What else do you see?"

Others chimed in, "A black dot."

The speaker asked, "Don't you see anything besides the dot?"

The audience responded with a resounding "No!"

"But you've overlooked the most important thing," the speaker replied. "You've missed seeing the sheet of paper!" He then went on to explain, "In our lives, we are often distracted by small, dot-like failures. They keep us from seeing the blessings, successes, and joys that are far more important than the disappointments that try to monopolize our energy and attention. I encourage you to focus on the big picture of what is right rather than the small view of what is wrong."

Are you so preoccupied today with what is that you've lost sight of what _can be?_ Step back, and see the bigger picture!

o o o o o

Faith is the substance of things hoped for, the evidence of things not seen.

HEBREWS 11:1 NKJV

Faith is daring the soul to go beyond what the eyes can see.

When I have God's approval, I . . .

...sible to please everybody all of
the ... ...rson can be immensely popular
on... ...virtually unnoticed the next.

... way to live is described in this
po...

...only one method of meetin' life's
...t:

...p on a-strivin' an' hope for the
...st;

...give up the ship an' quit in dismay;
... hammers are thrown when you'd
...ke a bouquet.

...world would be tiresome we'd all
...get the blues,

...the folks in it jest held the same
...views;

...nish your work, show the best of
...your skill,

...he folks won't like it, but other folks
...will.

—Unknown

...pop song of two decades ago seemed
...this sentiment in saying, "You can't
...everybody, you've got to please
...lf." However, a Christian is called to an
...igher standard: "Don't try to please
...dy other than the Lord. Follow in His
...eps, keep His commandments, and do
...best to fulfill His will for your life."
...ately, pleasing Him is all that matters.

o o o o o

*I don't know the secret to success,
but the key to failure is to try
to please everyone.*

_____.
_____.
_____.
_____.
_____.
_____.
_____.
_____.
_____.
_____.
_____.
_____.
_____.
_____.
_____.
_____.

"No one can serve two masters; for either
he will hate the one and love the other, or
he will hold to one and despise the other."

MATTHEW 6:24 NASB

Live in the Present

Today I need to focus on . . .

_____

_____

_____

_____

_____

_____

_____

_____

_____

_____

_____

_____

_____

_____

Sometimes we can become so preoccupied with the future that we lose all sense of the present! We can become so concerned about our next shot, our next match, our next game, our next project that we have no concentration or mental power left for the present moment. We become crippled in the now when we constantly live in anticipation of what's next.

Leon Lett learned that the hard way. A defensive tackle for the Dallas Cowboys, Lett hadn't scored a touchdown since he was in grade school. But in the 1993 Super Bowl, he got his chance. The Buffalo Bills' quarterback fumbled right in front of him, and Lett was there to scoop up the ball and head for the goal line.

Seeing no one between him and a sure touchdown, Lett threw out his arms when he reached the ten-yard line, thrilled at his uncontested sixty-four-yard scramble to the end zone. Unfortunately, he didn't hear Don Beebe, the Bills' wide receiver, in pursuit of him. At the one-yard line, Beebe lunged forward and knocked the ball from Lett's outstretched hand, stealing the touchdown from him.

Stay focused on the task at hand. Keep yourself in the here and now. Then you'll be better prepared for tomorrow when it comes.

o o o o

"Do not be anxious for tomorrow; for tomorrow will care for itself. Each day has enough trouble of its own."

MATTHEW 6:34 NASB

It is a mistake to look too far ahead. Only one link of the chain of destiny can be handled at a time.

Have I been given a warning I should heed?

, a corps of civil engineers went
to at a dam in Pennsylvania that
co waters of several streams that
flo toward a valley. Concerned by
w , they went to the town just
be m and reported to its officials,
" unsafe. The people of your town
a r."

ficials replied, "You're just trying
. The dam is all right. We've heard
"

all, the engineers revisited the dam
back again, saying, "We are warning
re in danger every hour."

, the people laughed as if to say,
if you can." In the spring, the
again went to the dam, and again
ned the townspeople. Their warning
issed.

teen days later, a boy on a horse rode
the valley at a dead run shouting,
r your lives! The dam has broken, and
ter is coming." The people only
d at him, certain he was only trying to
them. But in a few minutes, a wall of
water struck the town, and in less than
minutes, Johnstown was in ruins. More
thirty-seven hundred people died.

If you are warned you have a problem,
it that it exists, then don't delay in fixing
ake action to bring about a solution.

o o o o

None so deaf as those who will not hear.

Noah . . . trusted God. When he heard
God's warning about the future, Noah
believed him even though there was then
no sign of a flood, and wasting no time, he
built the ark and saved his family.

HEBREWS 11:7 TLB

A Willing Worker

What is my assignment in the body of Christ?

_____

_____

_____

_____

_____

_____

_____

_____

_____

_____

_____

_____

_____

_____

A crude little lifesaving station once stood on a dangerous seacoast known for shipwrecks. The station was only a hut with one small boat, but volunteers tirelessly kept their watch over the churning seas.

Some of those they rescued and others who admired their work began to volunteer. New boats were purchased. New crews were trained. Some of the members raised funds to build a bigger station with newer equipment and better lifesaving systems.

Over time, the station began to be less of a lifesaving station and more of a boat club, with only a few members actually involved in patrolling the seas and rescuing those in danger. Eventually, so few members of the station were interested in the lifesaving missions, they hired professional lifeboat crews to do it, but only when storms arose.

About that time a large ship experienced an explosion in its engine room and began to take on water. Its SOS signal went unnoticed in the lifesaving station—the regular members were too busy with other matters. The ship was already sinking by the time a lifeboat was launched. Many people died.

Would you hear an SOS call today, or are you just a member of a yacht club? Are you content with being a member of the body of Christ, or are you willing to share in the Great Commission? Discover the joy of being a coworker in the kingdom.

o o o o o

He said to His disciples, "The harvest is plentiful, but the workers are few."

MATTHEW 9:37 NASB

The world is full of willing people: some willing to work, the rest willing to let them.

... amson was a Welsh miner.
Eac... ...t in long, hard hours at the
min... ...in constant danger—just to
ear... ... wage. One day, the foreman of
the... ...e to him and said, "Thomas, I've
fou... ...er job for you above ground.
Yo... ...ss to do and earn more money.
A... ...rested?"

... ...s," said Thomas, "I'm very inter-
e... ...t, would you consider giving the
jo... ...end Tregony instead? He isn't as
s... ...m, and he's not able to work as
h... ...n. I fear the work below in the
... ...orten his life, and I will lose my
... ...t he have this job?"

...reman was moved by Thomas's
... ...and gave the job to Tregony.
... ...ntinued to work hard, and when
... ...oove-ground position opened, the
... ...gain approached Thomas about the
... ...ime, he accepted the offer. Thomas
... ...ny went on to work side by side for
... ...des.

...en you selflessly give for another
...ou build an honorable reputation.
...on will surely follow.

o o o o

*...o one is useless in this world who
...ens the burden of it to anyone else.*

Whose burden can I help lift today?

_____.
_____.
_____.
_____.
_____.
_____.
_____.
_____.
_____.
_____.
_____.
_____.
_____.
_____.
_____.

Bear ye one another's burdens,
and so fulfill the law of Christ.

GALATIANS 6:2

Do What You Love

What things have I always enjoyed doing?

_____

_____

_____

_____

_____

_____

_____

_____

_____

_____

_____

_____

_____

A designer in Dallas, Texas, was once asked by a client to build a large, elaborate model. It was one that called for several building interiors and hundreds of human figures. The model was to be created in a scale of one inch to five feet, which meant that each of the human figures was only a little more than an inch in height. Each one had to be hand-painted, using a brush with a single hair.

As the designer hunched over his table one day, painstakingly painting the figures and then carefully gluing them into place, one of his employees asked him, "Don't you find this tedious?"

The designer replied, "Tedious? My goodness, no! I've loved making and painting models ever since I made my first model airplane at age seven. I just can't believe someone is actually paying me to do this!"

Whether you work with your hands or your mind, loving what you do is the secret to having "fun" while you make money. Indeed, work will cease to be "work."

A kindergarten teacher once said about her class of five-year-olds, "They build and tear down and rebuild more in a day than most construction workers do in weeks, but they never call it work. They call it play!"

o o o o o

It is good and fitting for one to eat and drink, and to enjoy the good of all his labor in which he toils under the sun all the days of his life which God gives him; for it is his heritage.

ECCLESIASTES 5:18 NKJV

Find out what you love to do, and you will never have to work another day in your life.

...ones began his career as a clerk in a ... store. He soon gained a reputation ... a bright, ambitious employee—a yo... ...own for good work habits, fine m... ...an easy-going personality. The fo... ...ts people referred to when prais-in... ...however, were his honesty and t... ...ess. It was this reputation that c... ...attention of Henry J. Raymond, a ... ...ournalist, and together Raymond ... ...tarted the *New York Times*.

...nes continued to live up to his ... His loyalty to Raymond and his ... a businessman won him great ... New York City.

...the *Times* began a crusade against ...ed and his corrupt dynasty. Jones ... an under-the-table offer of five ...thousand dollars—a vast sum at the ...om associates of Tweed. All he had to ...retire to Europe. "You can live like a ...he rest of your days," the man making ...r said.

...t Jones replied, "Yes, and know myself ...day to be a rascal."

...clean conscience can't be bought. That ...t makes it so highly valued! Keeping a ...conscience is as simple as deciding to do ...ecide not to let tempting offers influence ...And remember, God is right there to give ...the strength to overcome any temptation.

○ ○ ○ ○ ○

There is one thing alone that stands the brunt of life throughout its length: a quiet conscience.

HOW committed am I to keeping a clean conscience?

_____ .
_____ .
_____ .
_____ .
_____ .
_____ .
_____ .
_____ .
_____ .
_____ .
_____ .
_____ .
_____ .
_____ .
_____ .
_____ .
_____ .
_____ .

If our hearts do not condemn us, we have confidence before God.

1 JOHN 3:21 NIV

Continue Setting Goals

What goals have intimidated me that I want to conquer?

. _____

. _____

. _____

. _____

. _____

. _____

. _____

. _____

. _____

. _____

. _____

. _____

. _____

. _____

. _____

After falling twice in the 1988 Olympic speed-skating races, Dan Jansen sought out sports psychologist Dr. Jim Loehr, who helped him find a new balance between sport and life, and who helped him pay more attention to the mental aspects of skating. Peter Mueller became his coach, putting him through workouts that Dan has since described as the "toughest I've ever known." By the time the 1994 Olympics arrived, Jansen had more confidence than ever. He had set a five-hundred-meter world record just two months before. That race seemed to be all his!

During the five-hundred-meter race, Jansen fell. He was shaken. Dr. Loehr immediately advised, "Start preparing for the one thousand. Put the five hundred behind you immediately. Stop reliving it." The one thousand! For years Dan had felt he could not win at that distance. He had always considered it his weaker event. Now it was his last chance for an Olympic medal. As the race began, Jansen said, "I just seemed to be sailing along," and then he slipped and came within an inch of stepping on a lane marker. Still, he didn't panic. He raced on and recorded a world-record time that won him the gold medal!

Once you reach a goal or master a skill, set your sights higher. As you approach each goal, set a new one. Don't be intimidated! Your toughest goal can become your greatest triumph.

o O o O o

I am bringing all my energies to bear on this one thing: Forgetting the past and looking forward to what lies ahead, I strain to reach the end of the race and receive the prize.

PHILIPPIANS 3:13-14 TLB

Unless you try to do something beyond what you have already mastered, you will never grow.

- ople are unreasonable, illogical,
  red, and arrogant, love them

- ople insist that your goodness
  selfish ulterior motives, do
  eds anyway.

- ou are successful, people may
  jealous of you. Succeed anyway.

- ou are honest and frank, some
  k to twist your words against
  honest and frank anyway.

- you do good deeds today, some
  get about them by tomorrow. Do
  eds anyway.

- you show yourself to be a big
  with great ideas, don't be surprised
  are opposed by small people with
  minds. Think big anyway.

- someone seeks to destroy
  ight what you have spent years
  ng, build anyway.

- Twain once said, "Always do right.
  gratify most people, and astonish

○ ○ ○ ○ ○

*When you soar like an eagle,
you attract hunters.*

How can I help my friends do the right thing?

_____ .
_____ .
_____ .
_____ .
_____ .
_____ .
_____ .
_____ .
_____ .
_____ .
_____ .
_____ .
_____ .
_____ .
_____ .
_____ .
_____ .

"Love your enemies, bless them that
curse you, do good to them that hate you,
and pray for them which despitefully
use you, and persecute you."

MATTHEW 5:44

Instead of judging others, I'll get busy . . .

_____

_____

_____

_____

_____

_____

_____

_____

_____

_____

_____

_____

_____

_____

President Theodore Roosevelt once said, "It is not the critic who counts, not the person who points out where the doer of deeds could have done better. The credit belongs to the person who is actually in the arena; whose face is marred by dust and sweat and blood; who strives valiantly; who errs and comes up short again and again; who knows the great enthusiasm, the devotion, and spends himself or herself in a worthy cause; who at best knows in the end the triumph of high achievement; and at the worst, at least fails while daring greatly; so that his or her place shall never be with those cold and timid souls who know neither victory nor defeat."

It actually takes very little effort to voice criticism. Judging others requires no degree, no expertise, no background, no qualifications. It requires no investment of time, resources, or self. In other words, it costs nothing. And because of that, criticism is usually worth just that: nothing.

On the other hand, a life well lived is one that has few apologies to make. It is highly invested with self, energy, resources, and time. It is rich in friends, associates, and good deeds. It is built by effort and morality. And because of that, it is beyond value.

o   o   o   o   o

"Do not judge, or you too will be judged. For in the same way you judge others, you will be judged."
MATTHEW 7:1-2 NIV

Those that have done nothing in life are not qualified to be judge of those that have done little.

Do I have a standing appointment with God? When is it?

In the introduction to Catherine Ma_____ _loser Walk, her husband of tw___ ___ years, Leonard LeSourd, writes ab___ ___ marriage in 1959:

> ___erine had huge adjustments to ___ sold her Washington dream ___ move to Chappaqua, forty ___ th of New York City, so that I ___ tinue to commute to my job at ___ s in the city. My children— ___ ; Chester, six; Jeffry, three—had ___ ough a deeply unsettling two ___ justing to a variety of house- ___ . They had mixed feelings toward ___ into a new house, and especially ___ "the new Mommie that Daddy's ___ home." Catherine's son, Peter ___ ineteen, was going through a ___ of rebellion at Yale. . . . Catherine ___ had so many things to pray about ___ e began to rise an hour early each ___ ing to read the Bible and seek ___ ers together. Her current journal lay ___ beside us in these pre-dawn prayer ___ , recording our changing needs, His ___ anging faithfulness.[24]

___ he more you have crammed into your ___ le and the more problems you have, ___ ore you have to pray about!

o o o o o

___on't pray when you feel like it. Have ___ appointment with the Lord, and keep it. A man is powerful on his knees.

_____ .
_____ .
_____ .
_____ .
_____ .
_____ .
_____ .
_____ .
_____ .
_____ .
_____ .
_____ .
_____ .
_____ .
_____ .
_____ .

> Evening and morning and at noon I will pray, and cry aloud, And He shall hear my voice.
>
> PSALM 55:17 NKJV

He Wants to Use You

What mission is right in front of me?

_____
_____
_____
_____
_____
_____
_____
_____
_____
_____
_____
_____
_____
_____
_____

Was God telling him to stay in London rather than go to China? Thomas Barnardo had come to London for missionary training, only to have a ten-year-old child show him a rooftop where eleven homeless boys were sleeping. Barnardo's heart was touched. He set about finding temporary lodging for the boys.

Other midnight tours of the area revealed many more homeless youth—as many as seventy-three in one night. China would have to wait. God had given him London. Barnardo sold some 30,000 copies of the Scriptures in the public houses and marketplaces to raise money for his work among the children. He was often rejected for defending them, even sustaining physical injury.

In one attack, he suffered two broken ribs. When a cholera epidemic hit London in 1866, he and others worked tirelessly, only to see thousands die. He eventually opened a "Home for Destitute Boys" and later, a "Village for Girls." Through the next several decades, he built numerous homes and villages that cared for some 60,000 abandoned children.

Barnardo's missionary desire was put to work by his being "The Father of Nobody's Children." And happily, he lived long enough to see seventeen of the youth he rescued take the Gospel to foreign lands!

o o o o o

"Truly, truly, I say to you, he who believes in Me, the works that I do shall he do also; and greater works than these shall he do; because I go to the Father."

JOHN 14:12 NASB

Attempt great things for God; expect great things from God.

Empowered by Him

ke dripping with perspiration;
her just broken. Her body was
ach e was completely drained. She
co gine speaking that night, and yet,
wl to do? She was the only
sp duled for the annual vacation-
cl ol adult class. To cancel would not
o eated somewhat of a crisis, but
s ould also reflect a failure of her
c ed faith that God helps and heals.
I anceling, she prayed.

ghout the day, Jane felt no better.
ring all the energy she had, she
d drove herself to the meeting.
minutes, she found herself thinking,
this. Only by God's help will I even
the lectern. Every step, every action,
najor effort. She could tell her fever
ned.

e behind the lectern, however, she
at she had energy to speak a
, and then another, and yet another.
ke with great vitality and clarity of
for nearly an hour. Upon return home,
r, she collapsed into her bed where she
nd slept for eighteen hours.

he later said, "What I could not possi-
e done in my own strength . . . I did in
ength."

○ ○ ○ ○

Anybody can do their best. God
helps us to do better than our best.

In what situations do I need to be empowered by God?

_____ .

_____ .

_____ .

_____ .

_____ .

_____ .

_____ .

_____ .

_____ .

_____ .

_____ .

_____ .

_____ .

_____ .

_____ .

Glory be to God who by his mighty
power at work within us is able to
do far more than we would ever
dare to ask or even dream of.

EPHESIANS 3:20 TLB

Don't Be Foolish

What is my responsibility, and what is God's?

_____
_____
_____
_____
_____
_____
_____
_____
_____
_____
_____
_____
_____
_____
_____

The story is told of a farmer who told a friend that he had decided he no longer needed to work. "God will do it for me," the man said.

"Oh, really?" the friend said. "What makes you think that?"

"Well," the farmer said, "do you remember that old shed I used to have? I've been meaning to tear it down for years, but lightning struck it last month and burned it to the ground, and then the wind came up and blew away all the ashes."

"And on the basis of that, you're going to let God do all your work?" the friend asked.

"Oh, no," the farmer continued. "Last weekend my wife asked me to wash our car, but a big rainstorm blew in before I got to it, and the rain washed the car clean."

The friend shook his head in dismay, and before he could say anything further, the farmer asked, "Do you know what I'm doing out here on my porch right now?"

The friend said, "No, what?"

The farmer replied, "I'm waiting for an earthquake to shake my crop of potatoes out of the ground!"

Don't expect God to do what He has empowered and enabled you to do.

o o o o

Some men are so lazy they won't even feed themselves!

PROVERBS 19:24 TLB

Shallow people believe in luck . . . strong people believe in cause and effect.

Have I been a good steward of my time?

...erday to tomorrow:
...was young like you,
...s fond of boasting
...meant to do.

...le I fell a-dreaming
...he pleasant way,
...I scarcely knew it,
...I was today!

...today, so quickly
...le course was run,
...not time to finish
...half the things begun.

...d I could try it over,
...can ne'er go back;
...sterday forever,
...w must be, alack!

...so, my good tomorrow,
...ou would make a name
...t history shall cherish
...on its roll of fame,

...all prepared and ready
...ur noblest part to play
...those new fleeting hours
...hen you shall be today.

—The Pacific

o o o o o

...st thou love life? Then do not squander
...e, for that is the stuff life is made of.

_____.
_____.
_____.
_____.
_____.
_____.
_____.
_____.
_____.
_____.
_____.
_____.
_____.
_____.

Remember how short my time is.

PSALM 89:47

Be the Person God Made You

What are the characteristics I most like about myself?

. _____

. _____

. _____

. _____

. _____

. _____

. _____

. _____

. _____

. _____

. _____

. _____

. _____

. _____

. _____

. _____

. _____

Pat loved children and was quick to volunteer when the call went out for a Sunday-school teacher for the five-year-olds. There, she met Andy. He was a likable boy, but he lacked confidence, and he rarely smiled.

One Sunday while the class was coloring a Bible scene, Andy became so frustrated he tore his paper in two, threw it on the floor, and crawled under the craft table. Pat thought, *I go where he goes!* And she immediately crawled under the table, where she found Andy muttering, "You're so dumb. You can't even color in the lines." He seemed surprised to see Pat join him under the table.

Pat quickly said, "Who said you always have to stay in the lines? Some of the smartest, most creative kids I've ever known didn't color inside the lines."

Andy stared at her. This was obviously a new idea to him. Then Pat said, "I like your picture. Can I tape it back together and keep it?"

Andy was stunned but finally said, "I guess." While Andy watched, Pat taped the pieces together and carefully put the picture in her satchel. As he returned to the craft table, Pat overheard him say, "I like coloring!"

Maybe you don't like to be squeezed into a box. You don't have to be! Just be the person God created you to be, and you will bring color to your world.

o o o o o

We are God's workmanship, created in Christ Jesus to do good works, which God prepared in advance for us to do.

EPHESIANS 2:10 NIV

Every human being is intended to have a character of his own; to be what no others are, and to do what no other can do.

Prepare and Do

In _____ *Hopefully,* Stan Mooneyham
wr_____ owing:

> _____ when—
> _____ e, after—
> _____ ey, but first—

_____ n always find reasons for delay,
a_____ nes they may even seem to be
v_____ s. A close friend of mine and I
v_____ to preach about the same time,
_____ nt to university together. I was out
_____ homiletics in rural Oklahoma
_____ uring those four years of study, but
_____ nsisted he wouldn't preach his first
_____ ntil he had received his Ph.D. That
_____ thirty years ago. I am still mutilating
_____ s, but my friend isn't preaching at all.
_____ did. Preparation is important, but
_____ an important part of preparation. . . .
_____ ld Testament we hear much about
_____ of "firstfruits." God's portion came
_____ the top. Nowadays we are more
_____ be known by and for our "lastfruits."
_____ ear the hold button on the hotline to
_____ , these classic words would be appro-
_____ "If not I, who? If not here, where? If
_____ ow, when?"[25]

○ ○ ○ ○ ○

_____ crastination is the thief of time, but it
_____ nuch more. It clutters up our lives with
_____ appalling number of half-done things.

What do I need to do *now?*

_____ .

_____ .

_____ .

_____ .

_____ .

_____ .

_____ .

_____ .

_____ .

_____ .

_____ .

_____ .

_____ .

_____ .

_____ .

_____ .

Don't procrastinate—
there's no time to lose.
PROVERBS 6:4 THE MESSAGE

Master Yourself

What must I master about myself?

. _____

. _____

. _____

. _____

. _____

. _____

. _____

. _____

. _____

. _____

. _____

. _____

. _____

. _____

. _____

Bobby Jones, one of golf's greatest players, was only five years old when he first swung a golf club. By the age of twelve, he was winning club tournaments. At the time, he was known for his hot temper, and he soon had the nickname "Club Thrower."

Jones became friends with a man named Grandpa Bart, who worked part-time in the club pro shop. Bart had been an excellent golfer but had retired when arthritis gripped his hands. After Bobby lost the National Amateur Tournament at the age of fourteen, he said, "Bobby, you are good enough to win that tournament, but you'll never win until you can control that temper of yours. You miss a shot—you get upset—and then you lose."

Bobby knew Grandpa Bart was right, and he set to work to improve, not his golf swing, but his mood swings. When Bobby won a major tournament at age twenty-one, Grandpa Bart said, "Bobby was fourteen when he mastered the game of golf, but he was twenty-one when he mastered himself."

Norms and records are always established in relationship to other people's performance, but the true "standards of success" are established within and then lived out in relationships.

o o o o

Forget your opponents;
always play against par.

He that is slow to anger is better than the mighty; and he that ruleth his spirit than he that taketh a city.

PROVERBS 16:32

Play to Win

... back victories by the Dallas
C... the Super Bowl in 1993 and
1... ask the fact that Jimmy Johnson,
th... egendary former coach, knew as
m... losing as he did about winning. In
... st season in Dallas, Johnson's team
... e win and fifteen losses! Yet this
... ing losing season was still slightly
... not as humiliating as his first year
... chool defensive coach, when his
... ed the season 0-10.

... son said about that first season in
... Ve had the worst team in the NFL,
... uldn't accept anything but being in
... r Bowl."

... nson kept a positive attitude. If a
... back had the ball, he shouted,
... t the ball," rather than, "Don't
... " To his field-goal kickers he'd say,
... this," not "Don't miss." After a loss,
... end his post-game time plotting the
... vin, rather than second-guessing what
... one wrong.

... The Cowboys responded and improved.
... k four seasons of hard work, but finally,
... r Bowl rings were on their fingers.[26]

... You may not win every contest you
... sue, but if you play to win, you have a
... ch better chance!

○ ○ ○ ○ ○

Never play not to lose;
always play to win.

HOW can I be more positive in my quest to win?

_____ .

_____ .

_____ .

_____ .

_____ .

_____ .

_____ .

_____ .

_____ .

_____ .

_____ .

_____ .

_____ .

_____ .

Thanks be to God, Who gives us the
victory [making us conquerors]
through our Lord Jesus Christ.

1 CORINTHIANS 15:57 AMP

HOW can I solidify my goal?

_____

_____

_____

_____

_____

_____

_____

_____

_____

_____

_____

_____

_____

_____

_____

After Dwight Eisenhower won the Republican nomination for president from Robert Taft in 1952, a reporter asked Taft about the disappointment that he surely must have felt in setting a goal and not reaching it. Taft admitted, "My great goal was to become president of the United States in 1953." But then he added, "Instead, I became a senator from Ohio!"

Ultimately, Taft's goal was to be elected to a political office and to serve his nation as a representative of the people. And in that he succeeded. If he hadn't run for an office, however, he would never have been elected to one!

That's true for the accomplishment of any real goal in life. You've got to throw your hat into the ring and start pursuing your goal—campaign for its accomplishment the best you know how, thoroughly brief yourself on the issues that are important, define your stance and stay true to it, and maintain a positive attitude even in the face of serious opposition.

You can't cross the finish line if you never leave the starting blocks.

o o o o

Saddle your dreams before you ride 'em.

Write the vision, and make it plain upon tables, that he may run that readeth it.

HABAKKUK 2:2

God Can Turn It Around

...s a great amateur boxer. He
po... ...at knockout power in both hands
an... ...ned to become a top professional
p... ...efore turning pro, he broke both
o... He would never be able to punch
v... ...ver he once possessed. Both his
... ...his manager told him he would
... ...me a world champion.

...Tunney didn't listen to them. He
...e could excel at his profession,
...e major obstacle he encountered.
...become a champion as a [power]
...he said, "I'll make it as a boxer."

...unney, knowing that he could no
...ely on his knockout power, set out to
...is boxing skills. He learned to bob
...ve and throw accurate—albeit less
...—punches.

...one of the biggest fights of his career,
...faced Jack Dempsey, known as the
...a Mauler, a man with feared knockout
... But, using the skills he might not have
...ped had he not had the injury, Tunney
...xed Dempsey and became the heavy-
...t champion of the world.

...Life might alter the path you take to
...ess, just as it did to Gene Tunney. But that
...sn't mean you can't still get to where you
...t to go.

o o o o o

*The great pleasure in life is doing
what people say you cannot do.*

Do I trust God to turn my defeats around?

_____ .
_____ .
_____ .
_____ .
_____ .
_____ .
_____ .
_____ .
_____ .
_____ .
_____ .
_____ .
_____ .
_____ .
_____ .
_____ .
_____ .

We know that in everything God works
for the good of those who love him.

ROMANS 8:28 NCV

Do I need to start anew in any areas? Which ones?

·_____
·_____
·_____
·_____
·_____
·_____
·_____
·_____
·_____
·_____
·_____
·_____
·_____
·_____
·_____

On the night of December 9, 1914, Edison Industries was destroyed by fire. The loss exceeded $2 million, and included the vast majority of Thomas Alva Edison's work. Edison was insured for only $238 because the buildings were constructed of concrete, which at that time, was thought to make a building fireproof. At sixty-seven years of age, Edison watched his life's work go up in flames.

The next morning, after firefighters had finally brought the inferno under control, Edison surveyed his charred dreams and crushed hopes. As he surveyed the scene, he said, "There is great value in disaster. All our mistakes are burned up. Thank God we can start anew."

Three weeks after the fire, Edison Industries produced the first phonograph.

In every setback one can find the seeds of a future success. Such a success, however, will not be automatic. One must plant those seeds with vision, fertilize them with hope and hard work, and continue to water them with enthusiasm.

o o o o o

An inconvenience is only an adventure wrongly considered.

We are hunted down, but God never abandons us. We get knocked down, but we get up again and keep going.

2 CORINTHIANS 4:9 TLB

You Are Responsible for Your Destiny

A Chicago bank once considered a young Bostonian for employment and decided to check out his references, one of whom was an officer at a Boston investment house, an investment executive who responded to the request for a reference saying the young man's father was a Cabot, his mother was a Lowell, in his background was a happy blend of Saltonstalls, Peabodys, and other members of Boston's first families. The man gave his highest recommendation without hesitation!

A few days later, the personnel manager of the Chicago bank called the man who had sent the letter and said, "We'd like to have a work reference from you before we hire this young man."

The executive replied, "I told you all about him. Didn't you receive my letter?"

The personnel manager replied, "Yes, but we are contemplating using this young man for work not for breeding purposes."

Your family tree may provide solid roots from which you can grow, but you alone are responsible for the fruit you produce in your life. Genuine purpose in life does not come because others set it up for you; it comes as you pursue what you desire to achieve and to be.

o o o o o

Destiny is not a matter of chance; it is a matter of choice. It is not a thing to be waited for; it is a thing to be achieved.

HOW can I be more responsible for my destiny?

_____.
_____.
_____.
_____.
_____.
_____.
_____.
_____.
_____.
_____.
_____.
_____.
_____.
_____.
_____.

Diligent hands will rule, but laziness ends in slave labor.

PROVERBS 12:24 NIV

Humor Heals Relationships

Am I sharing enough laughter with others?

_____

_____

_____

_____

_____

_____

_____

_____

_____

_____

_____

_____

_____

_____

Ludwig Bemelmans wrote in *My War with the United States* that among the many regulations published by the United States Army is a book that gives advice on practical matters to noncommissioned officers. One piece of advice tells an officer how to help soldiers who have quarreled become friends again. The men are to be assigned to wash the same window— one working on the outside, the other inside.

Writes Bemelmans, "Looking at each other, they soon have to laugh and all is forgotten. It works; I have tried it."

Laughter shared between friends is one of life's great treasures. Not only is laughter free, but it is a renewable resource and one with countless benefits. It restores a sense of balance to an oppressive day. It builds up energy in a flagging spirit. It helps lighten the load of sorrow, grief, and suffering. It tightens the bonds of relationships.

Laughter has an extremely high rate of return. It brings positive results when we are able to laugh with others.

○ ○ ○ ○ ○

Imagination was given to human beings to compensate them for what they are not. A sense of humor was provided to console them for what they are.

A merry heart doeth good like a medicine.

PROVERBS 17:22

...rs, *The Wide World of Sports* televi-
si... ...n had, as part of its opening
s... ...scene used to depict "the agony
o... ...he scene showed a skier heading
d... jump in good form, and then, for
... ...t reason, he tumbles head over
... ...e side of the jump, bouncing off
... ...rting structure. The scene caused
...ers to groan in sympathy.

...t viewers didn't know, however, was
...particular skier chose to fall rather
...nish the jump. He explained later, the
...face had become slick with ice—
...o fast for jumping. Midway down the
... realized that he was picking up so
...eed that if he completed the jump, he
...ery likely land beyond the sloped
...area and hit level ground, which may
...ell have been fatal. Although it looked
...and painful, by taking the alternative
...the skier actually suffered no more
... headache.

...Changing directions in midcourse may
...etimes be painful or difficult. Halting a
...ect that seems headed for failure may be
...enging and stressful, but that is
...etimes the wisest decision to make now
...rder to succeed later!

o o o o o

*Do not persist in folly. It is not
a badge of character to continue
down the wrong road.*

How can I tell when it's time to change plans?

———————————————————— .
———————————————————— .
———————————————————— .
———————————————————— .
———————————————————— .
———————————————————— .
———————————————————— .
———————————————————— .
———————————————————— .
———————————————————— .
———————————————————— .
———————————————————— .
———————————————————— .
———————————————————— .
———————————————————— .
———————————————————— .
———————————————————— .
———————————————————— .

The way of a fool is right in his own eyes,
But he who heeds counsel is wise.

PROVERBS 12:15 NKJV

More Beyond

Knowing there is "more beyond" makes me feel . . .

._____

._____

._____

._____

._____

._____

._____

._____

._____

._____

._____

._____

._____

._____

Spain once controlled both sides of the Mediterranean at the Straits of Gibraltar, a powerful position for any seafaring nation. With great pride, the Spanish minted a coin depicting the two Pillars of Hercules—the name given to the promontories of rock on either side of the passageway. Over the pillars, they placed a scroll that read, "ne plus ultra," which means "no more beyond."

One day, however, bold Spanish sailors made their way through the Straits of Gibraltar and headed for the high seas. They sailed south to Africa, then around its horn to Asia, and eventually across the Atlantic to the New World.

The Spanish wisely rethought their position and stamped a new set of coins. They resembled the old, except that one word had been left off—the word "ne." The new coin read "plus ultra"—"more beyond."

Regardless of your position today, take hope in the fact that there is "more beyond" for you. Life has greater blessings in store for you, and eternity holds the greatest potential for blessings you will ever know.

o O o O o

*When all else is lost,
the future still remains.*

Ask me and I will tell you some remarkable secrets about what is going to happen.

JEREMIAH 33:3 TLB

Don't Be Distracted

... of juvenile thieves had a well-
r... ...hod of operation. They would
e... ...e as a group. Then, one or two of
t... ...l separate from the rest of the
... others would move to a distant
... the store and start a loud
... causing enough commotion to grab
... on of the clerks and customers. All
... d be turned toward the distur-
... ving the one or two "roving" thieves
... tunity to fill their pockets with
... dise or cash and leave the store
... nyone suspected what had happened.
... vould be hours, sometimes even days
... fore the victimized merchant realized
... ere missing and called the police. By
... ne, the thieves were long gone, and
... vas no possibility of tracing or recov-
... vhat had been taken.

... emptation works the same way. It
... cts us by using the allure of fame,
... ne, power, or satisfaction of fleshly
... es. In the process, we are often diverted
... critical steps we need to take toward
... ccomplishment of our goals. When we
... our eyes off what is truly important in
... lives, we run the risk of losing it!

○ ○ ○ ○ ○

*No matter how many pleasures Satan
offers you, his ultimate intention is to ruin
you. Your destruction is his highest priority.*

What are the things that distract me from my goals?

_____.
_____.
_____.
_____.
_____.
_____.
_____.
_____.
_____.
_____.
_____.
_____.
_____.
_____.
_____.

"Satan hath desired to have you, that he
may sift you as wheat: But I have prayed
for thee, that thy faith fail not."

LUKE 22:31-32

Into whom would God have me plant a seed today?

_____

_____

_____

_____

_____

_____

_____

_____

_____

_____

_____

_____

_____

_____

A Christian man was walking to church one night when he encountered four boys loitering on the street corner. He invited them to go to the service with him. They did, and each of the boys also agreed to return to church with him the next Sunday. They became the nucleus of a Sunday-school class the man began to teach.

Years later, a group of the man's friends decided to try to contact the four boys to see what had happened in their lives and to invite them to write a special birthday letter to their teacher to be read at a surprise party. Their letters revealed that one of them had become a missionary to China, one was the president of the Federal Reserve Bank, one was the private secretary to President Herbert Hoover, and the fourth was President Hoover himself!

If you were to hold a handful of pine nuts in your hand today, you could not begin to predict which of the seeds might actually sprout and produce a giant tree. It is amazing that such a large tree might grow from such a small seed. The only way to tell which nuts have trees inside them is to plant them! When you plant acts of kindness and generosity to others, you never know what mighty tree may grow from that small seed.

o o o o

"The kingdom of heaven is like to a grain of mustard seed, which a man took, and sowed in his field: Which indeed is the least of all seeds: but when it is grown, it is the greatest among herbs, and becometh a tree, so that the birds of the air come and lodge in the branches thereof."
MATTHEW 13:31-32

When we do the best that we can, we never know what miracle is wrought in our life, or the life of another.

Earhart had a reputation for
gi   st to any task she undertook. It
w   d of diligence and pursuit of
e   hat led to her being the first
          Columbia University to attain the
          professor.

          she retired, she moved to
          n, DC, and became a parishioner at
          York Avenue Presbyterian Church.
          a member of the church's women's
          n asked Dr. Earhart to give a talk on
          of Job during one of the upcoming
          meetings. She agreed. No doubt the
          vho extended the invitation was
          ing the basic run-of-the-mill presenta-
          t she didn't really know Lida Earhart.

          da studied the Book of Job for two
          s. She researched the archaeological
          s of the time of Job and his contempo-
          and she read numerous commentaries
          alyses by biblical scholars. She deeply
          ered the book's theme. The result was a
          ntation that people were still talking
          t many years later.

          What was amazing to her pastor was
          she had done all that work for an
          dinary church meeting." Lida, however,
          n't know the meaning of ordinary.

          Leaders are made out of ordinary
          ople who choose to go beyond the
          dinary to the extraordinary. That's what
          ts them apart and makes them leaders.

o o o o o

*All excellence involves discipline
and tenacity of purpose.*

What ordinary things can I make extraordinary?

_____ .
_____ .
_____ .
_____ .
_____ .
_____ .
_____ .
_____ .
_____ .
_____ .
_____ .
_____ .
_____ .
_____ .
_____ .
_____ .
_____ .

Whatever your hand finds to do,
do it with all your might.
ECCLESIASTES 9:10 NIV

Share the Gifts God Has Given You

What lasting legacy will I leave?

._____

._____

._____

._____

._____

._____

._____

._____

._____

._____

._____

._____

._____

._____

._____

At age five, he wrote an advanced concerto for the harpsichord. Before he was ten, he had published several violin sonatas and was playing the best of Handel and Bach from memory. Soon after his twelfth birthday, he composed and conducted his first opera. He was awarded an honorary appointment as concertmaster with the Salzburg Symphony Orchestra and within a few years was hailed as the pride of Salzburg.

When he died at the age of thirty-five, he had written forty-one symphonies; fifty-seven arias, duets, tercets, and quartets with orchestral accompaniment; and more than a dozen operas. He is credited with some 600 original compositions in all!

Even so, Johannes Chrysostomus Wolfgangus Amadeus Theophilus Mozart lived most of his life in poverty and died in obscurity. His sick widow seemed indifferent about his death. A few friends made it to the church for his funeral, but a storm prohibited their going to the graveside for his burial. The location of his grave thus became virtually impossible to identify. No shrine marks his resting place.

What is Mozart's legacy? Not the life he lived but the music he gave. As with all of us, what we give to the world of our talent and creativity is what lasts.

o o o o o

> The godly are able to be generous with their gifts.
>
> PSALM 37:26 TLB

If you have a talent, use it in every which way possible. Don't hoard it. Don't dole it out like a miser. Spend it lavishly like a millionaire intent on going broke.

people for who and what they are.
and considerate.
a positive, can-do atmosphere.
sult or demean.
age others.
about past wrongs done to you.
smarter and wiser.
around with positive people.
on smiling at everyone.
lubs or programs at your school
or church.
that God loves you no matter what.
h as often as possible.
e a new friend.
jealousy in the bud.
en your mind to new ideas, new
friendships.
k up after yourself without being asked.
it insisting on being right all the time.
ach out to someone who is struggling.
retch your abilities.
alk about your goals to those who can
help you achieve them.
Uncomplicate your life.
Vindicate yourself by your upright
conduct, not excuses.
Wait to talk. Don't wait to listen.
Xerox (or photocopy on the machine of
your choice) a humorous quote,
and share it with someone.
Yank hurtful, hateful words from your
speech.
Zero in on what you need most to
accomplish, and do it!

o o o o

*He who stops being better
stops being good.*

Which of my ABCs do I need to work on today?

_____ .
_____ .
_____ .
_____ .
_____ .
_____ .
_____ .
_____ .
_____ .
_____ .
_____ .
_____ .
_____ .
_____ .
_____ .
_____ .
_____ .

Be careful how you act; these are
difficult days. Don't be fools; be wise:
make the most of every opportunity
you have for doing good.
EPHESIANS 5:15-16 TLB

What good has come from the "cracks" in my life?

. _____
. _____
. _____
. _____
. _____
. _____
. _____
. _____
. _____
. _____
. _____
. _____
. _____
. _____
. _____

> It is this God who has made you
> and me into faithful Christians.
>
> 2 CORINTHIANS 1:21 TLB

Long ago there were two jars. Each was carried by a king's waterbearer on opposite ends of a long pole. One jar was perfectly made. It was ornately decorated, with no cracks or chips.

The other jar wasn't much to look at. It was unglazed earthenware—with a crack at its base.

Daily, the waterbearer would walk to the river and fill both containers, then carry them back to the king's palace. Once inside the palace, the first jar offered its full contents into the king's cistern. The other had less to offer. Much of its water had leaked through the crack on the trek from the river to the palace.

Despondent, the cracked jar spoke to the waterbearer one day: "Please, sir, replace me. I try to contain the king's water, but I always fail. I spill so much that my offering cannot compare to what the perfect jar brings. I'm ashamed!"

The waterbearer smiled. "Have you noticed the hill we climb every day?"

"Well, no. I have been so preoccupied with my crack and the water dripping through it that . . ."

"Look now." The jar obeyed. All along the path over the hill bloomed beautiful wildflowers. "Haven't you seen me spreading seeds as I walk up the hill?" asked the waterbearer. "And those flowers you see now have grown from your loss, little jar. Flowers that please the king and all his people."

Like the pot in this folk tale, if you go about your life diligently, you will be able to survey the landscape and see the flowers of faithfulness that you have grown. Not because you are perfect, but because you were faithful to your task.

o o o o

Faithfulness is consecration in overalls.

Today I'll work on my relationship with God by . . .

_____ .
_____ .
_____ .
_____ .
_____ .
_____ .
_____ .
_____ .
_____ .
_____ .
_____ .
_____ .
_____ .
_____ .

...ensign had nearly completed his ...tour of duty when he was given ...ty to display his ability at getting ...er way. With a stream of crisp ...he had the decks buzzing with ...on the ship left port and was ...t of the channel.

...sign's efficiency had been remark-..., the deck was abuzz with talk that ...a new record for getting a ...under way. The ensign glowed at his ...ment and was not all that ...when another seaman approached ...a message from the captain. He was, ...a bit surprised to find that it was a ...ssage, and he was even more ...d when he read, "My personal ...lations upon completing your under-...paration exercise according to the ...d with amazing speed. In your haste, ...r, you have overlooked one of the ...en rules—make sure the captain is ...before getting under way."

...od's Manual for Life, the Bible, is our ...f instructions" for getting our lives ...way. But we must never become so ...d to the Book that we forget the Author ...and the relationship He desires to have ...us on the voyage.

o o o o o

*If at first you don't succeed,
try reading the instructions.*

Take fast hold of instruction; let her not go: keep her; for she is thy life.
PROVERBS 4:13

That Little Extra Touch

What little "extra" things can I do for others?

· _____
· _____
· _____
· _____
· _____
· _____
· _____
· _____
· _____
· _____
· _____
· _____
· _____
· _____

An Oregon schoolteacher went to Nordstrom's department store to buy a one-dollar booklet on how to tie scarves. A store employee told the teacher that, unfortunately, the store was sold out of the item. Four weeks later, the teacher checked her mail and, to her surprise, found two of the booklets—at no charge. That gesture made her a faithful Nordstrom's customer, even though the store didn't have what she wanted the first time around. But that's not the whole story. There is no Nordstrom's department store in the teacher's hometown. She drives 160 miles round-trip to shop at a store that took the time and effort to compensate her because they were out of a simple, inexpensive booklet.

You might not always be able to give teachers, customers, or coworkers exactly what they want. But the way you make up for an oversight, mistake, or shortage can build a greater sense of loyalty and satisfaction than merely meeting the initial request. What will teachers, customers, or bosses remember about you when you are not able to meet a request? The mere fact that you couldn't provide what they wanted? Or, the creative, service-minded way you responded to the situation and turned a negative into a positive?

o o o o

The difference between ordinary and extraordinary is that little extra.

"Whoever compels you to go one mile, go with him two."

MATTHEW 5:41 NKJV

Don't Fly off the Handle

person loses his temper, one of
th___ ___mmon expressions used to
de___ ___ situation is "fly off the handle."
T___ ___ refers to the head of a hammer
c___ ___e from its handle as the carpen-
t___ ___s to use it. Several things happen
a___

___he hammer becomes useless—no
___ good for work. In like manner,
___you lose your temper, you often
___our effectiveness. Anything you say
___ot be taken seriously and is likely to
___productive.

___nd, the hammerhead—twirling out
___ontrol—is likely to cause some type
___damage to anything in its path. When
___ lose your temper, you cause damage
___n if you don't realize it—perhaps
___sically to people or objects in your
___y and nearly always emotionally to
___ose who feel they are victims of
___ncontrolled wrath.

___hird, the repair of both the hammer
___nd the resulting damage takes time.
___When you lose your temper, you may
___ecover right away, but the one who is
the victim of a hot temper rarely recov-
ers as quickly.

Keep your temper today. Nobody else
___ts it.

○ ○ ○ ○ ○

*Your temper is like a fire. It gets very
destructive when it gets out of control.*

When I feel my temper rising,
I will stop it by . . .

_____ .

_____ .

_____ .

_____ .

_____ .

_____ .

_____ .

_____ .

_____ .

_____ .

_____ .

_____ .

_____ .

_____ .

He that hath no rule over his own
spirit is like a city that is broken
down, and without walls.

PROVERBS 25:28

God's answers to tough situations are always . . .

. _____
. _____
. _____
. _____
. _____
. _____
. _____
. _____
. _____
. _____
. _____
. _____
. _____
. _____
. _____

In the seventeenth century, Edinburgh was bustling with both aristocracy and peasants, all living in very close quarters. The Scottish city was built on a hilltop with many enclosed stairways leading down to the city gates below. Each stairway, or "close," was shared by numerous families whose front doors opened onto it. Each close had a gate at the top and one at the bottom that were locked at night for protection. But the plague still found its way inside.

As word reached Edinburgh that the plague was spreading through the low-lying countryside, the city gates were locked to all outsiders. But soon there was a small outbreak inside the city, in Mary King's Close. To prevent further spread of the disease, the city fathers decided upon a simple, yet heartless plan.

The gates to Mary King's Close were locked with all four hundred residents inside. They were given no food or water, and their cries of suffering were ignored, until finally there was only silence. Mary King's Close is locked to this day, a memorial to those whose deaths served as an easy solution.

When faced with a difficult decision, take time to make sure your solution is the best one, not simply the most expedient.

o o o o o

The wisdom that comes from heaven is first of all pure; then peace-loving, considerate, submissive, full of mercy and good fruit, impartial and sincere.

JAMES 3:17 NIV

There can be no such thing as a necessary evil. For if a thing is really necessary, it cannot be an evil, and if it is an evil, it is not necessary.

Reflections

Reflections

Reflections

Acknowledgments

Kin... owledge and thank the following people for the quotes used in this book: Martin Luther
...eodore Roosevelt (10,140), J. C. Penney (11), Dale Carnegie (12), Abraham Lincoln
(13... 33,290), Harvey Firestone (14), Edward Young (15), Ronald Brown (17), Calvin Coolidge
(18... ...minster Fuller (19), Robert Hall (20), Dorothy L. Sayers (22), Chinese Proverb
(23... Les Brown (24), John D. Rockefeller Jr. (25), Dr. Eugene Swearingen (26,28,151), Thomas
Jeff... ...64), Robert C. Edward (29), C. W. Wendte (30), John Bunyan (33), Kin Hubbard (34), Henry
W... ...r (35,126), John A. Shedd (37,46,159), Ralph Waldo Emerson (39,85,163), Dwight L. Moody
(4... Cole (42,143), H. E. Jansen (43), Descartes (47), Helen Keller (48), Seneca (49), Aristotle
(5... Williams (52), William A. Ward (53), Charles Simmons (54), Molière (56), Pope Leo XIII
(5... C. Noble (59), Eleanor Roosevelt (60), John Sculley (61), George Bernard Shaw (62),
B... ...nklin (66,226,269,303,353), Woodrow Wilson (67,179), Charles H. Spurgeon (68,169),
V... ...n Phelps (69), Bertha Munro (70), Terence (71), Cardinal John Henry Newman (76), Henry
V... Longfellow (77,131), Josh Billings (78), Hebrew Proverb (79), Jean Paul Richter (80,247),
N... ...man (81), Samuel Butler (82), H. P. Liddon (83), George Elliot (84), John R. Ricer (87),
P... ...,215), Thomas A. Edison (89,214,267,270), William Shakespeare (90,221), George Edward
V... (91), Bill Cosby (92), Winston Churchill (93), Thomas Wilson (94), Thomas Carlyle (95),
[... Bouhours (96), William H. Danforth (97), Denis Diderot (98), Publilius Syrus (99,162),
I... ...0), Louis D. Brandeis (101), Hannah More (102), Latin Proverb (103), Orlando A. Battista
...y Emerson Fosdick (105,250), Victor Hugo (106), David Dunn (107), Mark Twain (109,293),
...ch (110), Thomas Carlyle (112), Johann Wolfgang von Goethe (113), George Washington
...s Robinson (117), Oswald Chambers (118,203), Miguel de Cervantes (120,198), Ben
...(123), James Whitcomb Riley (124), Zig Ziglar (125), Builder (127), Diane Sawyer (132),
...zner (133), George P. Burnham (134), Frances J. Roberts (135), John Oxenham (136), Helmut
...(137), Dennis Rainey (139), Leo Tolstoy (141), Reginald Wallis (142), Henry Ford (144), George
...rdman (146), Jeremy Taylor (147), Margaret Fuller (148), Samuel Johnson (149), Gary Smalley
...Trent (150,152), Erastus Wiman (153), Henry J. Kaiser (153), Oliver Goldsmith (154), Albert
...158), Joseph Joubert (164,248), Comte Georges-Louis Leclerc De Buffon (167), Frank Borman
...ph Washington Sockman (173), Josiah Gilbert Holland (174), Sister Corita (176), Pablo Casals
...glish Proverb (181), William James (184), Elbert Hubbard (193,256,323), T. J. Bower (194,240),
...Swindoll (195), Benjamin Nathan Cardozo (196), Robert Green Ingersoll (197), Honoré de
...00), Michel Quoist (201), Saint John Chrysostom (202), Babe Ruth (205), Taylor Morgan
...,294), Confucius (207), Mary Kay Ash (209), Charles Schwab (210), William Cowper (213), Sir
...Fuller (216,274,282), Georg Hegel (218), Steve Prefontaine (219), Charles E. Hummel (220),
...th (222), Wayne Gretzky (223), Darrell Royal (224), Aldous Huxley (227), Edmund Burke (229),
...Jackson (230), Phillip James Bailey (232), Billy Graham (235), Lance Armstrong (237), Tertullian
...Mrs. A. J. Stanley (241), Edward Young (242), William Wordsworth (243), Jude Phelps (245,266),
...Smiles (246), Bernard Meltzer (249), Lord Chesterfield (252,265,271), George Herbert (254),
...Luther King Jr. (257), Olivia Kent (259,279), Kent Taylor (261), Jami Josephine (262), Madeleine
...(263), Roy Disney (264), Andrew Carnegie (268), Lord George Noel Gordon Byron (272),
...H. Fischer (275), American Proverb (276), Arabian Proverb (278), Madeline Bridges (280), Solon
...edd and Todd Hafer (283), Grandma Moses (284), Benjamin Lichtenberg (285), Greek Proverb
...Kenyan Proverb (287), Charlotte Bronte (288), Frances Havergal (289), Chamfort (291), Dwight
...enhower (292), William Penn (295), Arnold Palmer (298), Michelangelo (306), Jeremy Collier (307),
...ozer (311,327), George Macdonald (325), William Wolcott (329), Archbishop Anthony Bloom
...Thomas à Kempis (336), Matthew Henry (341), Charles Dickens (343), Diane Ravich (344),
...d E. Osborn (346), Corrie ten Boom (349), William Carey (350), William Ellery Channing (354),
...Cole (355), Walter Bagehot (359), Christian Nestell Bovee (364), Erwin W. Lutzer (365), John W.
...ner (367), Brendan Francis (368), Oliver Cromwell (369), Evelyn Underhill (370).

Endnotes

1. g Brian Larson, *Contemporary Illustrations for Preachers, Teachers, and Writers* (Grand Rapids, aker Books, 1996) number 156. First published in "Epic in the Making," in *Chicago Tribune* 1991) Sec 5, Page 1.

2. "In California City, Acts of Kindness Are Becoming Contagious," *Chicago Tribune* (October Also found in Craig Brian Larson, *Contemporary Illustrations for Preachers, Teachers, and* rand Rapids, Michigan: Baker Books, 1996) number 114.

3. ven R. Mosley, *God: A Biography* (Phoenix, Arizona: Questar Publishers, 1980) pp. 201-202.

4. aig Brian Larson, *Contemporary Illustrations for Preachers, Teachers, and Writers* (Grand Rapids, Baker Books, 1996), number 119. Based upon a Phillip Yancey article that first appeared in Today.

5. enn Van Ekeren, *Words for All Occasions,* (Paramus, New Jersey: Prentice Hall, 1988) p. 187.

6. inton T. Howell, *Design for Living* (New York: Grosset & Dunlap, 1970) p.39.

7. eader's Digest* (February 1994) p. 119.

8. 58) *Illustrations Unlimited,* James S. Hewett, ed. (Wheaton, Illinois: Tyndale, 1988) p. 185.

rthur Pine, *One Door Closes, Another Door Opens* (New York: Dell Trade Paperback, 1993) pp.

lustrations Unlimited,* James S. Hewett, ed. (Wheaton, Illinois: Tyndale, 1988) pp. 469-470.

Lloyd John Ogilvie, *Let God Love You* (Dallas, Texas: Word, 1974) pp. 139-140.

Craig Brian Larson, *Illustrations for Preaching and Teaching* (Grand Rapids, Michigan: Baker 1993) p. 7.

B. Eugene Griessman, *The Achievement Factors* (New York: Dodd, Mead & Co., 1987) pp. 54-55.

Illustrations Unlimited, James S. Hewett, ed. (Wheaton, Illinois: Tyndale, 1988) p. 469.

Nat G. Bodian, *The Joy of Publishing* (Fairfield, Iowa: Open Horizons Publishing Company, pp. 49-51.

Jokes and Anecdotes, Joe Claro, ed. (New York: Random House, 1996) p. 163.

Rewrite of Internet story from *goodstories.com,* attributed to *The Church Humor Digest,* ohis, Tennessee: Castle Books).

David K. Fremon, *The Holocaust Heroes* (Springfield, New Jersey: Enslow Publishers, Inc., 1998) -64.

4) Nat G. Bodian, *The Joy of Publishing* (Fairfield, Iowa: Open Horizons Publishing Co., 1996)

5) *Reader's Digest* (May 1994) p. 114.

7) *Good Housekeeping* (July 1995) p. 20.

2) Steven Carter and Julia Sokol, *Lives Without Balance* (New York: Villard Books, Random House, 1991) pp. 125,194.

33) *Illustrations Unlimited,* James Hewett, ed. (Wheaton, Illinois: Tyndale, 1988) p. 142.

49) Catherine Marshall, *A Closer Walk* (Ada, Michigan: Fleming H. Revell, 1986) p. 27.

55) Stan Mooneyham, *Traveling Hopefully* (Dallas, Texas: Word, 1984) pp. 90-91.

57) *Fortune* (May 1, 1995) p. 32.

References

Additional copies of this book and other titles
in our Devotional Series are available
from your local bookstore.

God's Little Devotional Journal
God's Little Devotional Journal for Women
God's Little Devotional Journal for Mothers
God's Little Devotional Book
God's Little Devotional Book, II
God's Little Devotional Book for Moms
God's Little Devotional Book for Dads
God's Little Devotional Book for Students
God's Little Devotional Book on Prayer
God's Little Devotional Book on Success

If you have enjoyed this book, or if it has
impacted your life, we would like to hear from you.
Please contact us at:

Honor Books
Department E
P.O. Box 55388
Tulsa, Oklahoma 74155
Or by e-mail at info@honorbooks.com

Tulsa, Oklahoma